# The Alteration & The Confusion

Two plays by

**Gerhard Waizmann**

published by

**Harald Osel**

First published in Australia by Aurora House
www.aurorahouse.com.au

This edition published 2023


Cover design: Donika Mishineva | www.artofdonika.com
Typesetting and e-book design: Amit Dey



ISBN number: 978-1-922913-37-1 (Paperback)

A catalogue record for this book is available from the National Library of Australia

Distributed by: Ingram Content: www.ingramcontent.com

Australia: phone +613 9765 4800 |
email lsiaustralia@ingramcontent.com

Milton Keynes UK: phone +44 (0)845 121 4567 |
email enquiries@ingramcontent.com

La Vergne, TN USA: phone +1 800 509 4156 |
email inquiry@lightningsource.com

# Contents

# Foreword from the Editor

The Austrian author, Gerhard Waizmann, who has since passed away, wrote two plays in Vienna in the 1970s or 80s - „Die Ablöse / The Alternation" and „Die Verwirrung / The Confusion" - which have so far remained unpublished. Possibly also because Gerhard Waizmann was not officially recognized as an author in his time.

"TheAlternation" is a play about a seemingly idealistic poet who wants to overthrow the dictator, Terra the Supreme Wise. As the play progresses it becomes more and more apparent that the poet is only presenting his humanitarian values - and his love for Terra's helper and paramour - to further his own ends. In alliance with the Council of Wise Men, that surrounds Terra - and with incredible brutality - the poet ultimately succeeds in becoming dictator himself. By then he does not differ in his means from Terra itself. Consequently, the replacement becomes an unfulfilled longing and remains a broken promise.

"The Confusion" is a play consisting of a large number of episodes, in each of which a dialogue represents the core of the episode. These dialogues take place between a variety of characters such as the two actors, the men in tails and top hat, the harlequin, the soldiers and the captain, the clown and the ballet dancer, the exotic actress and the director, the gentleman in a tropical suit, the scientist, and the dialogue between the nanny and the actors or the stagehand. Ultimately, "The Confusion" remains a collage of individually coherent but overall unrelated episodes. This piece thus becomes a description of self-centered, non-conversing conversations, which gets underlined as well by the subtitle making reference to the confusion of language during the building of the Tower of Babel.

Gerhard Waizmann lived in the second district of Vienna, at Halmgasse 3/23. I met Gerhard in the early 1980s through a mutual friend who, like all the other members of this group had a strong affinity to alcohol. Gerhard, who was a few years older than me, has shown at that time already what I think was a severe dependency on alcohol.

Gerhard had always openly professed his Judaism and although he expressed this visually as well, with his somewhat impressive beard, I still do not really believe that he lived his faith in a very orthodox way.

When I once asked him about his profession, he said that he was a set designer.

Since Gerhard didn't have his own car, I often acted as a 'chauffeur' on trips through Vienna. Once Gerhard jumped out of my car when I told him, my father was an officer in the Wehrmacht during World War II. (He was a flight engineer, i.e. a lieutenant, at the Fliegertechnische Schule 5 in Wischau).

Later I had the opportunity to tell Gerhard about my father's home visit during the Second World War, when he visited his mother in Vienna and stayed in the apartment building at Mollardgasse 25, which was owned by our family. During this visit – and that's how it was reported in our family - my father (who was in uniform at that time) met a group of soldiers whose job it was to arrest our Jewish tenant, Mrs. Fischer. At this point, my father seems to have shown civil courage when he confronted the soldiers and pointed out that Mrs. Fischer had never been guilty of anything and that there was no reason for her to be arrested. Subsequently this group of soldiers actually left. They may have also carried out their assignment reluctantly and might have thought: Well, let‘s just write “untraceable”. This circumstance made it possible for Mrs. Fischer to spend the Second World War in our house as a so-called “submarine”. I knew Mrs. Fischer personally, when I was a child - as a tenant in our house - before she passed away in the 1960s.

Later, when my father retired, he required vis-à-vis the Social Security Office a testimony for a period around World War II, which was otherwise poorly documented. Mrs. Fischer‘s son, Otto, who, it seems to me, worked at times in our family‘s transport company during this period, then submitted his statement to the Social Security Office.

At this point of my story, Gerhard made it clear to me that a similar incident also took place in his family, with a certain Pauker helping his father. It was The Pauker from Simmering-Graz-Pauker said Gerhard by then.

I’ve also lent Gerhard money again and again. At some point, I wanted it back. Instead, he handed me a bundle of paper on which two of his plays were written: “The Alternation” and “The Confusion”. I picked up this bundle of paper and said to myself, “Better than nothing. You‘ll never see the money again.” This was one of our last encounters. Not too long afterwards Gerhard has died.

Later I have accepted a new job, spending many years abroad as part of my work. Following my return to Vienna

- roughly 40 years after having met Gerhard first - his plays, which I had almost forgotten, fell into my hands again. It occurred to me that it might be appropriate to publish them by now.

At this point, I can only speculate why Gerhard did not publish his own plays back in the 1980s. Maybe his relatively early death and his poor health have contributed to that. However, publishing is certainly easier today than it was back then, and I believe that Gerhard would meet the idea with sympathy to ultimately do so by now.

The original version of these plays was written in German. At this point, I would also like to thank Linda Lycett from Aurora House for having encouraged me to come up with an English translation, as well as her relentless efforts to correct many of my mistakes.

Vienna, June 2023

# Vorwort des Herausgebers

Der mittlerweile verstorbene, österreichische Autor, Gerhard Waizmann, hat in den 1970/80-iger Jahren in Wien zwei Theaterstücke geschrieben – "Die Ablöse" und "Die Verwirrung" -, die bisher unveröffentlicht geblieben sind. Möglicherweise auch deshalb, weil Gerhard Waizmann in seiner Zeit nicht offiziell als Autor anerkannt wurde.

"Die Ablöse" ist ein Stück über einen scheinbar idealdenkenden Dichter, der den Diktator, Terra den Oberweisen, stürzen möchte. Im Verlauf des Stückes stellt sich jedoch immer mehr heraus, dass der Dichter seine humanistischen Ideen – und seine Liebe zu Terra's Gehilfin und Mätresse – nur vorgibt um an seine eigenen Ziele zu gelangen. Im Bündnis mit dem Rat der Weisen, der Terra umgibt, - und mit unglaublicher Brutalität - gelingt es dem Dichter letztendlich selbst Diktator zu werden, wobei er sich dann aber in seinen Mitteln durch nichts von Terra selbst unterscheidet. Damit wird die Ablöse zu einer unerfüllten Sehnsucht und bleibt vielmehr ein gebrochenes Versprechen.

"Die Verwirrung" ist ein Theaterstück, das aus einer Vielzahl von Episoden besteht in denen jeweils ein Dialog den Kern der Episode darstellt. Diese Dialoge finden zwischen einer Vielzahl von Charakteren statt, wie den beiden Schauspielern, den Herrn im Frack und Zylinder, dem Harlekin, den Soldaten und dem Hauptmann, dem Clown und der Balletteuse, der exotischen Schauspielerin und dem Regisseur bzw. dem Theaterdirektor, den Herrn im Tropenanzug, dem Wissenschaftler, sowie der Dialog zwischen dem Kindermädchen und den Schauspielern bzw. dem Bühnenarbeiter. Letztendlich bleibt "Die Verwirrung" aber eine Kollage von in sich schlüssigen aber insgesamt unzusammenhängenden Episoden, wobei auch nicht die eine mit der anderen im Zusammenhang steht. Auch gehen die einzelnen Episoden nicht gegenseitig aufeinander ein. Damit wird dieses Stück zu einer Beschreibung des auf sich selbst zentrierten, aneinander Vorbeiredens, was auch durch den Untertitel - mit dem Hinweis auf die Sprachverwirrung beim Turmbau von Babel - unterstrichen wird.

Gerhard Waizmann wohnte im zweiten Wiener Gemeindebezirk, in der Halmgasse 3/23. Ich habe Gerhard in den frühen 80-iger Jahren über einen gemeinsamen Freund kennengelernt, der so wie alle Mitglieder dieser Gruppe sehr stark dem Alkohol zugeneigt war. Gerhard, der um einige Jahre älter war als ich, hat zu dieser Zeit bereits Zeichen einer, wie mir scheint, ausgeprägten Abhängigkeit gezeigt.

Gerhard hatte sich immer offen zu seinem Judentum bekannt und obwohl er mit seinem einigermaßen beindruckenden Bart dies auch optisch zum Ausdruck brachte, glaube ich dennoch nicht wirklich, dass er seinen Glauben sehr orthodoxer gelebt hat.

Als ich ihn einmal nach seinem Beruf fragte sagte er, dass er Bühnenbildner wäre.

Da Gerhard kein eigenes Auto hatte fungierte ich, auf gemeinsamen Fahrten durch Wien, auch immer wieder als "Chauffeur". Einmal ist Gerhard dabei aus meinem Auto gesprungen, als ich ihm erzählt habe, dass mein Vater im Zweiten Weltkrieg ein Offizier der Wehrmacht gewesen ist. (Er war Fliegeringenieur, also Leutnant, an der Fliegertechnischen Schule 5, in Wischau).

Später hatte ich noch Gelegenheit Gerhard von einem Heimatbesuch meines Vaters während des Zweiten Weltkrieges zu erzählen, während dessen er seine Mutter in Wien besucht hat, und sich dabei in dem Mietshaus in der Mollardgasse 25 aufhielt, das sich in unserem Familienbesitz befand. Bei diesem Besuch (und so wurde diese Geschichte in unserer Familie erzählt) traf mein Vater – damals in Uniform - auf eine Gruppe von Soldaten deren Auftrag es war die in unserem Haus wohnende, jüdische Mitbewohnerin, Frau Fischer, abzuführen. An diesem Punkt scheint mein Vater Zivilcourage bewiesen zu haben, als er sich den Soldaten entgegenstellte mit dem Hinweis, dass sich Frau Fischer nie etwas zu Schulden hat kommen lassen und hier kein Grund zu einer Festnahme bestehen würde. Anschließen ist diese Soldaten-Gruppe auch tatsächlich abgezogen. Möglicherweise haben auch diese ihren Auftrag widerwillig ausgeführt und sich gedacht: Na‘ schreiben wir halt "unauffindbar". Dieser Umstand hat es Frau Fischer ermöglicht den Zweiten Weltkrieg in unserem Haus, als sogenanntes "U-Boot", zu verbringen. Ich habe Frau Fischer in meiner Kindheit noch persönlich gekannt – als Mitbewohnerin in unserem Haus - bevor sie dann in den 60-iger Jahren verstorben ist.

Später, als mein Vater in Pension ging, hat er bei der Sozialversicherung eine Zeugenaussage benötigt für eine Periode um den 2. Weltkrieg, die ansonsten schlecht dokumentiert war. Frau Fischers Sohn, Otto, der wie mir scheint in dieser Periode zeitweise im Transportunternehmen unsere Familie mitgearbeitet hat, hat dann bei der Sozialversicherung eine Bestätigung dazu abgegeben.

An dieser Stelle hat mir Gerhard zu verstehen gegeben, dass ein ähnlicher Vorfall auch in seiner Familie stattgefunden hat, wobei ein gewisser Pauker (der Pauker von Simmering-Graz-Pauker sagte Gerhard damals) seinem Vater Hilfestellung geleistet hat.

Ich habe Gerhard auch immer wieder Geld geborgt. Irgendwann wollte ich es zurückhaben. Da hat er mir stattdessen ein Bündel Papier in die Hand gedrückt, auf dem zwei seiner Theaterstücke aufgeschrieben waren: “Die Ablöse” und “Die Verwirrung”. Ich habe dieses Bündel Papier genommen und mir gedacht: “Besser als gar nichts. Das Geld siehst du ohnehin nie wieder”. Das war eines unserer letzten Treffen. Nach nicht allzu langer Zeit ist Gerhard gestorben.

Für die nächsten – ungefähr 45 Jahre – habe ich diese beiden Theaterstücke dann einfach in einer Schublade abgelegt.

Ich selbst habe dann einen neuen Job angenommen, wobei ich im Rahmen meiner Arbeitstätigkeit viele Jahre im Ausland verbracht habe. Nach meiner Rückkehr nach Wien – etwa 40 Jahre nachdem ich Gerhard zum ersten Mal getroffen hatte - sind mir seine Theaterstücke, auf die ich schon fast vergessen hatte, wieder in die Hände gefallen. Dabei kam mir der Gedanke, dass es wohl angebracht wäre diese nunmehr zu veröffentlichen.

Ich kann an dieser Stelle nur mutmaßen warum Gerhard nicht selbst seine Theaterstücke, bereits in den 80-iger Jahren, veröffentlicht hat. Mit Sicherheit ist es jedoch heute leichter ein Stück zu veröffentlichen, als dies damals der Fall war und ich glaube, dass es wohl auch auf Gerhards Sympathien stoßen würde dies letztendlich nun auch zu tun.

Das Original dieser beiden Theaterstücke wurde auf Deutsch verfasst. An diesem Punkt möchte ich mich auch bei Linda Lycett von Auror House dafür bedanken, dass sie mich ermutigt hat eine Übersetzung ins Englisch zu versuchen, sowie für ihre Ausdauer in der Korrektur vieler meiner Fehler.

Wien, im Juni 2023

# THE ALTERNATION!

## Die Ablöse

# THE ALTERNATION!

## Overview

The play takes place in an environment of a fictional, totalitarian state lead by a circle of men claiming to be the profoundly Wise men = Sages.

The leader of the sages – i.e. the dictator of this state - is called Terra. (His place of living is the central location in this play.) Instead of calling himself a supreme leader Terra is called The Supreme Sage.

Following an introduction the play continues with Terra starting an affair with his female secretary (Sec). While Terra goes to rest the Poet approaches the Sec to express his dismay about her affair with Terra just to confess to her subsequently that he is deeply in love with her. He takes here further into his confidence by telling her that he plans to overthrow Terra and would need her and her support to bring about a change to the better. At first the Sec is surprised, afraid and hesitant but ultimately agrees to exert her influence on Terra to lift the Poet into the inner circle.

When a prisoner – demanding freedom - is captured and brought to Terra for interrogation the poet becomes a witness to Terra extraditing the prisoner to two fellow sages for further interrogation. The two Sages torture the prisoner until he dies. When Terra comes to know about it he makes a big deal out of it accusing the two Sages of murder and manages to get them executed, while his real intention was to get rid of potential adversaries. The Poet is able to make use of this situation by raising the remaining sages against Terra. The male secretary (Secr.) – noticing the change – decides to join the side of the poet. After the Sages having ambushed and killed Terra the Poet shoots the male secretary dead with his own pistol, fearing he might become an opponent one day. At this point the Poet shows his true face and even more so when he pretends vis-à-vis the other sages that he actually doesn't really know the (female) secretary well.

With the acceptance of the other Sages the Poet ultimately becomes the successor of Terra, while his replacement actually closes the cycle without changing anything. The Alteration ultimately remains a déjà vu.

Cast:
Terra, the superior wise man; chief sage.
Poet (D.)
Secretary – female (Sec.)
Secretary – male (Secr.)
Orderly.
2 Guards (1W, 2W)
2 Prisoners (Gef.)
Makeup Artist (Ma.)
Director.
Maid / Cleaning women
Actress.
2 Wise Men (W.)
Plato.
About Io sage.

Guards, cameramen, lighting technicians, servants, stagehands, executioners, judges, cook, governess, children.

Setup:
Room in the Government Palace of the Wise. It is very spacious, more like a large salon. Right, left and center a marble covered door. (Heavy-duty clumsy marble.) Above each door is a gilded frame with a photograph of the superior Wise man. Actually, only his screaming mouth is visible on it. Below that, on the walls, are more photos – the busts of the other Wise men (the format is smaller). Next to them are gilded and silvered laurel wreaths with oversized sagging leaves. In the middle distance is a director's desk on which a black typewriter sits. (A sturdy behemoth with an old-fashioned hard touch.) Also, on the tabletop are telephones and glowing bell buttons of different colors. The huge desk is reminiscent of the command bridge of a spaceship. The floor is marble. Several chairs and armchairs (period furniture) are distributed throughout the room. Several long-stemmed ashtrays can be set up as desired although there is no need to do so. Overall facility: stately, ostentatious, pompous, impersonal, cold.

Terra the chief sage is a man in his "prime years". Slightly corpulent but could be described as stately.

A secretary, young, firm, naive charm.

A poet, slender, agile.

The secretary sits to the right of the desk. She is made up and fashionably dressed. Beside her stands the poet in a casual pose. Terra paces restlessly.

Terra: Could I have a cigarette?

Sec.: But you shouldn't...

Terra: I know, I know...

Sec.: *Stands up, and offers cigarettes, and gives a light.*

Terra: Thank you, very kind. (*Looks at her legs as she rocks back and forth to the desk. The viewer is left in the dark as to whether her rocking gait is conscious or unconscious.*)

... friendly prospects ...

Sec.: *standing still, half turn, coquettish*: Please?

Terra: Oh, nothing of importance.

Sec. sits down.

There is a knock at the door. (*To the viewer's right, i.e. to the left.*)

Terra: Come in! (male loud)

*The secretary, a small, slim man with glasses, enters. His face is yellow with correctness. Narrow nose, precise movements. Stubborn intelligence. Knows no scruples. Desk criminal. Dark, tight-fitting suit. He carries a folder under his arm.*

*Secretary standing to attention*: Long live the wisest!

Terra: What are you bringing me?

Secr.: Inconveniences.

Terra: I'm used to that.

Secretary: It is the concept for monthly support and maintenance of popular opinion.

Terra: Does it have to be now?

Secretary: Sorry, it cannot be postponed.

Terra: Fine, if I have to.

Secr. solemnly: One must repeat the truths until they are so self-evident that they are suckled by the children with the nurse's milk.

Terra to Poet: A competitor of yours?

Secretary polite: Don't worry, I'm not a poet, just an amateur. (*Opening the folder, reading.*) Our state is ruled by the Wise, you know (interrupts) … should I read everything?

Terra: Be as brief as possible.

Secretary: One of the Sages holds the office of senior sage. He is a brother of the other sages and exactly like them.

Terra: Stop! To brush! From - He is a brother - cross out. You write! At the head of the wise is the chief sage. (*secr. noted*) do you have that?

Secretary: Yes (*reading on*)...our system is based on justice, kindness and severity... there are choirs in the choreography meant to repeat this phrase... (*reading*) This state is the best of all states. Everyone is firmly in his or her place in the sun. Nobody can complain because there is nothing to complain about.

Terra: A bit naive. Do you believe that...

Secretary: Don't forget it's a folk festival. The speech has a popular character. Simple phrases are always very effective on big occasions. (*Reading*) Only our performance, which alone decides, has put us at the top of the nation after a hard struggle.

Our life is regulated in a more admirable way. The Wise men determine our partner, that's nice... choirs here again... The Wise men determine our partner and that's a good thing. Our children raised by the state are light, air and sun children. Our faith in you, oh wise ones, surpasses all. No question remains unanswered. Our fate is in your kind hands. And we won't ask either. How should we understand what you decide for our good?

Terra *yawns*: Sorry.

Secretary: I'm done right away, my Wise man. But we're diligently raising our patriotic hands without end.

Terra: That's enough.

Secretary: A parade of children in white dresses is planned. They sing the hymn, We love the wisest.

Terra: That's doing well.

Secretary: In the end, gymnasts use their bodies to form the slogan: Our wise leaders are the lifeblood of the state.

Terra: Very good.

Secretary: Thank you.

Terra: Is there free beer and sausages?

Secretary: Of course, as far as the financial situation allows.

Terra: Don't remind me. Good. As you know, hungry stomachs are not a solid basis for a feast. Bread and circuses - you know. Unfortunately, people are not as stupid as most people think.

Secretary: Yes, unfortunately.

Terra: Excellent.

Secretary: Don't forget, this rounds off a spectacular execution.

Terra: Great. The people can give free rein to aggression and let out its anger. Is that from you?

Secretary: I allowed myself...

Terra: Enough delinquents?

Secretary: In an emergency, we can still get some. There is no appeal against an accusation from the highest authority. (*Broad smile*.)

Terra: Yes, fun. You have a free hand.

Secretary bowing: Thank you very much. (*tight*) Long live the Wisest. (*away*)

Terra, *sternly*: Where did we stop?

Poet: You asked for a cigarette.

Terra: That's not what I mean.

Secr.: On the editorial for the weekly paper.

Terra to the poet: I'm curious about your manuscript.

Secr.: It's here (*holds it out to Terra*).

Terra: How many weeks are done?

Poet: Three.

Terra: Well, one more thing... then we're done with the month. I've got it up to there. (*Runs his hand across his neck*) ... play the lector ... you're not a machine. (*Hands the manuscript to the poet*.) I do hear.

Poet: Since we are the wise ones, the most dazzling luminaries in the spiritual firmament of this epoch - and that by virtue of our status, our birth and our genetic superiority - we have, as is well known, the right, even the duty, to make our decisions, their expediency only we alone can see, to communicate to the people without further possible confusing explanation. The state stands or falls with us. We are of the same permanent importance to you as the sun is to ...

Terra: Wait! Couldn't you include the whole cosmos right away?

Poet: Sun is more concise.

Terra: Do you think so? I was thinking the same thing. I see they are doing a good job.

Poet: Thank you.

Terra: That's enough. I'll read the sequel later.

Poet: It deals mainly with the love of the Wise for the people.

Terra: Dear... do you know the latest Count Bobby joke? … the Count leaves (whisper, one only understands the words "brothel, copulation, rectum")

Sec. with frozen face: But...

*Terra and the poet start laughing. Terra especially. His neighing starts right at the climax without building up and then slowly dies down to flare up again.* It must be contagious.

*Terra becomes aware of the sec's rigid face:* Well, isn't it a good one?

*Sec giggles to order.*

Terra to Poet: I don't need you right now...

Poet bowing: It was an honor.

Terra: I hope you appreciate your participation in my most intimate emotions.

Poet: Certainly (*leaving*)

Terra: Let duty be duty be my angel. (*He walks towards her in an exaggeratedly elastic manner.*) You have an adorable hairdo. Did I already tell you?

Sec: No. (*Smiles up at him, head tilted.*)

Terra: May I invite you for a little refreshment?

Sec. quietly: Yes.

Terra: You know I could do without polite phrases?

Sec: Yes.

Terra: That they are not necessary under our regulations?

Sec: I know.

Terra: You have a very honorable post.

Sec: Yes.

Terra: I don't like it when a lovely girl like you is prudish.

Sec: Yes.

Terra: I hereby offer you to be on a first name basis.

Sec: Very honorable. Yes, thanks.

Terra: Would you... would you please follow me to my private quarters?

Sec.: Yes ... gladly ... (*very hesitantly*)

Terra: Then come. (*Sec. gets up and approaches Terra. He puts his hand on her waist. Turns left to exit.*)

*The stage remains empty for a moment. It's getting darker. From the left the muffled voice of the two. Then hysterical giggling, loud smacking, and groaning. It must come as a surprise and sound like there is a stereo system on stage. Should only last a very short time and ends in background noise that is cut off with a loud crash. Silence.*

*Behind the opposite door (to the right, i.e. to the left) a quarrel can be heard, quietly but clearly. The voices sound metallic. (Metal wire singing far away.)*

No, that's impossible.

But we have folders...

I say it doesn't work that way.

Take care of your own business...

That's exactly what I'm doing, Sir...

You are orderly here, nothing more... we act on a secret mission that...

It is my task …

Nonsense, do you let us through now or not?

But... (*voices get louder, more natural*)

It's an urgent matter. We're supposed to get the guy to here at once, no matter what.

On your responsibility!

Well, you're finally seeing reason!

I take no responsibility!

OK. You don't need to do that.

*The right door is pushed open. Two gray-robed guards drag in a bleeding man. The prisoner's shirt collar is open. No shoe-laces, the buttons on the robe are missing. He's holding his pants with his hands chained together.*

1st Guard (1W), *calling to the back*: Our orders are binding!

2nd Guard (2W) *looking around, hesitating*: There's no one here. *(Full light again.)*

*Orderly, half visible in the doorway*: There you are! You're getting me in trouble!

1W: We know what we're doing. We can wait. We have time. We are used to waiting.

*Orderly, shaking his head*: You must know. *(Closes the door from the outside.)*

1W *pulls a packet out of his pocket, pulls out a cigarette and wants to put it between his lips.*

2W: Are you crazy?

1W: Excuse me... (*pushes the cigarette back into the pack*) ... I was so keen.

2W: Shall we sit down? (*Looks searching*)

1W: Let's stay where we are.

2W: I'm tired.

1W: We stop.

2W: As you wish.

1W *goes to the desk, picks up a cigarette butt from the ashtray and sniffs* it: Hmmm... expensive kind. (*Showing the stub from afar*): You see, smoking is allowed!

2W: That doesn't apply to us. We are on duty.

*The prisoner chokes.*

1W, *not without showing good nature*: Behave yourself, swine.

2W: He doesn't seem to know where he is.

*Prisoner, quietly*: I'm cold *(coughs convulsively)*.

2W: Don't spit on the floor!

1W: Don't mess up the boss's room! (*Pokes him*)

2W: And that's called an intellectual. Look how you look now. That's what you get for.

1W: The waiting is getting on my nerves. We should make ourselves known.

2W, *pointing to the left door*: Where does it go?

1W *reading with head bent*: Private.

2W: Knock once!

1W, *knocks*.

2W: Louder!

1W *bangs against the door (not too grotesquely)*: Nothing moves (*shrugs his shoulders).*

2W: Try again; (*with a look at the prisoner*). He's messing up the whole office.

You can hear footsteps (*very far away at first*) that are rapidly approaching. There is enough time for the two to strike a pose on either side of the prisoner.

Terra, *coming in and rubbing his hair, roars*: This is an infamy!

*Guards, at the same time*: Long live the wisest!

Terra, *standing still*: That impertinence could cost you your existence! Where is the faintest remnant of decency? How do you even get in? (*Briefly fumbling on the tie, maybe just a hand movement*) You owe me an explanation!

1W, *saluting*: We act at your express command oh Wisest. You said …

*Terra approaching them*: What did I say?

2W: We had orders for the anarchist...

Terra: The anarchist? Which …

1W: Yes, the anar...

Terra (*squeezing his face and stepping closer*): Oh yes... that's him ... this is an urgent case. However, is it common for you to break into someone's private rooms?

1W: *stuttering*: No...

Terra: You can read, can't you?

2W: We don't have private rooms.

Terra: What does it say? (*Points to the door*)

1W: Private.

Terra: There you go! I'm glad you're not illiterate (*calmer*), don't worry, I was busy elsewhere... you know your duties. Nevertheless, I thank you.

W. *confused*: At your service!

Terra to the prisoner: Now to you my darling. You finally got caught...

Terra: You're made-up red... I personally took care of you. You cost me sleepless nights. Do you know what it means to steal the sleep of the Chief Sage?

2W: You personally insulted Terra the Supreme Wise!

1W: Yes, that's what you did.

Terra *yelling*: How you dare causing me to waste my precious time on such subversive elements? Because decadent ideas grow in your stupid brain? Where would we be if we had to constantly fight for our livelihood? Because some hotheads don't like our order! Because the gentlemen think they are clever! You are a nobody! You are nothing! Do you even understand what you are doing? (*Loud but not yelling.*) That factual thinking is being replaced by childish sentimentality, especially in intellectual circles! (*To the guards*) Do you know what the pig preached and did?

1W: No. We just arrest. The reason is for us...

Terra: The creature declares the choice of mate an intimate matter. Ridiculous, huh?

*The guards laugh dutifully.*

1W: Ah, that's the kind of guy he is.

2W: That's something... (*shaking his head*)

Terra, *ironically*: Selfish love is dead, got it! A healthy state needs healthy children, and nobody can check that holding your views. Health to health and health gets checked by professionals... what do we have highly skilled computers for? Free choice of partner. The brainless old misery! In this way discipline and order never come into our system. Furthermore, marital ties rooted in sentimentalism distract far too much from work for the good of the state. But you and your friends don't want to understand that! (*silence*) How narrow-minded one can be! (*Pause*) Your whore sits in the hothouse of heroes. She is put to good use there. (*Pause - yelling*) She'll be fed to the heroes and many staunch patriots will be begotten. Why did you want to marry her? (*Turns to the guards with exaggerated perplexity.*) How can a sane person insist? The upshot of this unfortunate fact?

1W: He's stupid; (*purrs it down happily*).

Terra: What's having to happen, idiots?

2W: Malicious idiots who deliberately persist in their idiocy are handed over immediately to the court-martial for liquidation, according to Paragraph I, Section II of the Criminal Code, without any claim to direct or indirect legal protection, which would correspond to Section 555.

Terra: That`s the way it is.

*Prisoner screaming*: Hypocritical pig! (*Spits at Terra.*)

*1W hits the prisoner twice in the face with the back of the hand*: Down! (*The prisoner staggers.*)

Terra: The sow. (*Guard raises his hand for the third swipe.*) No stop! I can only see brutality on screen. I like to look just there. Otherwise, I'm sensitive.

1W: Excuse me... the excitement.

Terra: It's okay, you didn't hit (*runs sleeve over the front of the jacket, rubs*)... when I drive past the abomination sites I have to draw the curtains... I'm an aesthete too.

1W: I feel for you.

Terra: You're working day and night for the state and what does this maverick do? Make the floor dirty? He!

Prisoner: Terracotta Pig!

2W: Shut up (*pulls a crushed handkerchief from his breast pocket*)

Terra: Don't do that...

2W: Wait, we'll have that in a moment. (*Presses the cloth over the prisoner's face.*)

Prisoner, indistinctly: Pigs!

Terra: Go now... thanks, thanks, no formalities... (*Before they reach the door, sharp*) ... And how do you do it?

W: With the utmost discretion!

Terra: Good. His bacillus could be contagious. You are doing your duty in an exemplary manner, gentlemen.

1W *to prisoner*: Take this as an example.

2W: Yes, take an example; (*drags the prisoner out*). Long live the wisest (*almost incomprehensible*).

Terra: I'm too good-natured. I lack toughness.

W1, *almost at the door*: You're right there...

Terra: Get out!

W1: I've just confirmed your opinion. (*Trio exits*)

Terra, *calling after him*: Tell the cleaners, the room... the dirt must go...

W. *shouting from the corridor*: Yes...

*Terra exits through the left door; mumbles*: All schemers.

Silence. *The stage gradually brightens, bathing itself in brilliant light as the text begins.*

*A cleaning woman (housekeeper, maid) comes in with a bucket full of steaming suds. Her hands are in red rubber gloves. She is dressed simply but cleanly and smells like a hospital.*

Cleaning women: Stains again ... aaah yes ... (*kneels, takes a gray rag out of the suds, wriggles it out over the bucket and wipes it*) … if that (*wipes*) ... if someone had said that to me earlier (*wipes*) I would have … in his face … (*wrings out the rag*) Yes, I would have laughed in his face. My salary is wisely determined, I have the most necessary things. Oh, if that's wise, I'll eat a broom... They settled it in their favor. They are their own minions, but they have cheap labor in the likes of us... (*squirms*)... My children raise others. The smaller ones at least, and I'm dying alive. I have fool's freedom. Also, the room has no ears. I know that. But if I do, I have the freedom to fool. I don't get that much attention anymore. Poof over! (*Makes a movement with the rag.*) I was once in the temple of love and gave birth to children. That was a long time ago...

good material I was, said the doctors (*stretching*). They said I was good material. Loins ready to give birth, they said. A healthy uterus. Best soil, they said. Well, and then they just planted the pig boys. Well, it was disgusting at first. Later everyone was fine with me. You didn't get anything at all from artificial insemination. (*Rubbing the stomach.*) I preferred the other even more. How could I have defended myself? (*Let the rag splash back into the water.*) I was 18 years old at the beginning. And how wild were the wise men! They pounced on every young thing. Assault Force of Lust. Please, with the old ones, you had to do a bit... oh, what... the flower of youth spilled in antiseptic beds... I need fresh water. (*Gets up with a groan and carries the bucket a bit ... half-turned to the audience.*) We weren't doing badly in that damn dump, at least looking at it from the outside. We had air and hygiene. But heaven, heaven we had none. Just a little bit of open sky would have been enough. A fist-sized piece of hope. (*Puts the bucket down sluggishly and addresses the audience directly.*) Bullshit, there are facts you can't wash away. Even the cleanest prison is a prison. (*Strokes her hair and wipes her hands on her robe.*) Do you know that I was beautiful? (*Smiles youthfully.*) Yes, yes, that sounds ridiculous now. But I still have my education. You won't believe it, but I was an educated woman. And pretty. Are you waiting. (*Stepping close to the ramp and quotes, hands tightly closed, like a schoolgirl*):

The wild urge of passions.
Compulsion of duties and instincts,
you share with examining feelings,
with strict judgment according to the goal,
what nature on its great journey ...

I'm afraid I'm losing the thread. Thank you, thank you, thank you, thank you very much *(smiles, curtsies childishly and lifts the hem of the skirt)*. That was, yes, those were the days. I had fluffy peach cheeks. Very fluffy, you know. Yes, I had. (*Pause for several seconds, then it bursts out of her*): And no matter how much make-up you put on, ladies... (*despondent*)... you'll forgive... I... (*Stands a moment at a loss as if waiting for the text, then kneels again.*) ... oh, the never-ending cleaning... it's an honorable post... I don't want to complain... if I should have said something, please take it to my age's credit... (*pulls a few spray cans out of the various pockets and lines them up next to her. An overlong white cloth appears. She takes it out of her pocket like a magician. Nevertheless, it may only appear grotesque in hints of it. She takes a can, shakes it, and sprays the floor*) ... this substance is really good. Best of all. Makes black floors bright white. Of course, one could also say shining white. It convinced me and I've been happier since I've known it. Every young woman should have it. (*Shows the can to the audience*) Do you see, that simple and effective (*sprays*) ... isn't that a relief for the troubled housewife? (*Wipes*) Yes, I'm happy. (*Shows another can.*) And this is a model for mature ladies. It makes me particularly happy. I haven't had any problems since then. (*Sprays*) Believe me or not ... (*wipes*) ... the dirt ... blown away ... I ... I ... how would a poet put it? I'm wrinkled on my knees and there's frozen blood in my swollen veins ... it's all settled anyway (*wipes away the spray*). Besides, a good cleaning agent shines brighter than the sun. We say that strength must not be wasted. The main thing is that you stay quiet and even kiss and lick their hands afterwards. Sometimes I want to be like a shrike and impale them. There is a thorn ready for everyone in the thickets of my prickly heart. A curved, sharp thorn with barbed hooks ... I'd better shut up ... Shut up is the little man's watchword ... So, the dirt would be gone (*stands up groaning and holds her hips*).

*Terra emerges from the private quarters and clears his throat...*

Clerk: My Sage (*bows*)

Terra: Keep up the good work.

Maid: Am I disturbing you?

Terra: But no...

Maid: If so, I would like to...

Terra: That's not necessary at all. I must thank.

Note: Nevertheless...

Terra, sharply: Are you done?

Maid: I'm completely exhausted.

Terra: Then go.

Maid: Yes, right away (*goes off with her utensils, which she laboriously collects beforehand.*)

*Terra calling to the left into the private rooms*: Where are you? (*silence*) come on! Where were we? (*Lights a cigarette*)

Sec. *not yet visible*: Where?

Terra: Yes, where? Hurry up.

Sec. *closer*: At the love of the wisest for the people.

Terra: Alright, come on!

Sec. comes out of the private room, a little crushed. The clothes aren't quite right... maybe the bra or stockings are missing... you can see a change, which is also reflected in the clothes.

Terra: The way you look... look at your looks a bit... (*sec adjusts her pullover*) ... it doesn't have to be the same for everyone... you could really pay more attention to your looks. (*He rings one of the bells. It rings very loudly. Preferably behind the audience.*) Are you ready?

Sec: I think so.

Poet enters: You wish?

Terra: You can go on.

*Poet looking at the sec*: I think it's already over.

Terra: What?

Poet: The end of the article is already worked out.

Sec: Oh, I'm just pretty tired.

Terra: Check it out together. I'm freshening up now. (*away*)

Poet: I don't want to bother you unnecessarily with the manuscript. It is finished.

Sec: if you...thank you.

*sharp light.*

*Poet, looks at her, shakes her head and then goes to the desk. He plays with the briefcase and loose sheets.*: So, you too. (*pause*) Like everyone. I was wrong. Forgive me. (*Indicates a mocking bow.*) I should have known.

Sec: What is it? What do you want from me? Express yourself more clearly.

D.: That was clear enough. (*Points to the left*)

Sec: What's that to you? I do my duty.

D. ironically: Bravo, shall I applaud?

Sec: Paha (*shrugs*)

D.: Or do you prefer other forms of ovations?

Sec: What do you actually want? Leave me alone.

D.: Since when so squeamish?

Sec.: Say what you want. Or are they? ... no ... (*laughs cheerlessly*) ... no, that would be too funny ...

D.: What would be too funny?

Sec: That you are jealous. No, I do not think so. Jealousy is forbidden. We live in the age of reason.

D: Like that?

Sec: But yes, yes. That's obvious. That's quite clear.

D: Sure?

Sec.: Of course! Even fairy tales are told appropriately. Our educational program, you know how it is ...

D.: Yes, I know how it is handled.

Sec.: No more monkey-like pampering of the children. The program is: nursing homes, kindergartens, educators, trainers. Everything is based on common sense. Or do you have a different opinion? (*Takes a cigarette between his lips. D. gives her light.*)

D.: You dodge.

Sec.: No more nonsense. All sentimentality abolished. (*Tearing hand movement that tries to be bold.*) ... pfffft away ... (sobs)

D.: That doesn't sound very convincing.

Sec. *gulping tears*: No?

D: No.

Sec. *takes powder compact and lipstick from the right desk drawer.*

D.: So, you've already settled in?

Sec. *while she is putting on make-up, defiantly*: The post is good...isn't it? ... and Terra a nice person ... right? ... I mean, he could be different.

D.: So… Terra… just Terra. Officially, our honored sage does not like such salutations. Not even in his absence.

Sec: I mean he could be uglier.

D.: I continue to listen with devotion?!

*Second looking at herself in the hand mirror*: That's how it works. Don't you think so?

D.: You know very well that I only accept all humiliations because of you.

Sec: Is my hairstyle, okay?

D.: You know that!

Sec.: You child, doesn't that matter? (*Powders face*) You're funny. (*Opens cream jar and rubs hands*) You're really funny. (*Puts away the makeup*)

D.: Even if they find it funny. I love you.

*Sec blurts out hysterically*: Ha, ha... isn't that for you ... oh you smart aleck ... *(sobs, falling back into lethargy*). That is your problem. (*Takes pen out of pocket and draws eyebrows*) … (*while seemingly just concentrating on her work*): How much? (*Bursts out laughing again, which ends as if cut off*) Excuse me... I... (*Fixes the eyelashes with the brush.*) How much?

D.: More than you think.

*Sec. tucking away the pen and the brush*: I would have soon forgotten. By the way, I don't believe anything anymore.

D: I love you!

Sec: How much? (*Laughs*) let me, I have to calm down... (*sharp*) More than your life?

D: Yes

Sec. *hysterical*: Then prove it (*points left*) the bed is still open and I'm still warm. What I lack now can only increase your pleasure.

D.: You are crazy! ... was it really that ...

Sec.: Yes, it was the first time. (*Laughing*) Does that surprise you? More than his life... it looks like that... you're a coward... you coward!

D.: I'm not crazy, my sweet coo-coo. I understand your condition well...

Sec: My condition? What condition?

D.: I love you; do you understand? (*Takes her hand, which she leaves limp in his hands*) Do you understand what that means? What does that really mean?

Sec: You're a little late on this...

D.: I want to protect you ...

Sec: Now? (*swallows*) a little late...

D.: It's never too late. We invented the clock. We smash it and with-it time.

Sec: You are not my house poet.

D.: Your irony strikes me...

Sec: You confuse everything even more...

D.: I'm honest...

Sec: But Terra...

D.: That can also be done. Please stop crying. There you have a handkerchief. (*She sobs.*) It's not that bad. Believe me. We must be smarter than foxes, tails tucked, belly up and playing dead. It's not very funny, I know, but together...

Sec.: Together... I never thought that far. For what reason? It all came so suddenly. Something's broken... shattered inside me... though I'm aware of the honor...

D.: Don't panic. Whining is useless. We must work together. For now, you must woo for Terra's sympathy for me, brave girl, then you can... the rest will fall in place.

Sec: Like foxes? Smart as foxes?

D: Yes.

Sec: Foxes don't have tails. Your plan is absurd... if we...

D.: Why don't foxes have tails?

Sec.: They don't have just tails ... their rear end is actually a bushy tail ... you can also call it cauda …

D.: Oh, I'm not a hunter.

Sec.: You want to get rid of him... I understand that, but... I don't really know... And if so? What about the others? What about the other sages?

D.: The sub-sages are since long fed up with him. They just don't dare to open their mouths and have weak decision-making capabilities. But you can get them to get it done ...

(*responding to the sec's doubtful look*) ... I realize my role isn't very heroic. Intrigue and heroism don't mix well. Bad as fire and water...

Sec: Why are you doing this?

D.: Because of you, didn't I say that?

Sec: It's coming too fast.

D.: We must be mean for a while. (*Pushed into bubbling defense by the sec's doubtful looks.*) Do you think it's easy? I find it just as difficult as you. When the boss spits, I open my mouth, say thank you and swallow. I can't stand it much longer. And then there's the agony of seeing such an adorable creature as you between his paws.

Sec. *with naive coquetry*: Am I adorable?

D.: More than adorable!

Sec: Swear to me!

D: I swear!

Sec.: I don't think I'm very pretty. No.

D.: You are an enchanting woman for me. To me you are the loveliest woman in the world. I don't lie.

Sec.: I was afraid of the word 'world'. Those are phrases.

D.: How can you tell the difference? Lovers don't choose the words. The genuine often sounds more false than the construed. The most honest emotional exuberance can seem ridiculous. But what am I talking about. Terra must go. We cannot live otherwise. I'll take care of him. We'll take care of him.

Sec: These are bloody flowers... you bring a bloody bouquet to the first date... my hands stink of his sweat... I feel dirty...

D.: It was coercion.

Sec: Do you believe that? Does that matter?

D: No.

Sec: Do you actually like me? ...I don't care of anything.

D.: It wasn't you (*kissing her hands*).

Sec.: Leave it, I don't care.

D. *whispering*: I need your trust, your absolute trust.

Sec: You are a dreamer.

D.: I am a realist. I need you to gain his trust by your flattering. No, don't say anything... He makes two basic mistakes.

Sec: Which?

D.: He thinks he's wise...

Sec: And secondly?

D.: He thinks he's completely safe. He's infected with delusions of grandeur. The disease ends fatally for a politician.

Sec: I don't know yet... he hasn't done anything bad... he...

Whistle from the left. The two part. Terra comes in wearing a suit and smelling fresh.

Terra: Ready?

Sec: Yes.

Terra: What else is on the agenda?

Second: Today ... today ... (*checks the appointment book*) The television is waiting for your speech. (*Quick glance at the clock*) They should have arrived by now.

Terra *rings a bell*; *(male) secretary enters.*

Secretary: May I remind you...

Terra: I know...

Secretary: May I let the team in?

Terra: Immediately; (*to D. and Sec.*) You are not needed now. Wait a minute... (*searches at the desk*)

Sec.: Allow me... (*hands him a folder*)

Terra: That was what I was searching for. Thank you. (*Exit of the two*) Let the gentlemen come in!

*Secretary goes to the door, opens it*: Please.

*The team rolls loudly into the salon armed with cameras, lights, cables and other props. A throne chair with a high, narrow backrest stands out. (It should look serious and dignified; modernized, simplified Gothic is best.) The structure is made of wood. Four attached staircases lead up; surround the armchair like a tapering podium. It is placed in the middle of the stage. Lighting technicians, cameramen, directors, reporters, stagehands. Part civilian, part blue and white work coats. People work hastily and change the symmetry of the room in a matter of minutes. The choppy calls are not understandable.*

Director to Terra: We're almost there.

*Terra sitting behind the desk*: Please...

Makeup Artist (Ma.) to Terra: Would you please come to the light, wise man. (*Compliments him to a leather armchair in front of the desk*) May I make you up a bit?

Terra: Do your duty ... it's supposed to be like this ...

Ma.: The unfavorable influence of the light ... you would appear unnatural ... even an Apollo would have to be made up ... which I don't mean to say anything ...

Terra: Is it really not possible?

Ma: People would think you had jaundice ... please sit down. (*A mirror and a box are brought out. The makeup artist takes a white towel from it and ties it around Terra like a napkin.)*

Terra *to Secretary*: What's your speech today? The stimulating one or the encouraging, calming one...?

Secretary: The Hate Speech.

Terra: Uh...

Ma. *to the obediently waiting assistant*: The lipstick! A bit of blush... very pretty lashes... The make-up stick! ...

Terra: Leave the lips as they are... (*wipes his lips with the cloth*) ... I don't like it.

Ma. *whining*: My artwork... no, not that please...

Terra: Go ahead!

Ma.: Yes, I'm not saying anything.

Terra: Mainly the eyebrows!

Ma.: What an instinct! ... and now some more blue for the eye shadow ... (*stretches his arm rigidly backwards, shrill*) Violet! (*The assistant claps what he wants in his hand*) Enchanting... firm features... clear... tart-sweet lines ... enchanting maturity... good, very good.

Terra: Ready?

Ma.: Right away, just a little more emphasis on the bridge of the nose... now they look a lot more despotic... no, excellent! ... some people did not recognize themselves after my treatment ... they searched for their identity and did not find it ... (*Looks at his artwork*)

Terra: Let's begin!

Director: The chair a little more to the left, please! No, no; (*waves with his right hand*) a little more to the right, no, not that far to the right... we've practiced this so many times... we're always in the same position... yes... finally!

*The chair (throne) is now on the left not too far from center stage. During transport, he is half covered by the crowd of stagehands. Only at the destination does the view of it become clear. The lighting technicians adjust their lamps to him. (Bright white light) It's getting dark on the rest of the stage. The light (apart from the twilight) comes exclusively from the spotlights that are on the stage.*

*Terra goes to the throne and is caught by the light*: Where are the insignia?

*Four magnificently dressed heralds emerge from the darkness into the light. They solemnly wear the red ceremonial cloak. Behind them two more heralds with ceremonial batons and crowned helmets. The latter rests on a red cushion. They approach Terra and put the cloak on him. He takes the crown off the cushion, holds it up for a moment, then puts it on. The heralds crowd around him as he slowly climbs the steps. Only his torso and the heralds' shoulders are bathed in light. The ceremonial must be silent. Terra sits down and grabs the wand. The light has followed his torso. Two heralds stand on either side of him. (On the bottom step of the podium.)*

The insignia. The crown: basic form/=tiara.

*From the tiara, which has a knob (above), gently curved bundles of gold wire, each about half a meter long, grow at head height to the right and left. (This is variable) They strive upwards and end up in the horizontal. Wide bands woven with gold hang from them (on the outside) down to the floor. They are decorated with thick gold fringes and can be dragged on a bit.*

1st Variant: Mixture of tiara and flattened Napoleon hat. Full golden semi-circle about 1 m in diameter (in width; depth must not be more than 3 cm) above which the tip of the tiara rises. The two parts of the semicircle are to be attached laterally; (dissected sun disk) bands as above.

2nd Variant: The flat semicircle is openwork or consists of wire mesh! Rosettes, chains, glass plates. The tapes stay. The staff is taller than a man is and should not necessarily be reminiscent of an episcopal staff. Both objects are richly set with stones. The coat: Large-scale pattern in the form of one (or two) mythical creatures/right/possibly only gemstones.

The presentation should look fantastic and expensive.

Clothing of the heralds: doublets with puffed sleeves (perhaps pulled), wide breeches, high shoes. The robe is embroidered all over with silver and gold sequins. In between there are also larger plates made of glass and silver. Silver shall prevail. The tall, otherwise undecorated hats have feathers. White silk bows. The presentation must not appear ridiculous.

Director: It is Time (*muffled*).

Makeup artist, quiet: A bit of shadow over the lashes...

Voice: Pssst...

Terra: Is the manuscript visible?

Director: No, you appear to speak freely.

*In the twilight that falls before Terra, a man in a white work coat kneels and holds up the manuscript. The light now also encompasses Terra's knees. On them lies the cloak in picturesque folds. Everything else is plunged into darkness. Even the man in the work coat only appears in outlines.*

Director: One, two, three – tail slate.

Terra; *his voice is too loud (microphone)*: Terra the High Wise speaks to you! We are a nation of Sages, heroes, soldiers and workers. This ideal state did not come about by chance. No, we brought it with blood and tears and paid for it! Thanks to our joint efforts, work is provided for our hardworking, upright people. To this, we can only say an open "YES" with a glowing heart and with a full throat. (*Indicates to the man to hold the manuscript closer. This needs to be done discreetly.*) Nevertheless, I have a request for you. (*The light becomes reddish and increases to red.*)

I. Suggestion: Change the red constantly during the speech.

II. Suggestion: Wavy movements of the light.

III. Suggestion: Only illuminate the cloak and insignia in bloody red and illuminate the face in white.

IV. Suggestion: Scattered over the robe and insignia, small red lightbulbs should glow alternately.

Terra continues speaking: Frail individualism must be eradicated forever! Healthy, hard and always with a wet snout is the motto! I love you citizens! As long as brain, hand and foot can still say "yes", I love you. Woe, however, to the narrow-chested, fear-gasping individuals. These myrmecophilous parasites, with their criminal physiognomy, inherited freedom, - with bestial hatred of our order - they seek to undermine! You who hate our grace. The word mercy shall be written all over their faces. They who hate this mercy will still whine and drool for this very mercy. Yes, folk comrades, I mean that filthy empire that bathes the full breasts of its white dairies in the blood of our people! That is only concerned with raising its own seed and does not care for its fellow citizens, no, only fattens its own fat body. This stinking mishmash of corruption and self-interest that it tries to hide behind the mask of humanity, albeit without success. I hurl my "no" at them a thousand times! Those poisoners of the nation who seek in vain to manipulate your opinion with anarchist roars: (*waves to turn the page*). Dealing with them only induces moral and psychological damage. The sanatoriums are full of them. Moreover, even now my anger falls on those who call our golden army the scourge of God and call the glorious pillars of the state murderers! However, I will be merciless! As merciless as it gets! Say firmly "no"! An open "no" becomes a questionable yes. Therefore, "no" and again "no"! The ties of blood can no longer count! Friendship has to stop there! Hatred must cry out to heaven and shatter the firmament. The wound has to be cauterized, detoxified and sterilized! No, there is no more hesitation! (*Breathing air.*) We are not burnt offerings at the altar of intellect! It is entirely in line with their concept that they repeatedly point out with false eloquence that this is not a burnt offering. (Yelling) It is one! (*Quickly*) Hundreds can come and thousands afterwards I will still shout in their face:

It is a burnt offering! (*Pause*) We all sacrifice. (*Screaming the words*) However, no burnt offerings! (*More calmly, matter-of-factly*) The enemy within must be defeated wherever it appears. Under whatever pretense he approaches. It is our most sacred duty to put a stop to this rabble. The slightest human sympathy would be out of place, because the hand that our sincere fellow citizen stretches out to them brings him down himself. That's why they bring arguments that initially sound reasonable to the uninitiated. Thank God it has got to the point that most fellow citizens are disgusted by their pseudo-intellectual ramblings. That their words fizzle out in the air. Nevertheless, the fight must be continued! Forever and ever. Only the constant state of struggle can free the healthy body of the people from the mites of doubt! (*Pause*) On you who are true to the idea, we scatter merciless mercy, and no one can say that we are not true to our word. (*Head movement. The spotlights go out. At the same time stage light, work light that slowly brightens.*)

*Everyone applauds.*

Terra *takes off the crown, climbs down, and wipes the sweat from his forehead*: Have I been well in the picture?

Sec.: You were great!

Terra: Take that! (*Gives the crown to the director. He hands it to a subordinate.*) Phew, that is hot! (*Opens the cloak clasp. A stagehand takes the cloak from him and throws it over a chair where the crown is already lying.*)

Terra: It is always very tiring. You would have to invent something. Maybe an imitation that weighs less...

Stagehand to another: Take that one away too (*points to the staff still leaning on the throne*) and put it with the rest!

Other B.: Yes, right away...

Director to Terra: You know, that is the art of language...

Stagehand to the other: I am telling it to your face; you will never make it...

Sec: The speech was brilliant. Clear structure, good speaking technique...

Stagehand: Do that, you braggart!

Other: I am not saying anything...

Director: I am touched...

Stagehand: Hit in the center ...

Terra, *reaching for the towel*: Damn it! Could the public see that?

Ma.: It didn't bother me...

Terra, upset: Impossible! (*Tears off the cloth.*)

(Male) Secretary: If I may say so, it didn't bother me. Your face came more into play as a result.

Director: Pure whit creates underlines …

Terra: No way do I want to be ridiculous ...

Ma.: Quite the opposite. The head of John on Herodias' tablecloth ... the characteristics of your features were better illuminated.

Terra: I hope so because of you!

Orderly enters, saluting at attention: My wise man!

Terra: What's up?

Orderly: May I speak to you alone for a moment (looks around doubtfully).

Terra: Of course.

*The two retreat to the corner. The TV crew fiddles about noisily, coiling cables, pushing the throne chair, conversing with the heralds and looking at the insignia (lifting it, testing it in secret, stealing glances at Terra and being hindered by ones that are more serious).*

*Terra and the Orderly approach the foreground.*

Orderly: They ordered me to report it immediately.

Terra: Good. Where is? Ah, there! (*To the director*) Don't hurry, I might still need them.

Director: stop, stop, stop...

Terra to (male) Secretary: Please convey the following request to my wise brothers. They should blow their nose, comb their hair and put on clean institutional clothing. The prisoner should put on the medals. Nonsense, of course I mean it the other way around. Repeat!

Secretary: The prisoner shall appear in clean condition. The revered Sages may put on their medals.

Terra: Make it quick! (*Secretary exits.*) Terra, to himself: This is the opportunity. (*To the team*) Gentlemen, I ask for a moment's patience. You will soon be witnesses of a historic moment. (*To the director*) Well, I still need the throne chair. Put it there! (*Points to the right*) Stagehands obey the wish.

B: This way?

Terra: Yes, good. (*To the Heralds*) Put your robes in order.

Herald: Very well. (*Fiddling with the robes. Helping each other.*)

Terra: Brush the coat or shake it, as you like...

Herald: Of course (*dealing with the coat*)

Ma.: Shouldn't I once more...

Terra: What?

Ma.: Retouch your appearance...

Terra: Nonsense...

Sec. *entering*: We are ready.

Terra: Show them in!

Orderly opens the right door. Two guards lead a man in. He wears clean blue-grey clothes. His hair is cropped short. Two men who look similar to Terra follow. They are in civilian clothes. The chest is paved with medals and a medal ribbon hangs around the neck. The resemblance to Terra must be striking, but not too strong.

Terra: My dear ones! I greet you, dear brothers. (Gives them his hand. To the prisoner.) You look clean. Although, you were brought to here in a disheveled state. (To all) Because these individuals resist a just arrest! Then they talk about our brutality. Do you know what kind of theses he spreads? Theses, despite their ridiculousness, are very dangerous! He speaks of the equality of men! (*Quiet laughter*) Yes, he is actually talking about it. Can you name a form of government or a political system where this absurd idea was brought into reality? Can you name a country, no matter what time, in which there were no social classes and no leading personality? Give me one example in human history and I will be grateful! Anyone who claims something like that must have the moral status of a pig! Stands morally just on the level of a sod! Wait, however, I'm going to turn you inside out! (*To the fellow wise men.*) What do you say about this human being, if one can still call this product of complex views a human being at all?

First Sage: Incredible!

Second Sage: Disgusting!

First Sage: It was high time.

Second sage: This leveler!

Terra: Yes, look at this leveler (*points to the prisoner*) look at him closely. There are several more of this kind.

First Sage: Unfortunately.

Terra: I suffer too. Given the timeliness of the incident. (*Takes one of the sages by the sleeve and drags him to the ramp, the other follows them.*) I would like you to personally... gently pull the worms out of his nose. We need everyone who is infected! All accomplices! ... Treat him as usual.

*The director waves to the TV crew to move backwards. Rolling their eyes and lifting their hands skyward, the team retreats to the background.*

Director: But please, please ... (*to the wise men and the prisoner*) … please to here gentlemen … if you please ... (*to the team*) … hop, hop ... a little faster ... (*to the wise men*) … please to here gentlemen ... chief Sage please also move a bit closer to them ... like that, yeah ... good ... very good ... overhead lighting on that guy... badass ... a gangster … he is supposed to look like a gangster.

Terra: The camera pans from me to the prisoner and back. Roger that? I will leave the details to your talent.

Ma.: We have to make up the prisoner and the respected gentlemen. You know, at least a little...

Terra: Why should I only endure everything. Of course, of course...

Director: Is something?

Terra: Make up the sod and my fellow brothers... (*To them*) I would like to see you in the role of victim for once.

First Sage: How can you be so malicious (*laughs*).

Prisoner: No (*screaming*) No!

Terra: We will see.

*Several guards rush in to hold the prisoner down. Their gray block glues the man to the chair. Attempts are made to clean him and make him up. Two newly added make-up artists (Ma.) are by now dealing with the sages. Clear contrast in the treatment.*

Ma. *to the prisoner*: Be good darling. Nothing will happen to you. Keep still! (*To Terra*) It doesn't work like that ... I can't possibly work like that...

Terra: A syringe!

*The prisoner resists desperately. The TV crew stands there waiting. You only hear the wheezing and groaning of the wrestlers. A guard comes in with a vial, slides up the prisoner's sleeve, and administers the syringe. Everything is done in a very complicated way according to the situation.*

Terra: Well?

Ma.: He's getting calmer. (*Gets to work*) It works. If that's not progress ... well ... well ... yeah, like that ... like that ... now he's looking more like a cur ... (*stepping back*) … satisfied?

Terra: Yes.

Director: Please get back to your seats!

*The guards retreat. The wise men sit on either side of the prisoner. Terra puts on the crown. The heralds hang the cloak around him, this time yellow in color. Terra takes the throne. Bright bluish stage light. Warm yellow rays fall from the fly loft to enfold Terra.*

Director: Attention ...

Terra: We can ...

Director: Recording!

Terra: The man – with who's pitiable sight I have to bother you - is a traitor to the people. I do not want to mention the number of his offenses nor their nature. There could be young people among the viewers who would suffer moral damage as a result. So, I shall not try. Of course, I could call him a poor stray, a stray sheep, if I wanted to, but his crimes are too great. We will try to put him on the right path, taking into account his battered soul. It's always terrible for me when I see a man destroying himself. (*Addresses the wise*) I commend this unfortunate case to you, building on your experience. Treat him with the utmost consideration. That is my personal request to you. I know it's unnecessary, but I say it anyway. I do know only too well the quality of their therapeutic treatment and therefore I have complete confidence in them. I know that, as always, they will proceed with consideration and gentleness. He will enjoy all the comforts with us. There is no doubt about it. I can clearly see your indignant faces now, your fists raised, I hear you shouting: Get rid of that sputum! However, it is not our job to avenge crime with crime, no, we want to heal and help. Therefore, repress your anger, lock it up in the most secret corners of your heart. Forget it! We will bring him back into the human community. I thank you.

*The lamps go out. The made-up people get cleansed. A sense of new beginnings.*

*Terra; he has discarded his crown and is dragging his cloak*: We must … his buddies ... by any means... as gently as ... (*louder*) you know, dear sir, gently.

First Sage: I got it.

Second Sage: You can't tolerate that. See you soon. (*Exeunt*) *The TV crew is also about to leave.*

Orderly: Any further orders?

Terra: No.

Orderly leaves with a stiff salute.

Terra: I got rid of two dogs. (*Rings.*)

Poet, entering: My wisest one!

Terra: Record the interrogation immediately! That is between us! Roger that?

Poet: I am ...

Terra: Hurry! That is more important than what your cerebellum allows you to dream.

Poet: Yes (*exeunt*)

Terra: The word "gentle" could be heard by all ... Torture! A cabinet of horrors! Potential sadists! Behind their clean façade ... I'm being deceived ... such devilry behind my back!

Poet: Things are going!

Terra: Good. They are ... I trip over them too often. You carry them around like rubbish ... Don't you? ... Did you say what?

Poet: I don't give a damn.

Terra: They became an albatross, nothing else.

Poet: That is clear.

Terra: The damn makeup. The stuff sticks. I have to wash up. I place great trust in you; (*goes away*).

Poet: Asshole.

Sec entering: Be careful!

Poet: I don't give a damn.

Sec: Please!

Poet: Your affection makes me strong. I could yell!

Sec.: In the kennel?

Poet: It doesn't have to be very loud.

*Sec laughs.*

Poet: You're laughing again! I like to see you laugh. Yes, I like to see you laugh. By the way, did you know that this is the only room without bugs?

Sec: Bugs?

Poet: Yes, bugs.

Sec.: Ah, bugs. I didn’t even think of that.

Poet: Could I talk like this otherwise?

Sec: I didn’t even think about that. We have a little time...

Poet: I don’t just love your body, I love you!

Sec.: Quiet, it’s so easy to talk ... did you … put … on the line?

Poet: The part I have been waiting for! However, judging by your upbringing, it should honor you.

Sec: Cynic!

Poet: First, we need a healthy basis.

Sec: Base.

Poet *gently embracing her*: Calm, serenity... laugh!

Sec.: How nice you say that.

Poet: Keep your head cool; otherwise, your head will go for a walk alone.

Sec.: I will...

Poet: Pull yourself together!

Sec: Yes.

Poet: You women are natural talents. You all are.

Sec: Me? Do you think I’m pretty?

Poet: More than I can prove at moment.

Sec: Do you like my makeup?

Poet: Could be more decent.

SEC: Terra wishes it to be so.

Poet: That will pass. Without hormone injections, he is half a man. You confirm him.

Sec: Me?

Poet: That is your most important function.

Sec.: I don't want to anymore...

Poet: I say we must (*with a sharp voice*) and you will hold out, my poor little sacrificial lamb. Me at mine and you at your post.

Sec.: Everyone at their ... we're actually gloriously banned.

Poet: That's us.

Sec.: But... he doesn't have anything... besides, Terra is a nice name, or don't you like it? I mean he has something.

Poet: Terra. Do you know his real name? Aloysius Hundsburger. Simply Aloysius Hundsburger!

Sec: That is very sobering. It is ... but will it ... no, I never thought of that. One more question … will it really go well?

Poet: That's almost a hundred percent clear.

Sec: I trust you... and hope...

Poet: I think he is coming.

*Terra enters*: My little poet ... yes, what did I want to tell you? Oh yes, your presence is not required. Have a pleasant time. You will find something else to do. Afterwards ... we will see.

*Poet exits with a silent bow.*

Sec.: The children have to arrive in a few minutes.

Terra: Yes, yes, the provincial grimaces want to look at me. See the wise man once in a lifetime. Nice what? The cute little rascals with the tiny snub noses and the red apple cheeks ... you get sentimental straight away. (*Strokes the sec.'s face briefly*) I like children. Yes, that is a weakness of mine. They also increase popularity ... I like to mix business with pleasure.

Sec: Always?

Terra: Almost always. Sit there (*points left*); yes.

*He takes a seat behind the desk. Rings a bell. Chirping, hoarse shrilling.*

Orderly: Is it time, my chief Sage?

Terra: Let the buds go to the gardener ... let the kids in.

Orderly: At your command. (*Away*)

Terra *to sec.*: How is the poet, actually? He seems bland, is he stupid? Or is he faithful? Or is he both? That would be a good mix.

Sec: Loyal!

Terra: Is he stupid?

Sec.: A lion...

Terra: Excuse me?

Sec: Totally committed. He's attached... attached to you with a naive love.

Terra: So stupid. I like impartial people. Where are the kids?

Sec: You're impatient!

Terra: You? Oh, ... but from now on please call me by my title, my angel ... and I ask you to keep it that way in the future ... namely in public ... or when other people are nearby ...

Sec: Excuse me my chief Sage.

Terra: Not so formal ... keep mediocrity! … I need powers I can trust. The poet... are you certain, he is good?

Sec: Absolutely.

*Guard entering, at attention*: The children ask to be received! (*From afar singing*.)

TERRA, *with exaggerated enthusiasm*: Where are they? (*Rising*) … where are the tots? (*Strictly to sec*.) Is everything ready?

Sec: How? Oh yes, just now, yes.

*The children march in, in stiff columns of two. They bandaged their mouths with white cloths. The cloths stretch tightly over lips and noses and are knotted at the nape of the neck. Uniform clothing. All of the children's sounds, including the poem, are broadcast from a loudspeaker. (Louder than average.) They sing the following hymn, which only ends after they have squared in front of Terra. Two austere, dry women in austere garb command the children with nervous hand gestures and buck every time they believe they are in Terra's perspective. Terra nods, seemingly touched, throughout the whole thing.*

The Anthem:

Oh, my wisest one.

Oh, you clever one.

Oh oh oh oh.

Oh you my all sort of things.

Lovely child-shawm.

Oh oh oh oh.

And we believe in you.

Life and death is

just oh oh oh...

A boy with a bouquet of flowers in his hand steps forward. Monotonous droning from a speaker (sound may fluctuate).

Let the rays of your grace

don't pass us by.

Let, oh wisest of all

Not leave us just in the dark

Let' ... let' ... (crying from the loudspeaker)

*The governess takes the bouquet and hands it over to Terra.*

Vitriolic, to the child: Fool!

Terra: The excitement... (*Pats the boy.*) It's okay ... that's understandable... (*The boy follows the teacher's outstretched hand and finds his place again.*)

Teacher: Please...

Terra, *with a majestic wave of the hand*: Not at all ... psst ... (*turning the flowers around*)... picked for me? ... very good ... (*to sec.*) Aren't they cute? (*Gives the flowers to the sec.*)

Sec: Very!

Terra: You are adorable children! Do you want chocolate? (*clapping*) Where's the chocolate?

Servant (*entering*): Certainly, Sir … the chocolate.

Terra: And a lot of it … (*timid laughter from the speaker*) … all must be taken care of by your wisest. What are you holding in your hand?

Child, *timidly (very loudly)*: A whistle...

Terra: May I? Or do you not allow it? (*He whistles*) Good sound. Does it always sound this good?

Child, shy (*very loudly*): Yes, wisest.

Terra: So awesome ... but I would not have acted any differently if I were you. No, not at all differently. I'm full of joy... Why? Because you love me … because we all love each other. Nevertheless, that has to be the case ... but I can also be strict. With such obedient children, of course not ... do you always follow the instructions of the teachers?

Children: We are soooo nice.

*Child with a sweet child's voice, delightfully, cheeky*: We are the goody-two-shoes of them all!

Terra, *laughing*: So young and already so smart. When I was that big (*points towards the height*) I played with tin soldiers, piff, puff...

Children: We want to be good soldiers.

Terra: That's clear... and shoot the enemies of the fatherland, right? Boom... away with them. Are you laughing? The sun rises on your faces, my poet would say. Poets always say something like that. (*Angry*) Where is the chocolate? Right away, dear ones.

*Servant enters. He distributes chocolate from a large basket among the children, who bow silently, like marionettes. After receiving the treat, they stand there rigidly.*

Terra: How that tastes, hmm. Now I have to take care of the welfare of the State again. Off you go! March in rows of two! (*Snaps his fingers.*)

Teacher: It was a great honor for us, oh chief Sage. You have greatly supported our pedagogical efforts with the reception.

Terra: You have given me great pleasure.

*All but one of the children walk off singing the anthem. The servant follows them.*

Child, *in a normal tone*: Your autograph, please!

Terra: For once (*writes*) ... but only to you. (*Slaps the child at its butt. The child runs after the others but is caught halfway by the teacher and dragged to the group. The door is closed.)*

Terra to Sec: How was I? Well, right?

Sec: Very.

Terra: Do you love children?

Sec: Of course.

Terra: Good show, don't you think?

Sec: You've outdone yourself.

Terra: That's hardly possible.

Sec: Yes.

Terra: Can't you disagree? You just nod ... I am for obedience but sometimes you might disagree. You are free to do that.

Sec: It's a bit much...

Terra: I understand your confusion...

Sec: It's something ...

Terra: It's best if you relax a bit ... send me the dreamer in!

Sec: Is he one?

Terra: Temporarily.

*Sec off.*

Terra: The two roast on the spit of my love.

*Sec enters with poet.*

Poet: My Sage! I heard that your humble self...

Terra to the sec.: You should not spill everything! (*Threatening jokingly.*) Besides, I have not said anything specific yet...

Sec.: Sorry, I thought ...

Terra: So, you thought. Coincidentally, you have guessed correctly. (*To the poet.*) My dear friend, I place my trust in you to an even greater degree than I have until now. From now on, you take over the responsibility for my personal protection. It is more of a formality. I would also like to entrust you with a position in the Ministry of State Security, but that is not yet up-to-date, the post is still occupied ... I am also raising you to the rank of staff officer with the appropriate privileges and dues ... yes, that would be all.

Poet: Your grace kills me. I hope I am up to the task.

Terra: Good. Time will tell. (*To the sec.*) You can freshen up. (*Sec off.*) You are surprised at my confidence, but I have no complications with you ... you are loyal to the idea. I do hear only good things about you. Not that anyone could harm me, but I do need people I can rely on 100%.

Poet: I hope to justify your trust. I am fully aware of the responsibility.

Terra: What about the prisoner?

Poet: He lies flat.

Terra: So fast?

Poet: He had a delicate constitution.

Terra: Sorry. Sad and mean. Where is the recording?

Poet: On the spot (*goes to the door, opens it and drags in a suitcase-sized machine. It can certainly look a bit utopian due to the protruding bunches of wire and antennae*) Please!

Terra: You faithful soul!

Poet: I am just doing my duty.

Terra: Of course, you do hear and see what I want...

Poet: And love what you love.

Terra: I almost want to call you a little brother.

Poet: Shall I let the voices dance?

Terra: Quick, I want to hear the male dogs barking.

Poet: They will suffocate in their own poison...

*He handles the phone. A squeaking that unpleasantly drags through the room. (It must be embarrassing for the listener.) The poet plays for a while, looking for the right note, the sound changes a few times accordingly. Then voices that slowly gain clarity. These voices are getting louder and softer, sometimes coming from behind the auditorium, sometimes from the side. In between, exaggerated panting.*

1st Sage: We shall treat you gently. That is the opposite of gentle. In our language at least. We do custom work. It's about our existence. (*clapping*).

Terra: In their language...existence.

2nd Sage: We'll squeeze you like a lemon. Wise Brother wants you to chatter ... and you will, you cretin. We want names, names ... nothing else. It's so simple. First names and surnames. Not more.

Prisoner, *indistinctly*: I don't know anything ... no, no, no ... (*The screaming turns into a gurgle that is very loud but soon dies down to an indefinable noise*.)

Terra: What? They make fun of me!

1st W.: We are not petty … (*very loud whimpering*) … increase the pressure! … (*Buzzing, both dies down*)

2nd W.: Gently, my dear, we'll kill him ... well, little one, do you know the torture of a hundred days? ... look at the store of pretty toys ... all at your service ... (clank of metal) … so spit it out … (*you hear the sound of a drill.*)

Terra: A meanness.

Poet: Incredible.

1st W.: Open your eyes! The middle ages and modern times do meet here. Lots of ticklish nightmares. Renaissance methods anyone? On the other hand, something Chinese? A little good will and everything becomes a tool of torture. Finally open your mouth! (*Moan*) Fair enough? Well? All right? (*Roaring*) Do you like that better? I think he has something against electricity. (*Splashing*) Water refreshes my angel. Come on ... come on … (*clapping*) … your wish is our command and today is a sellout. Once you'll chatter, anyway. You‘re struggling for nothing. How he sweats!

2nd W.: Well? Shall we get tougher? It hurts us as much as it hurts you. We are no sadists! We are sensitive people. None of that would be necessary. We could have a nice chat with each other. A chat, from person to person. You don't seem to care that privileged people talk to you like that ... I almost speak like an equal ... (*whirring, roaring*) ... poor fingers ... but we have good doctors, they will put everything back together ... do you play the piano? … What?

1st W.: Does he play? ... That will be over ... oh that should be oiled ... anyway the dust ... that has to be cleaned again otherwise we will be sued for poor hygiene. (*Laughter*) ... the guy is stubborn...

2nd W.: A confession makes it easier ... you have a soft spot for such old things ... the method is too direct for me. I prefer electricity...

*The prisoner, inarticulate*: No ... I cannot say anything ... (*long howling*)

Terra: Turn off I am getting sick. Those rascals! (*Poet switches off the apparatus.*) What else did they do?

Poet: They worked themselves into a frenzy. Hence the fatal outcome.

Terra: These dogs! (*Rings.*)

Orderly: What can I do for you?

Terra: I want to see the judges right away.

Poet: They are waiting. Everything is prepared. The recording has been made available to all.

Terra: Good. The executioners!

Orderly: I go and open the door to the wise men, the judges, the executioners. (*Opens the middle door.*)

*The called come in in rows. The judges wear red gowns.*

Terra: I salute you, gentlemen.

All: Long live the wisest.

Terra (*approaching the captives, quickly*): You will atone for that! (*Both are dressed only in shirt and pants, one is wearing riding boots. Shirt collars are open. They are not tied.*) I gave specific orders to treat the prisoner gently. Before witnesses! That is a scandal! This is outrageous!

1st W, *screaming*: This is a plot!

Terra: What did you think?

1st W.: You ... you said softly as always.

Terra: Right. Gentle as always.

2nd W.: Exactly, as always. If you drag this into the public eye, you will suffer the most, ha...

Terra: That's a real cheek! (*Roaring*) That is an absolute impertinence!

1st W.: You know the methods very well, you have yourself ...

Terra: What? This is the outright impudence! Can you find words for that?

2.W.: With your approval...

Terra: You want to mock me? What becomes of good civil servants when they are given free rein? They become murderers!

1st W.: But we have been dealing with the issue for a long time, and by joint decision ...

Terra: For a long time? For a long time? ... Maybe for years? ... Moreover, I am clueless! ... tsss ... no idea ... don't know anything about it ...

2nd W.: That is a mean thing! I object! I will prove...

Terra: What are you raising? Objection? (*To the guards*) Shut him up!

1st W.: You cursed sod!

*The mouths of the two get stuffed with white cloths.*

*They wrestle with the guards, to no avail.*

Terra: Who would have come up with such an idea? That goes against common sense! A torture chamber in our basement. Something you have to picture! This is incomprehensible! I am certainly to blame for my credulity. Did you, however, know? We have criminals among us! Did you know that? Such a crime! What impression do we make on the people? For my part, I did not know anything. I can only hope that you too have a clear conscience. (*Sharp voice*) I can only hope so! The death sentences signed by our government are regular. However, torture, Gentlemen, torture! Unbelievable! I cannot believe it! (*To the poet*) Do you have the headlines for the press yet?

Poet: Yes, please. (*Pulls a note from his coat pocket.*) The trust of the chief Sage betrayed in the most shameful way! No one knows the names of everyone involved! Will more heads roll?

Terra: That comes in bold! Do you understand, Gentlemen?

Poet: Please calm down!

Terra: I still cannot believe the horror! Undermine my authority! Do beasts surround me?

Poet: Calm down!

Terra, *to the judges*: Do you still need evidence? What is your decision?

Chief Justice: The case is clear. You are doomed you two wise men!

2nd Judge: Your guilt weighs like a rope...

Terra: The verdict?

Chief Justice: Death by hanging.

2nd Judge: You will be hung by the neck until death occurs.

*First wise man after desperate efforts tears himself free, flees into a corner, sinks to his knees and screams*: This is madness. You cannot do that to us ... stop the comedy! (*To the audience*) You have to stop... please ... that's it ... (*the guards circle him*)... don't you dare touching me!... (*jumping up, roaring imperiously*). You don't seem to know who I am! (*The guards pounce on him at Terra's motion*). Let go, that is a command; (*his mouth shuts up*).

Terra: Thank you. Disgusting. There will be investigations that are more rigorous. Embarrassing. Thank you.

*The two wise men are dragged out. At the door, the guards silently bow to Terra. The judges, other wise men and executioners form in rows of three and follow with dignity. Also a silent bow. The orderly closes the door from the outside.*

Terra: Two less and still too many.

Poet: You could rationalize that.

Terra: You could do that ... use your imagination … we need crimes and accomplices ... (*pushing a bell; sad buzzing sounds*). This has to go (*points to two photos; to the entering servant*). Put these photos away! Those two there.

Servant: These people?

Terra: Yes, the dead ones. Off to the junk room.

Poet: To the coming corpses.

Terra: You got me.

*Servant takes the pictures and their laurel wreaths from the wall and sneaks out.*

Poet: May I congratulate you?

Terra: Not yet, that's just...

Poet: The beginning.

Terra: Right. One should not count the chickens before they hatch.

Poet: I admire you.

Terra: And I am hungry. (*Looks at the clock.*) Dinnertime! Where is the chef?

Knocks. The chef, an inviting person, enters: You...

Terra: Why are you only coming now?

Chef: Sorry, I didn't mean to disturb you. It was such heavy traffic ...

Terra: Oh...

Chef: ... and I didn't want to disturb you. What does my chief stage desire to dine?

Terra: What do I want to eat? I'd like mushrooms, foie grass, tartar sauce... you know, savory, please. Yes and burgundy wine. Fruit for dessert and... well, you already know that.

Chef: Of course (*drops a curtsy; off*).

Terra: Do you actually eat as well?

Poet: Sometimes... intermittently...

Terra: When?

Poet: When time permits.

Terra: The philosopher is scheduled for audience. His name is Plato. Do you know him?

*The food is brought in on silver platters.*

Poet: Yes, that's one of them too...

Terra: Leave that now. Let's move on to something happier.

Poet: Please.

*Terra nervously poking around in his plate*: Where are the celery roots?

Chef: Sorry, immediately (*off*)

Terra: Celery roots ... do you love celery roots?

Poet: I love them very much.

*The salad is brought in.*

Terra: Cooked in that way as well?

Poet: Very tasty.

Terra *with a full mouth*: If you have bread, you will find a knife. (*Chews*) Isn't it? (*To the poet, who has sat down in some distance; not too far away.*) Do you like as well?

Poet: If I may ask.

Terra: There (*reaches his hand to the plate and swings a large piece of liver at the Poet. It almost has to be thrown and should not be a prop. Poet catches it with both hands.*)

Poet: Thank you.

Terra: Do you like it?

Poet: Excellent!

Terra: I value good food!

Poet, *bolting*: Excellent!

Terra: What? … Yes …

Poet: Excellent indeed!

Terra: That's what you said already ...

*They speak. One does not understand anything because of the smacking and chewing noises. That must not take too long.*

Terra: And that ... (*throws again*).

Poet: Thank you!

Terra: How do you like the position?

Poet, *swallowing*: Very much.

Terra: How do you like the post?

Poet: How?

Terra: How do you like the post?

Poet: A good job. Well worth a prince to cope with it ... between child rhetoric and being a man, murder ... he lies there as a greedy youngling.

Terra: You piglet. There. (*Hands him a bite.*)

Poet: Too kind.

Terra: You know my dear ... it beats the... nothing beats eating regularly. Almost all of modern man's ailments are due to an irregular diet. Gastritis, heartburn and other stomach complaints ... there you have it (*now Terra actually throws and the poet has to catch*) ... have their origins in an irregular and wrong diet.

Poet, *munching*: Sure.

Terra: Have that (*slowly hands him a piece*).

Poet: Thank you.

Terra: A sound mind in a sound body. One must not gobble the food or eat it too hot or too cold. The organism suffers.

Poet: Sure.

Terra: Exactly. The sauce is superb. You certainly have to taste it. There, you have the rest. (*Gives him the plate*).

Poet, *licking*: Very delicious ...

Terra: Just lick. Do you like it?

Poet: More than good.

Terra: How about the philosopher?

Poet: Plato is one ... thank you (*puts the plate back*) ... of those who are thrown out the door and march in again at the window.

Terra (*wiping his mouth*): What does he want?

Poet: Spreading his ideas...

Terra: What ideas?

Poet: The same ones that our system is based on. He just has no power.

Terra: Powerless tyrants are jokers. Does he breed mice?

Poet: Mice?

Terra: Or rabbits, or dogs...

Poet: Dogs?

Terra: He could bully them. As dogs or mice king.

Poet: I ... I don't think so.

Terra: Then you can't help him. (*Rings the bell. Very euphonious and rich sound.*) That tasted good. (*To the entering chef*) You have outdone yourself. My compliments.

Chef: Thank you. (*Clears the table together with servants.*)

Terra: I'll ask Mr. Plato.

Servant: As our chief sage wishes. (*off*).

*A requesting "please" from the anteroom. Plato enters. He wears a long robe. A kind of Greek dressing gown. His demeanor is nervous.*

Plato, *theatrically*: I salute you Sage. I applaud the regime and bow down. Oh, my apprentice (*approaching Terra*). Still you make mistakes, yes still.

Terra: Is he drunk? What do you want?

Plato, *laughing bitterly*: The pupil denies the teacher ... such is the world!

Terra: What is wrong with him?

Poet: Offended need for recognition.

Terra: I cannot console him. So what the hell does he want?

Plato, *whispering*: My congratulations ... my warmest congratulations ...

Terra, *mimicking*: What joy, what joy... (*with a sharp voice*) ... What are you congratulating me on?

Plato singing: Healthy children, regular life. The people bow before the state and the state is wise.

Terra: And you want to share the cake?

Plato: Snacking? I only understand "cake".

Poet: You got the idea. However, the crowd has to kowtow and for us you belong to the crowd. There would be otherwise many applicants.

Monotonous voice: But since the guards are supposed to be the best, don't they have to be best guarded?

Terra: That's right.

Monotonous voice: All of you in the state are brothers, so we will tell, but the educating God mixed gold at birth with all of you who are capable of ruling, which is why those are also the most honored ...

Terra: Dead right.

Monotonous voice: Yes, it's just like you say. In our state, too, we have subordinated the helpers like dogs to the rulers as shepherds of the state.

Terra: Good!

Monotonous voice: But it is up to the founders of the state to know the forms in which the poets should tell sagas and which no poem may violate, but they do not have to write sagas themselves.

Terra: I am for censorship. (*To the poet*) That goes to you.

Voice: So, obviously, we must first supervise the writers of legends and accept a beautiful legend that they write and reject an ugly one. Nevertheless, we will persuade the wet nurses and mothers to tell to the children the accepted legends and to educate their souls through the legends even more than what educates their bodies through their hands. So, are we going to allow the boys to hear common legends and legends invented by common people, which are planting ideas into their souls; contrary to what we think they should hear when they grow up? We won't.

Terra to Plato: What else have you to say?

Plato: Mistakes have been made ...

Terra: Every ideal suffers in its realization. You have to consider human weakness.

Poet: We thank you and give you the reward of the wise. Our boredom and nothing else. Not even our hate! Thanks!

Terra: Leave with applause!

Plato: I thought you, the noblest...

Terra: You think we act. A (*to the poet*) what? ...

Poet: Ideal complement.

Terra: There you have it. I was very happy...

Plato: I ...

Terra: Should I call the guards?

Plato: Not the guards, not the guards. This is beneath my dignity; (*bucks backwards*).

Terra: So, that got rid of him.

Poet: Yes, forever I hope.

Terra: People are incredibly annoying.

Poet: Yes, they are.

Terra: I'm taking a nap now. The morning was exhausting. It's best for you to rest too. By the way, what did the philosopher write?

Poet: The State.

Terra: Well, well...

Poet: The state or the ideal dictatorship. It comes down to the same thing.

BREAK

The following scene does not necessarily have to be recorded in one piece from beginning to end.

*Stage as first. Poet sits very close towards the center of the desk. Terra emerges from the private chambers. He seems relaxed.*

Poet: Did you rest well, oh chief sage?

Terra: Thanks, it has worked; (*pulls a cigarette out of his breast pocket*). Please, give me a light.

Poet: Please; (*hands him a lighted match*).

Terra: Thank you (*inhales*).

*There is a knock on the right door.*

Terra: This constant knocking drives you crazy. In!

*Male Secretary enters*: The censors threw us a play...

Terra: What is it again?

Secretary: Sorry. The censors handed a play over to us. The question is whether to warn the author, revoke his license or arrest him immediately. The department thinks the man is dangerous, but wants to leave the decision up to you. I myself dare not judge and ...

Terra *to Poet*: That's within your competence.

*Secretary gives the poet the manuscript.*

Terra: My decision is rest! The days pass in haste, one like the other. Roger that?

Secretary: Yes; (*stops waiting*).

Poet: The subject?

Secretary: An old couple arguing.

Terra: It can't be that wild.

Sec.: It depends on the perspective.

Poet: One would have to see it.

Terra: That's an idea! Couldn't that be arranged? At least one Act, I believe.

Secretary: I am a member of an amateur theater. My humble hobby. I would be able to play that stuff. As an amateur, of course.

Terra: Would you be able? That's great! (*To the poet*); what do you say to that? At least that would be a change. (*To the secretary*) I didn't even know you were an artist.

Poet: We have enough time. There are no more appointments for today.

Terra: There you go! However, where do we get the old woman?

Secretary: That can be done.

Poet: Yes, the censorship department has its own department for actors.

Secretary: You check the text just like the other censors. It's just about word painting or onomatopoeia.

Poet: It is about whether plays contain words or passages that could be treacherously emphasized. Like cabaret, you know.

Terra: Then the problem is solved. Have the scenes already been taught-in?

Secretary: I know the beginning by heart. The negative side of it captivated me. The colleague playing the old women could keep the script.

Terra: I'm a musical person. Fine, get what you need. (*Secretary exits with a bow.*)

Terra: I haven't needed fun like that for a long time. In addition, from time to time it is necessary for a head of state to intervene personally in literary intellectual life. Don't you think so?

Poet: That is very good.

Terra: I have good judgment in this regard.

Poet: I am convinced of that.

*Noise from the right. A small shabby podium is pushed in. It rolls loudly in the middle of the stage.*

Secretary *screaming*: I still need a small table - shabby please - two armchairs, also shabby, bottle of wine - half full please - a water glass, leftover chicken, a plate, the former cleaning lady!

Terra: Cleaner!

Secretary: In the play, of course.

*What was desired is brought in. A dirty tablecloth has further been added. The secretary dictates everything into place.*

Terra: Do you know that in China, there were plays in honor of certain river gods?

Poet: Why?

Terra: To cheer them up.

Secretary: No, no tablecloth!

Terra: Where is the old woman? Do we even have old employees?

Secretary: Wait a minute. Where's the chicken … chicken bones please! (*A servant exits.*)

Terra: It's going to be a folk play...

Secretary: I dare to doubt it...

Terra: A little rough humor, huh?

Secretary: I fear a...

Terra: You make me curious...

*Servant comes, the poor thing full of chicken scraps.*

Secretary: You've gone insane, a little bit.

Servant: A small one?

Secretary: Yes, a little. (*The secretary rips a piece out of what the servant holds in his arms and throws it on the table. The servant drops some remains, which he clumsily tries to pick up. More pieces slip out of his hands.*)

Secretary: Pick that up and get out!

*Colleagues help the servant ... get off the stage ... collecting.*

*An old woman enters; (abbreviated below as Be.). She resembles the cleaner in the first act.*

Be.: There I am. Striving old bones. You have funny ideas. However, it's an honor... an honor...

Secretary: You will play an old hag and be a prima donna at the same time.

Be.: I'm old myself...

Secretary: There is her text (*gives her the script*).

Be.: But I can (*chuckles*)...

Secretary: You'll probably still be able to read ... where it says old, it's your turn.

Be. greasy curtsy: I'm honored (*chuckles*).

Secretary: You are a born heroine.

Terra: Is that possible? How low a human can sink. Is she really part of our staff? Fired immediately!

Secretary: You should take a closer look. (*Laughing heartily to the cleaner.*) You are unbeatable.

Be. *pulls off a flexible, incredibly natural rubber mask from her face and reveals herself to be a young woman (pretty). With graceful fresh voice*: Long live our chief Sage. Please forgive me the little joke. I beg your pardon; (*folds her hands affectionately*).

Terra: That's an enchanting surprise! You'd still have to be punished.

Secretary: Indeed, she should. You will give us a double sample of your talent as punishment. You will be punished to play an old cleaner playing an old cleaner. From now on, you are a nonprofessional. Did you understand?

Actress: I think so and I suppose so.

Secretary: I'm just getting ready a bit.

Terra, *to the actress*: How did you come up with this adorable gag?

Actress: I should look as real as possible. That was a test.

Terra: Still, I'm relieved. It's a pity that you have to play an old woman. In addition, in … in a quasi-double role.

Actress: It won't take long. After that, I'll be entirely at your disposal.

Terra: I'll get back to that.

*Secretary approaches the middle of the stage. Thinning white wig ... rosy scalp shimmering through ... wrinkled white face ... an old jacket.*

*Those present laugh.*

Terra to the actress: Your dearest husband!

Actress: Unfortunately. One moment; (*puts on the mask*). We do harmonize better that way. (*To the secretary*): Are you sticking to your punishment?

Secretary: Yes.

*Cleaner/Actress/Be., with a still young voice*: Don't you think the piece suffers as a result?

Secretary: Since when are you so squeamish?

Be., still youthful: Well, as you wish.

*Secretary (old man) takes the cleaner by the hand and leads her to the podium*: Here is your place. (*Be. sits down stiffly and stares straight ahead.*)

Secretary: Sloppy, sleazy, more real ... but don't acknowledge it ... in either role.

Be.: No. (*The last juvenile word.*) What kind of life is it ... I would have preferred a juicy life ... (*stops*) ... a juicy roast (*stops*) ... you're your Highness ... what an un ... unfortunate coincidence that just me, just me has ended up here ... (*collects herself*) ... am ...

Secretary: Next!

Be.: ... and not through my own fault ... not really not ... no nobody can say that ... the e ... the evolution ... the ... (*to the secretary*) is that what it's called? I can't read that ... no ... really stupid ... sorry (*chuckles*). Evolution has bypassed me. (*To the secretary*) Right? And I'm old without having gotten old. That's only on the outside ... old age only sits on the outside. And I'm ... actually … just young ... just aged young. I'm (*moving with the finger down the line*) huh? ... just an old child ... stupid (*to the secretary*) ... sorry, I can't do that ... an old child who doesn't want to see the fact ... the superiors, yes, they can ... age ... but it is also ... made easy for them ... (*removing the mask to the secretary*) ... how am I?

Secretary: Miserable!

Terra: But please.

Actress: He's right. But the role...

Secretary: I'll accept that as a rehearsal ... but briefly, the scene. Please, may I just a moment (*takes the manuscript from the actress' hand*) Yes, there. (*To Terra, the poet, and to the audience.*)

*Room in the middle of which is a decrepit table at which an elderly couple is sitting. It's surrounded by a cheap, seedy establishment. The man is gaunt, the dry bones covered with bloated skin of a drunkard. The woman is a flabby lump of fat. She really doesn't have any female forms anymore but is just a plump something that grows fat in all directions. She pushes the remains of a chicken between her glossy lips. A glass of wine is in front of the man. He stares gloomily ahead. Either in the glass or past it. His movements melt away staggering after wasting languid energy. No matter how hopeful the beginning, concentration soon wanes and becomes blurred. (In brackets; like pigeons mating, i.e., without staying power. Bracket closed.) Bright lighting. Bright light falls on the podium.*

Terra: That doesn't sound very funny.

*The rest of the stage sinks into darkness. Actress puts on the mask.*

Secretary to the operator: There you have it; (*gives her the script*).

Be.: Thank you; (*curtsy, as far as possible in a sitting position*).

Secretary, softly: Eat them!

*Be. holds the chicken bones in front of his face.*

Secretary, *hissing*: Eat them!

Be.: Excuse me (*to the audience*) I can't do that spontaneously, although I was an educated woman...

Secretary: Stick to the text!

Be.: Excuse me (*curtsy again*).

*Secretary, in the role of the old man*: How she gulps. No wonder if she's strong, she can eat ... yes, yes ... just gobble ... (*to her*) wipe your mouth! (*Quietly as secretary*) the bone in the mouth! Pinch, suck!

Be., *startled*: Immediately ... (*tracing a line with her index finger*) Woman, ... no (*safer*) as soon as I'm done.

Secretary: My God, how she eats (*drinks*) it's so disgusting when you can't swallow a bite yourself.

B: Hmm?

Secretary: And her fat hands, her poor fat hands, even if they had nice fingers ... they wouldn't attract me anymore ... no, not in the slightest ... but like that, the worn-out cripples, even if it was work, does that make them prettier? Not a bit! Don't eat so loud!

Be.: The melting one to her husband...

Secretary: You don't need to read that ... da capo ... again ... don't eat so loud!

Be., defiant: It tastes good!

Secretary: Is that why you must insult me? (*Drinks*) Lovely little paws she had back when the world was green ... why do I always think of lovely hands? ... I was once a human. Yes, even a wise man. Yes, yes, I was actually human. I believe it ... that I was like that back then ... hard to believe. You don't even chase an old dog in this rain, in this darkness, in this eternally pouring rain. Before it rained so, so gray and incessant, the sky was charmingly clear. You didn't see the smallest cloud ... but what should she do other than eat? It's not her fault that it all turned out like this. No, she is not to blame for this twilight.

She was sharp as fresh horseradish back then ... but the years. The years are bad buddies. You desecrated the bitch. And the humidity. The rising humidity has caused them to swell. Yes, one would have to be rich, dull, and eternally young.

Be.: That would be a bargain …

Secretary: You're throwing me off!

Be.: Sorry.

Secretary: Dying slowly is mean (*drinks*).

Be., *chewing*: Do you think I'll die faster?

Secretary, *ignoring the remark*: A unique vulgarity.

Be.: Watch out for the tablecloth!

Secretary: Where is it?

Be, *angrily*: In the laundry, where else?

Secretary: Wash, wash, wash ... everything has to be washed. The moon, the stars, the carcass of a dog, the roofs, the walls, the people. Permanently cleaning up to complete wear. Just wash! But when you wash out your bin, don't be under any illusions, it'll stay greasy.

Be.: You old rotter!

*Terra laughs affectedly.*

*Actress takes up the mask and bows in his direction.*

Secretary: The imperfection is perfect. We want to live in eternal perfection - perfection from our point of view. So, no plague, no ailments, no dictatorship, no old age, no death, no hunger, no taxes, no natural disasters, no ugliness. Only one side is perfect for us. We deny any addition. The backside.

Be.: What are you complaining about? Wasn't I pretty?

Secretary: I didn't talk about that. If you're going to listen, you better listen, fatty! (*To himself*) from time to time she plays along ...

Be.: Fatty, fatty, ... once (*dreamily*) you were very nice.

Secretary: Oh you...

Be.: Besides, I don't understand that you men always have to lug the entire cosmos to here for some trivial thing, because of a stomach ache, for some ridiculous reason, because I eat and you hate eating. Strange.

Secretary: Weird? Very funny! And what are you carrying? Motherhood, prevented motherhood, forced motherhood, burdensome motherhood, Charité Centers, the eternal feminine, then roses, carnations, lavender and other weeds, the birds of the sky, plumes of clouds, rosy whispers, cockchafers, maggots, people, daughters and sons.

Be.: You were once very nice.

Secretary: Once is never and means nothing. Why can't we get out of our skin? Why don't we lie in a fragrant garden wrapped in a yellow sun? This twilight kills. Or do I already see badly? To be honest, my eyes have never been better.

Be.: You need glasses. Yes, you definitely need glasses! You've needed glasses all your life!

Secretary: Shut up!

Be.: You will never see properly. I didn't mean to hurt you, but it's the truth. I'm not saying that my eyesight is better.

Secretary: Didn't I say, shut up!

Be.: Yes, yes, calm down ... the old man has to ...

Secretary: This is for me!

Be.: Sorry.

*Secretary, stands up - stage directions; the old man must now take a book from the shelf and quote it.*

Terra, *impatient*: Carry on!

*Secretary gets up, fishes an imaginary book off the invisible shelf, blows away the dust and sits down: Watch out! (reads)*

Autumn winds have torn my mouth

I broke and flowed into the sluggish sewer sea

Lead is the color of light

that strangles the mountain of folds

and the sky laughs as if it hadn't seen anything

... but you don't care about that. (*Slams the book on the table. You hear the bang. Gets up and puts the book on the shelf. Coughs, blows the dust away.*)

Be., *chewing lazily*: What?

Secretary: You don't give anyone the slightest pleasure ... There (*blowing, dust everywhere, nothing but dust, runs his hand over the books and shows them to the Be.*) Is that okay?

Be.: Such poems lack the soothing sweetness ... (*turns to the next page of the script*). Sweet mouths should be poems, lips covered with foam. They shall sweeten the fog. You know that fog?

*Secretary fills the glass and laughs bitterly.*

Be.: Don't drink so much!

Secretary: Look at yourself!

Be.: A woman always has to look at herself ... I was once in the love temple of the heroes and I ... don't stare so stupid!

Secretary: Whore!

*Terra has jumped up. A thin, white ray falls from the rigging loft and attaches itself to him. He raises his hands like he has a submachine gun and aims at the secretary.*

*Terra, chases the sheaf across the old guy's body... Ratatatatat (or Brakakatatata). You can see Terra's shoulders shrug under the recoil. The old man staggers off his chair and falls flat under the force of death.*

Terra: That pig has deserved it.

Poet: Bravissimo

Secretary, *raising his head*: I'm finished.

*Everyone claps, applaud each other.*

Secretary: Should I continue?

Terra: Now I want to poison myself. Do what you can't resist. (*The beam of light suddenly goes blind.*)

Secretary, *bowing elegantly*: Thank you (*sits down*) ... that was not so ... it was meant to be so and it was not ... you are innocent ... nevertheless, it offends me ...

Be.: Those are old things...

Secretary: If you couldn't arrange it the way you wanted, certainly within the realms of possibility, if only real talent were at the helm ... charlatanry ... to hell's ass with it ... to eternally red hot blood farting hell's ass with it ... let them choke on their own vomit ... those bastards.

Be.: You're just jealous because you didn't get anywhere.

Secretary: Does that say anything? That says nothing in the least. Forget it ... I have proof, half the bookcase is full of my notes. But it does not matter. Look, billions of years from now, our "Eternal Values" won't matter at all.

Terra: I protest!

Secretary: This is the text. Pardon.

Terra: So, on (*to the poet*) Moral degeneracy!

Secretary: For now ... it's just habit that binds us...

Be.: Of course, I would be more interesting for you as a young woman.

Secretary: Yes, complain. I know the litany ...

Be.: That's the truth.

Secretary: How does that change the fact? Don't smack!

Be.: How else should you eat a chicken?

Secretary: Different or not at all. Don't choke on the bone!

Be., *mischievously*: Do you want me to save it for you?

Secretary: I know that your gums are firm ... you eat without dentures ... they are in the drawer, I do know that ...

Be., *chewing*: So, what, why are you crying?

Secretary, *yelling*: The bones!

B.: Oh...

Sec: Do you always have to remind me about my weaker gums?

Be.: Pure envy!

Secretary: No, disgust.

Be.: How did you first say it so beautifully theatrically? ... oh yes ... up the ass of hell with her ... in the eternally red hot, farting ass of hell with her ... wasn't that meant for me, kiddo? Yes, yes and still choking on your own vomit, my God you are cute.

Secretary: I spoke of charlatans.

Be: We wear each other down. The friction increases with indifference. We rub each other like we have sandpaper between us.

Secretary: Shut up!

Be.: Kill me! ... you feel ... (*turns the page*) my existence is a burden to you ... you gall my food, the air, my life ... you keep me dead silent, you almost only talk to yourself ...

Secretary: If you eat, yes...

Be.: Because you are ill and can no longer ... you can't even do that anymore ...

Secretary: Down!

Be.: You as well; (*minutes of silence*)

Terra *whispering*: What now?

Poet, *whispering*: An artificial break.

Terra: Waste of time.

Secretary: We live in the best of all worlds. Do you know how much I care about it? I don't give a fuck.

Terra (*jumping up, his chair falls over*): Outrageous!

*The lights come on, on the stage.*

*Secretary, taking off the white wig, with a slight bow*: Vulgar … a vulgar monstrosity.

Terra: Humans are not like that. They are not that trivial and selfish.

*Actress taking off her mask*: I think so too.

Terra, *to the Secretary*: What have they done to me?

Poet: Low-brow, vulgar monstrosities!

Terra: I can't find the words!

Actress: Me neither!

Poet: I wanted to say the same thing.

Terra: Isn't it? Even in the biggest shit there is no such tone. Humans must remain humans. Basta!

Actress: I don't give a fuck about roles like that. I only did it for you.

Terra: You were excellent, my dear, my compliments. (*To the secretary*:) And you too my dear.

Secretary: Thank you, it was only a modest achievement.

Poet to actress: You spoiled us. I'm literally floating.

Terra to the actress: Did you suffer a lot?

Actress: It's okay.

Terra: See you soon and thank you again.

Secretary, to the servants who enter: Take away the junk.

Actress: Goodbye.

Terra: Kiss your hand, madam. (*Secretary and actress exit*)

Poet, *to the servants*: A little faster, please!

Terra *to the poet*: Well, what do you say to that?

Poet: A salivation of human nature...

Terra: No trace of the beautiful and noble. Inner states! Can I afford that luxury? Nonsense!

Poet: Exactly.

Terra: What complications! I love clarity The state doesn't need people like that. These soul teasers and skinners can drive you nuts! The author needs to be locked away!

Poet: In addition, the structure was bad from a dramaturgical point of view. The performers must move, move, and move again. That's tradition. Whether it makes sense or not. The audience needs to see the director's work. This is so common.

Terra: Right!

Poet: In the epilogue, which I skimmed over briefly, it is said that the two still love each other.

Terra: More complications.

Poet: If I had covered the subject...

Terra: Yes?

Poet: … would initially be shown a nice, neat home. In front of it two elderly, well-groomed people seated at a modest but graceful table. Her white hair surrounded by the halo of purified calm.

Terra: Good!

Poet: The old people feast contemplatively and chat while doing so. The mother asks anxiously: How is our patron doing? We're so happy, but he ... meanwhile, the father: Which patron? ... This ignorance would be very humorous.

Terra: So, so.

Poet: So, the old man says: What patron? The old woman then: Well, him! The old man meanwhile: Which … him? I don't know any him! The old woman then: Well, our sage! The old man on the other hand: What? Which sage? The old woman soothingly: Well, ours, what else?

Terra: Isn't that a bit juicy?

Poet: Just a moment... The old man, self-satisfied: Ah, you mean him, he'll take care of us anyway.

Terra: Good. You just have to properly illuminate a topic.

Poet: It depends. Yes, and banners must be hung from the rigging loft - you know a favorite remedy - with aphorisms similar to: We have aged in the light of the wisdom of the wise one who has put our restless hands to rest. The reward of work is the fairest crown of old age ... or ... the heyday requires strong old men.

Terra: There should be a fair bit of success on the base. A few hearty but harmless jokes ... well, and so on ... that overlay the educational content.

Poet: Yes.

Terra: Take my burdens to your faithful heart for a few hours. My brain needs relaxation and the sweet sting of calm. A padded door will shut me off from the noise of life. Cotton in my ears makes me forget the singing of the air. How was it?

Poet: Pure poetry.

Terra: I'm chief art appraiser. Don't forget that!

Poet: I find you ...

Terra: Please, it wasn't entirely mine.

Poet: Still ...

Terra: We need pieces that sing about my wisdom, my absolute infallibility. I as a gigantic brain placed in this world. A brain that masters everything ... sympathy for the supreme sage, whose strong, fragile soul, defying all storms of fate, holds the rudder of the state firmly in his hand ... the divine task of course ... and so on... can you do that?

Poet: Nothing better than that.

Terra: Then police angels, men who defend our paradise with iron fists. Against the naked, women, children, and old people.

Poet: You really are a novelist manque.

Terra: Yes, I have talent ... I have ...

Poet: It is difficult to avoid this impression ...

Terra: I'm getting more and more sympathetic to you!

Poet: Thank you.

Terra: Not so formal, please. I also want to share my weaknesses with you. You are a poet. Hence a sensitive person. Can't you tell me something soul reviving for the night? Something that puts me to sleep.

Poet: You have blue eyes.

Terra: And?

Poet: You have bright eyes, like forget-me-nots boiled in milk.

Terra: Forget-me-nots cooked in milk? But, but compliments like that are paid to a woman.

Poet: You are my boss.

Terra: That's right again ... but do I actually have eyes like that?

Poet: It doesn't matter if it's a compliment.

Terra: Yes, yes, of course ... sure.

Poet: Do you want to hear anything else?

Terra: No, that's enough. I go to rest. The workload is overwhelming. Governing is no honey licking. I will sleep deeply. The cotton in my ears makes me forget the singing of the air; (*yawns*). Good evening; (*away*).

Poet: Likewise. (*Slouches behind the desk.*) It suits me. (*Hits the tabletop.*) Matches my complexion. The old idiot. The sentimental minx. The crow flies high and rests on a pig. One erects pyramids of rotting skulls. Another one writes a brilliant play and both go down in history. The consequence? You must stink skillfully. In whatever way. Whether as a skull pyramid builder, smelly skull pyramid builder of a smelly skull pyramid, or as a poet, as a poet of genius. You can do whatever you want, eternity, of course limited eternity, can only be achieved if you attract attention. Man grows through crime. That's crystal clear. And if it's just crimes against mediocrity...

*There is a knock at the right door*; Poet: Come in!

(Male) secretary: Excuse me... I wanted...

Poet: What do you want?

Secretary: A trivial matter, a signature... I...

Poet: Paper, what else?

Secretary: Nothing else.

Poet: Nothing else. So. Terra is sleeping. Have you seen a sleeping tyrant yet? Have you seen a snoring bully yet?

Secretary: No.

Poet: But it is not an uplifting spectacle.

Secretary: No.

Poet: Who do you serve?

Secretary: To the mightiest.

Poet: The actually most powerful or the most powerful as a concept?

Secretary: To the truly powerful.

Poet: I like you boy.

Secretary: I kiss your hand.

Poet: Soon ... (*bitter*) and only see these fingers in front of your eyes? (*Raises hand and spreads fingers.*)

Secretary: One recognizes the stars and follows them ... you know ... a flatterer must never lose his patience ...

Poet: Logically thought.

Secretary: The old universe gives birth in agony to new stars.

Poet: You change your opinion quickly.

Secretary: I don't have any.

Poet *stretching out his hand*: I sign!

Secretary: A distinctive handwriting.

Poet: Like that? ... Hm ... what do you say about my poetry?

Secretary: A full, yes!

Poet: Do you know any?

Secretary: Not exactly, but I'm totally on your side.

Poet: Very correct...

Secretary: It's an honor. I am your man.

Poet: If a horse had something to say, it would talk.

Secretary: Like ... sure ... of course ...

Poet: You know?

Secretary: I allow myself...

Poet: You are mute. Your mouth is like...

Secretary: Bonded.

Poet: Yes.

Secretary: Yes.

Poet: Come when the time comes!

Secretary: Yes! (*Exit with bow.*)

Poet.: That works. The puppets are dancing!

(Female) Sec quietly entering from Terra's private room: May I?

Poet: Shhhst!

Sec quietly closes the door.: I ... is it time ... I'm afraid. Darling, I'm afraid.

Poet *with dignity*: You were listening!

Sec.: As far as I could.

Poet: Your distrust offends me!

Sec: I'm suspicious because I ... because I love you ... I'm not suspicious ... I love you.

Poet, *taking her in his arms*: Your lips are damp as ... like morning dew; (*pets her*).

Sec: Next!

Poet: You are my day. Without you it's night. (*Breaks away from her.*) Go, the night is falling!

Sec: You've been better.

Poet, impatient: Go on!

Sec: You were already much better ...

Poet: Maybe I'm not in shape.

Sec: Do I have to?

Poet, *brusquely*: You must.

Sec: Kiss me!

Poet: Yes (*quickly kisses her*) please go!

Sec: As you wish. But you underestimate me. I'm not such a small, unreasonable so-and-so as you think. My motives are different. I love you. Yes … that means I'm still unreasonable. Yes, I am.

Poet: Please go!

Sec: As you wish. I ... I ... (*tiptoes to the door*) ... I can't say what I want ...

Poet: I understand you too ... we understand each other, don't we?

Sec: Yes (*closes the door*)

Poet: A blind horse will soon fall into the ditch. (*Wipes his mouth with a white handkerchief.*) Well. (*Goes to the right door and opens it.*) Gentlemen? (*Mumbling*) Are ... are ... are you there? Come!

*The wise men, about ten, pour into the room.* (*Silent, as if pushed.*)

Poet: Quiet!

First Wise Man: Don't push!

Second Wise Man: Psst!

*It's getting dark in the room.*

Poet: So, are you ready?

*Silence.*

Poet: That you have endured this state up to now.

*Silence.*

Poet: Given your intelligence, that surprises me.

*Silence.*

Poet: Didn't you ever come up with this simple solution?

First Wise Man: Good Lord, it's not that easy. That's a very bold decision.

Poet: That's right. But we are all dissatisfied. You and me. What is he providing you with? Very little. He is …

First Wise Man, *whispering*: His megalomania.

Poet: You are on a par with him. Yes, he is even inferior to you. At last, the abyss between us is filled with whispered assurances. We dance on a sword blade. You walked over it without cutting your soles. I would have … you would of course have … that shows my honesty. How did we deserve this treatment?

Well then? By nothing! And what raises the old man above us? Nothing! He eats, gives his orders, washes himself and goes to sleep. He is a guest on this earth like we are. But I don't want to philosophize. A guest is like the rain. If it lasts too long, it becomes a burden.

*From now on, the ones speaking are going to be illuminated alternately.*

First Wise Man: How should we do it?

Poet: As discussed.

First Wise Man: That seems impossible to me. It's easy to say ... but ...

Poet: Let's drop the syllable "im" and it becomes possible.

Another sage *whispering*: But the people?

Poet: They hardly know him. You know the doll on the throne. I play him. It's okay with a little make-up. Also, even sages can die a natural death. Well? (*Pause*) You're really scared. He can of course also have a state funeral.

Another Wise Man: We would prefer that.

Poet: I'll do whatever you want ... He and I have noses on our faces and have grown straight. My teeth are better, but that's not noticeable. I'll be as fat as him soon. That's just in case we make him disappear. A state funeral spares us the comedy.

Another Wise Man: I find the state funeral cheaper. With six black horses in front of the hearses ...

Another Wise Man: You mean in front of the carriage ... of course, I mean the funeral carriage.

Poet: We can discuss details later.

Another Wise Man: It all sounds very tempting, but it's not that straightforward ... maybe they're just testing us and vice versa, we're testing them, very weird ... that's why we came ... for fun.

Poet: My fun is bloody serious.

Another Wise Man: We do believe you. But maybe he's just pretending to be asleep.

Poet: He sleeps and feels safe. An unforgivable mistake.

Another Wise Man: God grant him more.

Another Wise Man: I'm tired.

Another Wise Man: I have heartburn.

Another Wise Man: It's like before a trip.

Another Wise Man: You must forgive us, we have been living in panic fear for a long time.

Another Wise Man: We may already be surrounded and meowing like dogs in a kennel.

Poet: Excuse me?

Another Wise Man: Meow...

Poet, sharp: Since when do dogs meow?

Another Wise Man: Of course, not exactly.

Poet: But indirectly they meow, don't they?

Another Wise Man: Why do you insist on the point?

Poet, nervous: It doesn't matter, it doesn't matter ... he's clueless as a baby. The longer a blind person lives, the more he sees.

Another Wise Man: That makes sense. But we shy away from any form of brutality. We are good-hearted people. You know that.

Poet: I, too, abhor violence. That is why we must combat his violence. No one has ever been as autocratic as he is. His so-called "wisdom" is a moral crutch he relies on to commit crimes. We are idealists. One man's heaven can be another man's hell. Push open the gate and we are in heaven.

Another Wise Man: And he in Hell.

Poet: Or somewhere else.

Another Wise Man: The guards? What about the guards?

Poet: There are no guards. I sent them on leave or bribed them. By virtue of my office, the old man lets me rule and rule. Sleeping dictators are bad dictators. He's been very tired lately. We will redeem him.

Another Wise Man: Right now?

Poet: Right now!

Another Wise Man: And the staff?

Poet: What is the staff supposed to do? It does not have the right to enter the room. It consists of muzzled sheep. You won't be afraid of them, will you?

Another Wise Man: Of course not. If so …

Another Wise Man: We're not butchers ... we're not used to it.

Poet: Don't carve … kill ... just kill.

Another Wise Man: We've never done that before.

Poet: My God, then you'll just have to relearn.

Another Wise Man: Let's hurry ... so it's over.

Poet: Do you have the knives?

Another Wise Man: Yes.

Poet: Your enthusiasm is limited.

Another Wise Man: No, we are very excited.

Another Wise Man: Yes.

Another Wise Man: I have a question! Aren't you an artist?

Poet: Yes.

Another Wise Man: Exactly. I love a picture and I don't know whose it is. It represents the following: A small room, on the right a window through which light falls. On the left is a half-open wooden door. In the middle of the room, in front of a simple, roughly worked table, a beggar breaks bread. All light gathers on him. He just breaks bread. A farmer's wife and her child stand devoutly next to him. They stare in disbelief, almost lurking, at the man who is surrounded by haloes ... of course it's just the light ... the beggar, he looks ragged but serious and noble ... very noble ... I mean ... do you know that?

Poet: No, I don't know the picture. Throw away that kitsch.

Another Wise Man: I don't have it, but I remember it clearly. When I was a child …

Poet: Are you drunk?

*The other sages chuckle.*

Another Wise Man: No. Childhood memories, you know.

Poet: Just don't get hysterical. Extreme concentration gentlemen! (*To the speaker*:) Or don't you want to participate?

Another Wise Man: Yes, yes, I just meant...

Poet: You'll get that picture! I promise you! And one more thing ... don't cut yourself gentlemen!

Another Wise Man: Can't we garrote him?

Poet: That's even more cruel.

Another Wise Man: Oh right.

*Poet goes quickly to the door that leads to the private room and knocks*: Bastard Terra, you bastard wake up!

*The wise gather in a dark group.*

*Denser, louder*: Terra, your little hearts are waiting for you! They have brought spiky wishes for you. Sharp gifts for you.

Terra's sleepy voice. Struggling to sleep … frightening the wise men: What is it … what the hell is it?

Poet: Aloisius Hundsburger come at last! We've got a bone to pick! Come on you old blood sow!

Terra, *enters barefoot and dressed in a dressing gown*: What is so urgent to disturb my sleep? (*To the poet*) How can you allow that?

*Silence.*

Terra: Since I'm so sensitive! (*Rubbing his eyes.*)

Poet: We were just talking about that.

Terra: About what? (*Paralyzing silence, it becomes very light.*) ... about what?

Poet: It was very interesting.

*Silence.*

Terra, *unconfident*: Why are you standing so stiffly? (*I hear, puts his hand to his ear.*) Nothing? Where are my slippers. (*Seeks, while bowing down.*) Where are they?

Poet snaps his fingers. The Sages press each other against Terra. One of them stabs the stooped man and quickly steps back.

Terra, *sitting up with a groan and grasping the wound*: Strange, kidney pain ... wet (*looks at his hand*). That's blood, isn't it? Where does … (*screams*) blood (*stares in bewilderment at the wise men*) blood (*he holds out his hand to them.*)

Poet: Come on, don't wait!

*The Sages fall upon Terra and butcher him. They form a fermenting knot, only the poet stands apart.*

Terra, *choked ... out of the crowd*: Gaaards ... Gaaards ... police ... (*rushes bleeding towards the poet*).

Poet: The walls have no ears.

*The sages catch up with Terra and stab him.*

Terra, *collapsing*: No ... dear ones ... dear ones ... no ... please ... (*whimper*).

*The wise men keep stabbing him.*

Poet: Bravissimo. You've missed your profession. (*The Wise Men stop the slaughter and look around uncertainly.*) You are bloody and stink of sweat, dear ones. My hands are clean; (*lifts them*). You must be born for being a butcher. (*The wise men look at their hands in bewilderment.*) That ... that ... gets rid of it ... (*kicks Terra's corpse*) ... well ... it'll be soon!

Another Wise Man: We?

Poet: Heck, who else? Or do you want to wait until it starts walking by itself? Should I get dirty?

Another Wise Man: Calm down.

Poet: I'm sick anyway. (*Goes to the private rooms, choking and throwing up.*)

Another Wise Man: That can happen.

Another Wise Man: The nerves.

Another Wise Man: Sensitive people act very sensitive to such things ...

Poet entering: It's alright (*wipes his mouth with a cloth*) thank you ... it's much better ... the excitement ...

Another Wise Man: Me too (*chokes*) me ... (*covering his mouth with his hand and running to the left.*)

Poet: Take that away … a sensitive person must throw up.

*(Male) Secretary coming from the right*: Is it time? Already over? My congratulations. The state is saved. (*The wise men hide the knives.*)

Poet: The gentlemen is in the know.

Secretary: I congratulated you gentlemen!

*The wise men hesitantly*: Thank you ... thank you ... sincere thanks ... thank you very much ...

Poet: Why so embarrassed, gentlemen? You are heroes!

Secretary: It's a feat!

*Terra, rattles.*

Poet to Secretary: Did you say something?

Secretary: Me? No.

Poet: Then the barking of the passers-by knocks against the floor.

Terra, gasping: The coup de grace ... give me the coup de grace ...

Poet: He's still alive ... (*retrogresses*)

Secretary: Please. (*Pulls a pistol from his pocket and shoots Terra.*) One has to be human ... pity, that's all ... (*puts the pistol away.*)

Poet: Do you always have it with you?

Secretary: Only on important occasions ... only for emergencies if something should go wrong...

Poet: That is very perceptive.

(Male) Secretary: For you … nothing is too expensive for me.

Poet: You clever person. Give me the gun. I want to look at it. (*Holds out his hand to the secretary. He puts the pistol into his hand. The poet shoots him.*) Too smart or too stupid ... I don't need cowboys like that. (*To the Wise Men*) You have nothing to fear gentlemen.

*(Female) Secretary storming in*: Finally! (*With a look at Terra*) It doesn't look nice.

Poet: What do you want?

Sec: It's terrible, but we're free ... even if the surrounding circumstances smell like a slaughterhouse.

Poets to the Wise Men: His mistress!

Sec: He's dead ... that's what counts ...

Poet: I understand your pain, miss, but I have to ask you to leave the room.

Sec: How long have we waited! Now we don't have to pretend anymore! Hug me! (*Approaches the poet.*)

Poet: Stop! (*Holds out his arm defensively; she stops.*) What are you allowing yourself? I understand your confusion, but this is definitely going too far!

Sec: I will laugh again darling ... we will sit in the garden under lilac bushes ... as we dreamed ...

Poets, to the wise: She is mad! I have no intention of inheriting her. I don't use his aftershave, neither his clothes, nor his bedding, nor his mistress! (*To the sec*:) Your game is up!

Sec: I don't understand that ... what's the matter with you? Tell me! What is it?

Poet: Don't play the theatre! Given the circumstances ...

Sec: That's not true ... no, no ... let me explain that ... it's not like that... no, you're pretending ... (*laughs tormented*) you're pretending ... (*looks around in a circle and lets her arms hang down*) ... you know … he is pretending. That makes the habit ... no ... maybe I don't look good in this light ... but that will work out (*reaches for the hairdo*) surely that will work out ... I ... I love you! Yes, I slept with Terra, gentlemen, that's true... (*points to the poet*) … but when his fat body slid over me, all I thought about was him. I've gritted my teeth and ...

Poet: You have opened your mouth so that his tongue might find the way. Thought of me? Don't make me laugh! If one man is not enough for you, I recommend a brothel! There you can satisfy your nymphomaniac desires.

The wise men laugh.

Sec: No ... you're not like that ... please stop the comedy ... even if you're a poet, please stop the comedy! ... me, I've been a little hysterical lately ... (to the Wise Men) ... He, he's kidding!

Poet: Stop addressing me on first name terms! (*To the wise men*:) How perverted this woman is! A dead friend seems to increase her drive.

Sec, *screaming*: That was all for us!

Poet, *cold*: That's new to me. (*To the wise men in utter amazement*:) Did they know about it? (*The wise men laugh*) She's crazy (*tapping his forehead*) completely crazy.

*Two Sages hold her in place.*

Sec, *screaming*: Why then? Why?

Poet: The last mercy, the last merciful answer. I watched Terra eat and it occurred to me to eat as well … as much as I wanted. (*To the wise men*:) And we all don't want that? (*Laughter*)

Wise man: That's how carelessness takes revenge, Miss.

Sec: I don't believe in anything anymore.

Poet: Take her to safety.

Sec, *as she's being dragged out, sobbing*: Believe me ... it's just the light ... the unfavorable light ... it's just the unfavorable light...

Poet: That disturbs. (*Points to the corpses.*) Clean up, gentlemen!

*The bodies are dragged out.*

Poet: The happy ending is here. Countries, continents, yachts, private planes, I'll eat. Also, camels laden with gold and ivory, secretaries, political prisoners, the state, the people, religion, the poets, the benefactors of humanity. Everything is going to be absorbed. (*Half to the wise men, half to the audience, which he has fixated already at the beginning of his speech.*) I thank you.

END

# DIE ABLÖSE!

Terra, der Oberweise.

Dichter (D.)

Sekretärin (Sek.)

Sekretär (Sekr.)

Ordonanz.

2 Wachen (1W, 2W)

2 Gefangene (Gef.)

Maskenbildner (Ma.)

Regisseur.

Bedienerin (Be.)

Schauspielerin.

2 Weise (W.)

Plato.

Etwa Io Weise.

Wachen, Kameramänner, Beleuchter, Diener, Bühnenarbeiter, Henker, Richter, Koch, Erzieherin, Kinder.

Zimmer im Regierungspalast der Weisen. Es ist sehr geräumig, gleicht schon eher einem großen Salon. Rechts, links und in der Mitte eine von Marmor umfasst Tür. (Schwer lastender plumper Marmor.) Über jeder Tür gleist ein vergoldeter Rahmen mit der Fotographie des Oberweisen. Auf ihr ist eigentlich nur dessen schreiender Mund sichtbar. Darunter an den Wänden weitere Fotos – die Brustbilder der übrigen Weisen. (Das Format ist kleiner.) Daneben vergoldete und versilberte Lorbeerkränze mit überdimensionalen schlaffen Blättern. Im Mittelgrund ein Direktorenschreibtisch auf dem eine schwarze Schreibmaschine hockt. (Ein robustes Ungetüm mit altmodisch hartem Anschlag.) Auf der Tischplatte befinden sich auch Telefone und leuchtende Klingelknöpfe von verschiedener Farbe. Der riesige Schreibtisch kann an die Kommandobrücke eines Raumschiffs erinnern. Der Fußboden ist aus Marmor. Im Raum verteilt mehrere Sessel und Fauteuils (Stilmöbel). Es können nach Belieben mehrere langstielige Aschenbecher aufgestellt werden. Eine Notwendigkeit besteht nicht. Gesamteinrichtung: Staatlich, protzig, pompös, unpersönlich, kalt.

Terra der Ober- oder Hauptweise ist ein Mann im "besten Alter". Etwas korpulent, könnte aber als stattlich bezeichnet werden.

Eine Sekretärin, jung, fest, naiver Charme.

Ein Dichter, schlank, wendig.

Die Sekretärin sitzt rechts vom Schreibtisch. Sie ist geschminkt und modisch gekleidet. Neben ihr steht der Dichter in lässiger Haltung. Terra geht unruhig auf und ab.

Terra: Könnte ich eine Zigarette haben?

Sek.: Aber sie sollten doch nicht …

Terra: Ich weiß, ich weiß …

Sek.: aufstehend, Zigaretten anbietend und Feuer gebend: Bitte!

Terra: Danke, sehr lieb. (Schaut auf ihre Beine während sie zum Schreibtisch zurückschaukelt. Der Zuschauer bleibt im Unklaren darüber, ob ihr schwingender Gang bewusst oder unbewusst ist.)

… freundliche Perspektiven …

Sek.: stehenbleibend, mit halber Drehung, kokett: Bitte?

Terra: Ach nichts von Bedeutung.

Sek. setzt sich. An der Tür wird geklopft. (Vom Zuschauer aus rechts also links.)

Terra: Herein! (männlich sonor)

Der Sekretär, ein kleiner schmaler Mann mit Brille, tritt ein. Sein Gesicht ist gelb vor Korrektheit. Schmale Nase, abgezirkelte Bewegungen. Sture Intelligenz. Kennt keine Skrupel. Aktenmörder. Dunkler, knappsitzender Anzug. Unterm Arm trägt er eine Mappe.

Sekr. Stramm: Lang lebe der Weiseste!

Terra: Was bringen sie mir?

Sekr.: Unannehmlichkeiten.

Terra: Daran bin ich gewöhnt.

Sekr.: Es handelt sich um das Konzept für die monatliche Unterstützung und Aufrechterhaltung der Volksmeinung.

Terra: Muss das jetzt sein?

Sekr.: Bedaure, es ist unaufschiebbar.

Terra: Gut, wenn es sein muss.

Sekr. Feierlich: Man muss die Wahrheiten solange wiederholen bis sie so selbstverständlich sind, dass sie bereits die Kinder mit der Ammenmilch einsaugen.

Terra zum Dichter: Ein Konkurrent von ihnen.

Sekr. höflich: Keine Angst, ich bin kein Dichter, bloß Amateur. (Die Mappe aufschlagend, vorlesend.) Unseren Staat regieren die Weisen, das wisst (unterbricht) … soll ich alles lesen?

Terra: Fassen sie sich so kurz wie möglich.

Sekr.: Einer der Weisen bekleidet das Amt des Oberweisen. Er ist ein Bruder der anderen Weisen und ihnen völlig gleich.

Terra: Stopp! Streichen! Ab – Er ist ein Bruder – streichen. Schreiben sie! An der Spitze der Weisen steht der Oberweise. (Sekr. notiert) haben sie das?

Sekr.: Ja (weiterlesend) … unser System beruht auf Gerechtigkeit, Güte und Strenge … da sind Chöre gedacht, die den Satz wiederholen … (lesend) Dieser Staat ist der beste aller Staaten. Jeder steht fest auf seinem Platz in der Sonne. Niemand kann sich beklagen, weil es nicht zu beklagen gibt.

Terra: Etwas naiv. Glauben sie das …

Sekr.: Vergessen sie nicht es ist ein Volksfest. Die Rede hat volkstümlichen Charakter. Einfache Formulierungen sind bei großen Anlässen immer sehr wirksam. (Lesend) Nur unsere

Leistung, die allein entscheidet, hat uns nach mühevollem Ringen an die Spitze der Nation gestellt. Unser Leben ist in bewundernswertere Weise geregelt. Die Weisen bestimmen unseren Partner, das ist schön … hier wieder Chöre … Die Weisen bestimmen unsere Partnerin und das ist gut so. Unsere vom Staat erzogenen Kinder sind Licht, Luft und Sonnenkinder. Unser Glaube an euch ihr Weisen übersteigt Alles. Keine Frage bleibt offen. Unser Geschick liegt in euren gütigen Händen. Und wir werden auch nicht fragen. Wie sollten wir verstehen, was ihr zu unserem Wohl beschließt?

Terra gähnt: Pardon.

Sekr.: Ich bin sofort fertig mein Weisester … Wir aber regen voll Fleiß ohne Ende unsere vaterländischen Hände …

Terra: Das genügt.

Sekr.: Eine Parade der Kinder in weißen Kleidchen ist vorgesehen. Sie singen die Hymne: Wir lieben die Weisesten …

Terra: Das macht sich gut.

Sekr.: Am Ende bilden Turner aus ihren Körpern die Parole: Unsere weisen Führer sind der Lebensborn des Staates.

Terra: Sehr brav.

Sekr.: Danke.

Terra: Gibt's Freibier und Würstchen?

Sekr.: Natürlich, soweit es die finanzielle Lage zulässt.

Terra: Erinnern sie mich nicht daran. Gut. Sie wissen ja, hungrige Mägen sind keine solide Grundlage für ein Fest. Brot und Spiele – sie wissen Bescheid. Leider sind die Leute nicht so dumm, wie man meistens glaubt.

Sekr.: Ja, bedauerlicherweise.

Terra: Ausgezeichnet.

Sekr.: Dass ich nicht vergesse, das Ganze rundet eine spektakuläre Hinrichtung ab.

Terra: Großartig. Das Volk kann der Aggression freien Raum lassen. Tobt seine Wut aus. Ist das von ihnen?

Sekr.: Ich habe mir gestattet …

Terra: Genug Delinquenten?

Sekr.: Im Notfall können wir noch welche besorgen. Gegen Anschuldigung von höchster Stelle gibt es keine Berufung. (Lächelt breit.)

Terra: Ja, spaßig. Sie haben freie Hand.

Sekr. sich verbeugend: Verbindlichsten Dank. (Stramm) Lang lebe der Weiseste. (ab)

Terra streng: Wo waren wir stehengeblieben?

Dichter: Sie baten um eine Zigarette.

Terra: Das meine ich nicht …

Sek.: Beim Leitartikel für das Wochenblatt.

Terra zum Dichter: Auf ihr Manuskript bin ich neugierig.

Sek.: Es ist hier (streckt es Terra hin).

Terra: Wie viele Wochen sind erledigt?

Dichter: Drei.

Terra: Also eine noch … dann haben wir den Monat hinter uns. Ich hab‘ das bis da oben über. (Fährt sich mit der flachen Hand quer über den Hals) … den Lektor spielen … man ist ja keine Maschine. (Reicht dem Dichter das Manuskript). Ich höre.

Dichter: Da wir die Weisen sind, die blendendsten Leuchten am geistigen Firmament dieser Epoche – und das Kraft unseres Standes, unserer Geburt und unserer genetischen Überlegenheit – haben wir, wie allgemein bekannt ist, das Recht, ja sogar die Pflicht, unsere Entscheidungen, deren Zweckmäßigkeit nur wir allein einsehen können, dem Volk ohne weitere vielleicht verwirrende Erklärung, mitzuteilen. Mit uns steht und fällt der Staat. Wir sind für euch von der gleichen, permanenten Bedeutung wie die Sonne für …

Terra: Moment! Könnte man nicht gleich den ganzen Kosmos miteinbeziehen?

Dichter: Sonne ist prägnanter.

Terra: Finden sie? Das dachte ich auch. Wie ich sehe, leisten sie gute Arbeit.

Dichter: Danke.

Terra: Das genügt. Ich lese mir die Fortsetzung später durch.

Dichter: Sie handelt hauptsächlich über die Liebe der weisen zum Volk.

Terra: Liebe … kennen sie den neuesten Grafenwitz? … der Graf geht (flüstern, man versteht nur die Worte “Bordell, Kopulation, Mastdarm)

Sek. mit erstarrtem Gesicht: Aber …

Terra und der Dichter lachen los. Terra besonders. Sein Gewieher setzt ohne Aufbau direkt am Höhepunkt ein und ebbt dann langsam ab um erneut aufzuflammen. Es muss ansteckend wirken.

Terra auf das starre Gesicht der Sek. aufmerksam werden: Na finden sie ihn nicht … ??

Sek. kichert auf Bestellung.

Terra zum Dichter: Ich brauche sie momentan nicht …

Dichter sich verbeugend: Es war mir eine Ehre.

Terra: Ich hoffe sie wissen es zu schätzen, dass sie an meinen intimsten Gefühlsregungen teilnehmen dürfen.

Dichter: Sicherlich (ab)

Terra: Lassen sie den Dienst, Dients sein mein Engel. (Geht übertrieben elastisch auf sie zu.) Sie haben eine bezaubernde Frisur. Sagte ich ihnen das schon?

Sek.: Nein. (Lächelt mit schiefem Kopf zu ihm empor.)

Terra: Darf ich sie zu einer kleinen Erfrischung einladen?

Sek. leise: Ja.

Terra: Sie wissen, dass ich auf höfliche Floskeln verzichten könnte?

Sek.: Ja.

Terra: Dass sie nach unseren Bestimmungen nicht notwendig sind?

Sek.: Ich weiß.

Terra: Sie haben einen sehr ehrenvollen Posten.

Sek.: Ja.

Terra: Ich habe es nicht gerne, wenn ein so reizendes Mädchen wie sie prüde ist.

Sek.: Ja.

Terra: Ich biete ihnen hiermit das “Du” an.

Sek.: Sehr ehrenvoll. Ja, danke.

Terra: Würden sie … würdest du mir bitte in meine Privaträume folgen?

Sek.: Ja … gerne … (sehr zögernd)

Terra: Dann komm. (Sek. steht auf und geht auf T. zu. Er legt die Hand um ihre Hüfte. Nach links ab.)

Die Bühne bleibt einen Augenblick leer. Es wird dunkler. Von der linken Seite her die gedämpfte Stimme der Beiden. Dann hysterisches Kichern, lautsprecherstarkes Schmatzen und Stöhnen. Es muss überraschend kommen und klingen als würde sich auf der Bühne eine Stereoanlage befinden. Darf nur sehr kurz dauern und mündet in Störgeräusche, die mit einem lauten Krach abgeschnitten werden. Stille.

Hinter der gegenüberliegenden Tür (rechts also links) hört man leise aber deutlich verständlich einen Streit. Die stimmen klingen metallisch. (Weit entfernt singender Metalldraht.)

Nein, das ist unmöglich.

Aber wir haben Ordner …

Ich sage so geht das nicht.

Kümmern sie sich um ihren Kram …

Genau das tue ich Herr Kollege …

Sie sind hier Ordonanz weiter nichts … wir handeln in geheimer Mission, die …

Es ist meine Aufgabe …

Quatsch, lassen sie uns jetzt durch oder nicht?

Aber … (Die Stimmen werden lauter, natürlicher)

Es ist ein dringender Fall. Wir sollen den Kerl sofort und unter allen Umständen herbringen.

Auf eure Verantwortung!

Na, endlich nehmen sie Vernunft an!

Ich stehe für nichts ein!

O.k. das brauchen sie auch nicht.

Die rechte Tür wird aufgestoßen. Zwei graugekleidete Wachen schleppen einen blutenden Mann herein. Der Hemdkragen des Gefangenen steht offen. Keine Schuhbänder, am Gewand fehlen die Knöpfe. Er hält mit den aneinander geketteten Händen die Hose fest.

1. Wache (1W), nach hinten rufend: Unsere Befehle sind bindend!

2. Wache (2W) sich umsehend, zögernd: Da ist ja niemand. (Wieder volles Licht.)

Ordonanz, halb sichtbar im Türrahmen: Na sehen sie! Sie bringen mich in Unannehmlichkeiten!

1W: Wir wissen was wir tun. Wir können warten. Wir haben Zeit. Wir sind warten gewohnt.

Ordonanz, kopfschüttelnd: Sie müssen es ja wissen. (Schließt die Tür von außen.)

1W zieht ein Päckchen aus der Tasche fischt eine Zigarette heraus und will sie zwischen die Lippen stecken.

2W: Bist du verrückt?

1W: Entschuldige … (schiebt die Zigarette ins Päckchen) … ich hatte solche Lust.

2W: Sollen wir uns setzen? (schaut suchend)

1W: Bleiben wir lieber stehen.

2W: Ich bin müde.

1W: Wir bleiben stehen.

2W: Wie du willst.

1W geht zum Schreibtisch, hebt einen Zigarettenstummel aus dem Aschenbecher und schnüffelt daran: Hmmm … teure Sorte. (Den Stummel von Weiten zeigend): Du siehst man darf rauchen!

2W: Das gilt nicht für uns. Wir sind im Dienst.

Der Gefangene würgt.

1W, nicht ohne Gutmütigkeit: Benimm dich anständig, Schwein.

2W: Er weiß anscheinend nicht, wo er sich befindet.

Gefangener, leise: Mir ist kalt (hustet krampfhaft).

2W: Spuck nicht auf den Fußboden!

1W: Versau nicht das Zimmer vom Chef! (stupst ihn)

2W: Und sowas nennt sich Intellektueller. Schau nur wie du jetzt aussiehst. Das hast du davon.

1W: Die Warterei geht mir auf die Nerven. Wir sollten uns bemerkbar machen.

2W, auf die linke Türe zeigend: Wo geht es da hin?

1W mit vorgebeugtem Kopf lesend: Privat.

2W: Klopf einmal an!

1W, klopft.

2W: Lauter!

1W pumpert gegen die Tür (nicht zu grotesk): Es rührt sich nichts (zuckt die Achseln).

2W: Versuch es noch einmal (mit einem Blick auf den Gefangenen) er verdreckt die ganze Kanzlei.

Man hört Schritte (erst sehr weit entfernt) die rasch näherkommen. Es bleibt Zeit genug für die Beiden sich rechts und links vom Gefangenen in Positur zu werfen.

Terra, eintretend und sich übers Haar streichend, brüllt: Das ist eine Infamie!

Wachen, zugleich: Lang lebe der Weiseste!

Terra, stehenbleibend: Diese Impertinenz kann sie ihre Existenz kosten! Wo ist der leiseste Rest von Anstand? Wie kommt ihr überhaupt herein? (kurzes fingern an der Krawatte, vielleicht nur eine Handbewegung) Sie sind mir eine Erklärung schuldig!

1W, salutierend: Wir handeln auf ihren ausdrücklichen Befehl Weisester. Sie sagten …

Terra auf sie zugehend: was sagte ich?

2W: Wir hatten die Order den Anarchisten …

Terra: Den Anarchisten? Welchen …

1W: Ja, den Anar …

Terra, sich übers Gesicht fahren und nähertretend: Ach ja … der ist das … dieser dringliche Fall. Trotzdem, ist es bei ihnen üblich in die Privaträume einzudringen?

1W: stotternd: Nein …

Terra: Sie können doch lesen oder nicht?

2W: Wir haben keine Privaträume.

Terra: Was steht denn da? (Zeigt nach der Tür)

1W: Privat.

Terra: Na also! Freut mich, dass sie kein Analphabet sind (beruhigter) Schwamm drüber, ich war anderwärtig beschäftigt … Pflichten wissen sie. Trotzdem danke ich ihnen.

W. durcheinander: Zu Diensten!

Terra zum Gef.: Nun zu dir mein Herzchen. Endlich hat man dich erwischt …

Terra: Du bist ja rot geschminkt … ich persönlich habe mich um dich gekümmert. Du hast mir schlaflose Nächte gekostet. Weißt du was es bedeutet Terra den Oberweisen den Schlaf zu stehlen?

2W: Sie haben Terra den Oberweisen persönlich beleidigt!

1W: Ja, das haben sie.

Terra, brüllend: Wie komme ich dazu meine kostbare Zeit an solch subversive Elemente zu verschwenden? Weil in deinem blöden Hirn dekadente Ideen wachsen? Wo kämen wir hin, wenn wir dauernd um unsere Existenzgrundlage raufen müssten? Weil irgendwelchen Hitzköpfen unsere Ordnung nicht in den Kram passt! Weil sich die Herren für klug halten! Sie sind ein Niemand! Sie sind ein Nichts! Haben sie überhaupt begriffen was sie tun? (laut aber nicht brüllend) Dass gerade in intellektuellen Kreisen sachliches Denken durch kindische Gefühlsdudelei ersetzt wird! (Zu den Wachen) Wissen sie was das Schwein gepredigt und ausgeführt hat?

1W: Nein. Wir verhaften nur. Der Grund ist uns …

Terra: Die Kreatur erklärt die Wahl der Partnerin zu einer Intimangelegenheit. Lächerlich, was?

Die Wachen lachen pflichtbewusst.

1W: Ah, so einer ist der.

2W: Sowas … (kopfschüttelnd)

Terra, ironisch: Die egoistische Liebe ist tot, kapiert! Ein gesunder Staat braucht gesunde Kinder und das kann bei deinen Ansichten niemand überprüfen. Gesundes zu Gesunden und die Gesundheit überprüfen Fachkräfte … wozu haben wir hochqualifizierte Computer? Freie Partnerwahl. Das hirnlose alte Elend! Auf diese Art und Weise kommt nie Zucht und Ordnung in unser System. Außerdem lenken eheliche Bande, die auf sentimentaler Basis wurzeln, viel zu sehr von der Arbeit zum Wohl des Staates ab. Aber du und Konsorten wollen das nicht begreifen! (Schweigen) Wie man nur so borniert sein kann! (Pause) Deine Dirne sitzt im Treibhaus der Helden. Dort findet sie gute Verwendung. (Pause – brüllend) Die wird verfüttert und viele stramme Patrioten zeugen. Weshalb wolltest du gerade die heiraten? (Wendet sich mit übertriebener Ratlosigkeit an die Wachen.) Wie kann ein vernünftiger Mensch darauf bestehen? Das Fazit dieser betrüblichen Tatsache?

1W: Er ist blöd (schnurrt es beglückt herab)

Terra: Was passiert, Idioten?

2W: Bösartige Idioten, die absichtlich in ihrer Idiotie verharren werden laut des Strafgesetzbuches § I Absatz II ohne Anspruch auf mittelbaren oder unmittelbaren Rechtsschutz, der dem § 555 entsprechen würde, sofort dem einzuberufenden Standgericht zur Liquidation übergeben.

Terra: So ist es.

Gef. Schreiend: Scheinheiliges Schwein! (spuckt nach Terra)

1W schlägt dem Gefangenen mit der verkehrten Hand zweimal ins Gesicht: Kusch! (Der Gef. Taumelt.)

Terra: Die Sau. (Wache hebt die Hand zum dritten Schlag.) Nein aufhören! Ich kann Brutalitäten höchstens auf der Leinwand sehen. Da sehe ich gern hin. Sonst bin ich sensibel.

1W: Entschuldigen … die Erregung.

Terra: Schon gut, er hat nicht getroffen (fährt mit dem Ärmel über die Rockbrust, reibt) … wenn ich an den Stätten des Gräuels vorbeifahre muss ich die Vorhänge zuziehen … ich bin auch Ästhet.

1W: Ich fühle mit ihnen.

Terra: Da schuftet man Tag und Nacht für den Staat und was tut das Vieh? Beschmutzt den Fußboden! Er!

Gefangener: Terrakotten-Schwein!

2W: Halts Maul (zieht ein zerdrücktes Taschentuch aus der Brusttasche)

Terra: Lassen sie das …

2W: Warten sie das werden wir gleich haben. (Drückt dem Gefangenen das Tuch vors Gesicht.)

Gefangener, undeutlich: Schweine!

Terra: Geht jetzt … Danke, danke keine Formalitäten … (Bevor sie die Tür erreichen, scharf) … Und, wie tut ihr es?

W: Mit der größten Diskretion!

Terra: Gut. Sein Bazillus könnte ansteckend wirken. Sie erfüllen vorbildlich ihre Pflicht meine Herren.

1W zum Gefangenen: Nimm dir ein Beispiel.

2W: Ja, nehmen sie sich ein Beispiel (schleifen den Gefangenen hinaus). Lange lebe der Weiseste (fast unverständlich).

Terra: Ich bin zu gutmütig. Mir fehlt es an Härte.

W1, schon fast bei der Tür: Da haben sie Recht …

Terra: Verschwindet!

W1: Ich habe doch nur ihre Meinung bestätigt. (Trio geht ab)

Terra, nachrufend: Benachrichtigen sie die Reinigung, das Zimmer … der Dreck muss weg …

W. vom Gang her: Ja …

Terra geht durch die Linke Tür ab. Murmelt dabei: Lauter Intriganten.

Stille. Die Bühne wird allmählich heller und badet sich gegen Anfang des Textes in strahlendem Licht.

Eine Aufräume-Frau (Raumpflegerin, Bedienerin) kommt mit einem Kübel voll dampfender Lauge herein. Ihre Hände stecken in roten Gummihandschuhen. Sie ist einfach aber rein gekleidet und riecht nach Spital.

Bedienerin: Schon wieder Flecken … aaach ja … (kniet nieder, nimmt einen grauen Fetzen aus der Lauge, windet ihn über dem Kübel aus und wischt) wenn das (wischt) … wenn mir das früher jemand gesagt hätte (wischt) ins Gesicht hätte ich ihm (windet den Fetzen aus) ja ich hätte ihm ins Gesicht gelacht. Mein Lohn ist weise bestimmt, ich hab‘ das Notwendigste. Ach, wenn das weise ist, fress‘ ich einen Besen … Günstig zu ihren Gunsten haben sie's geregelt. Ihre eigenen Günstlinge sind sie, aber dafür haben sie an unsereins eine billige Arbeitskraft … (windet) … Meine Kinder erziehen andere. Die kleineren zumindest, und ich krepier lebendig. Ich habe Narrenfreiheit. Außerdem hat das Zimmer keine Ohren. Ich weiß das. Aber wenn auch, ich habe Narrenfreiheit. So sehr beachtet man mich nicht mehr. Pfutsch vorbei! (Macht mit dem Fetzen eine Bewegung.) Ich war doch auch einmal im Liebestempel und hab Kinder geboren. Das ist lange her … gutes Material war ich sagten die Ärzte (sich streckend). Sie sagten ich sei gutes Material. Geburtsfreudige Lenden sagten sie. Eine gesunde Gebärmutter. Bester Boden, sagten sie. Na, und dann haben sie halt gepflanzt, die Schweinekerle. Na ja, anfangs war‘s widerlich. Später war mir jeder recht. Von der künstlichen Befruchtung hat man ja überhaupt nichts gehabt. (Streicht sich über den Bauch.) Da war mir das andere noch lieber. Wie hätte ich mich auch wehren können? (Lässt den Fetzen ins Wasser zurückplatschen.) 18 Jahre war ich am Anfang. Und wie wild die Weisen waren! Auf jedes junge Ding stürzten sie sich. Stoßtruppe der Lust. Bitte bei den Alten musste man schon ein bisschen … ach was … Die Blüte der Jugend in antiseptischen Betten verschüttet … ich brauche frisches Wasser. (Richtet sich stöhnend auf und trägt den Kübel ein Stück … halb zum Publikum gewandt.) Es ging uns ja nicht schlecht in dem verdammten Kaff, äußerlich besehen zumindest. Wir hatten Luft und Hygiene. Aber Himmel, Himmel hatten wir keinen. Nur ein kleines Stückchen freier Himmel hätte genügt. Ein faustgroßes Stückchen Hoffnung. (Stellt den Kübel schleppend hin und wendet sich direkt ans Publikum.) Blödsinn, es gibt Tatsachen die kann man nicht wegwaschen. Selbst das sauberste Gefängnis bleibt ein Gefängnis. (Streicht sich übers Haar und wischt die Hände im Gewand ab.) Wissen sie, dass ich schön war? (lächelt jugendlich) Ja, ja das klingt jetzt lächerlich. Aber meine Bildung hab ich noch. Sie glauben es nicht, aber ich war eine gebildete Frau. Und hübsch. Warten sie. (Tritt knapp an die Rampe und zitiert mit eng geschlossenen Händen, wie ein Schulmädchen):

Der Leidenschaften wilden Drang.

Der Pflichten und Instinkten Zwang,

teilt ihr mit prüfendem Gefühle,

mit strengem Richtspruch nach dem Ziele,

was die Natur auf ihrem großen Gang …

Ich glaube mir ist der Faden ausgegangen. Danke, danke, danke, ich danke ihnen vielmals (lächelt, knickst kindlich und hebt dabei den Rocksaum). Das war, ja das waren noch Zeiten. Ich hatte flaumige Pfirsichwangen. Sehr flaumige, wissen sie. Ja, die hatte ich. (Sekundenlange Pause, dann aus ihr hervorbrechend): Und wenn sie noch so viel Schminke auflegen meine Damen … (verzagt) … sie verzeihen schon … ich … (steht einen Augenblick ratlos als warte sie auf den Text, kniet sich dann wieder hin) … ach die ewige Putzerei … dabei ist es ein ehrenvoller Posten … ich will mich nicht beklagen … falls ich was gesagt haben sollte halten sie das meinem Alter zugute … (zieht einige Sprühdosen aus den verschiedenen Taschen und reiht sie neben sich auf. Es folgt ein überlanges weißes

Tuch. Sie holt es aus der Tasche wie ein Zauberer. Trotzdem darf es nur andeutungsweise grotesk wirken. Sie nimmt eine Dose, schüttelt sie, und besprüht den Boden) … das Mittel ist wirklich gut. Das Beste von allen. Macht schwarze Fußböden strahlend weiß. Selbstverständlich könnte man auch leuchtend weiß sagen. Es hat mich überzeugt und ich lebe glücklicher seitdem ich es kenne. Jede junge Frau sollte es haben. (Zeigt die Dose dem Publikum) Sehen sie so einfach und wirksam (sprüht) … ist das nicht eine Entlastung für die geplagte Hausfrau? (Wischt) Ja, ich bin glücklich. (Zeigt eine andere Dose) Und das ist ein Modell für reifere Damen. Es macht mich besonders glücklich. Ich habe seitdem keine Probleme mehr. (Sprüht) Ob sie es mir glauben oder nicht … (wischt) … der Dreck … wie weggeblasen … Ich … ich … wie würde sich ein Poet ausdrücken? Ich bin gefältelt in die Knie gegangen und in meinen geschwollenen Adern steht gefrorenes Blut … alles eh geregelt (wischt den Spray weg). Nebenbei ein gutes Mittel glänzt heller als die Sonne. Kraft darf nicht vergeudet werden sagt man bei unsereins. Hauptsache du kuscht und schleckst ihnen nachher noch die Hand ab. Manchmal möchte ich ein Würger-Vogel sein und sie aufspießen. Für jeden ist im Herzgestrüpp meines Stachelherzens ein Dorn bereit. Ein gebogenes, scharfes Dörnchen mit Widerhacken … am beste ich halt den Mund … Maul halten ist die Parole des kleinen Mannes … So der Dreck wäre weg (steht stöhnend auf und hält sich die Hüften).

Terra tritt aus den Privaträumen und räuspert sich …

Bedienerin: Mein Weiser (verbeugt sich)

Terra: Machen sie nur weiter meine Beste.

Bed.: Störe ich?

Terra: Aber nein …

Bed.: Falls es so ist möchte ich mich …

Terra: Das ist gar nicht notwendig. Ich habe zu danken.

Bed.: Trotzdem …

Terra, scharf: Sind sie fertig?

Bed.: Ich bin vollkommen fertig.

Terra: Dann gehen sie.

Bed.: Ja, sofort (Geht mit ihren Utensilien, die sie vorher mühevoll einsammelt, ab.)

Terra nach links in die Privaträume rufend: Wo bleibst du denn? (Stille) kommen sie schon! Wo waren wir stehen geblieben? (zündet sich eine Zigarette an)

Sek. noch nicht sichtbar: Wo?

Terra: Ja, wo? Beeilen sie sich.

Sek. schon näher: Bei der Liebe des Weisesten zum Volk.

Terra: Gut, komm endlich!

Sek. tritt etwas zerdrückt aus den Privatzimmern. Die Kleidung ist nicht ganz in Ordnung … vielleicht Fehlen des BHs oder der Strümpfe … man merkt jedenfalls eine Veränderung, die auch durch die Kleidung auszudrücken ist.

Terra: Wie du aussiehst … schau‘ ein bisschen auf dein Äußeres … (die Sek. zieht den Pullover zurecht) … es muss ja nicht jeder gleich … sie könnten wirklich mehr auf ihr Aussehen achten. (Er betätigt eine der Klingeln. Es läutet sehr laut. Am besten im Rücken der Zuschauer.) Sind sie soweit?

Sek.: Ich glaube.

Dichter tritt ein: Sie wünschen?

Terra: Sie können weitermachen.

Dichter mit einem Blick auf die Sek.: Ich glaube es ist schon zu Ende.

Terra: Was?

Dichter: Das Ende des Artikels ist schon ausgearbeitet.

Sek.: Oh, ich bin nur hübsch müde.

Terra: Schaut es euch zusammen durch. Ich mache mich inzwischen frisch. (ab)

Dichter: Ich will sie nicht unnötig mit dem Manuskript belästigen. Es ist fertig.

Sek.: wenn sie … danke.

Scharfes Licht.

Dichter, betrachtet sie, schüttelt den Kopf und tritt dann zum Schreibtisch. Er spielt mit der Aktenmappe und losen Blättern.: Sie also auch. (Pause) Wie alle. Ich habe mich getäuscht. Verzeihen sie. (Deutet spöttisch eine Verneigung an.) Ich hätte es wissen müssen.

Sek.: Was ist denn? Was wollen sie von mir? Drücken sie sich deutlicher aus.

D.: Das war deutlich genug. (zeigt nach links)

Sek.: Was geht sie das an? Ich tue meine Pflicht.

D. ironisch: Bravo, soll ich applaudieren?

Sek.: Phaaa (zuckt die Achseln)

D.: Oder sind ihnen Ovationen in anderer Form lieber?

Sek.: Was wollen sie eigentlich? Lassen sie mich doch in Ruhe.

D.: Seit wann so zimperlich?

Sek.: Sagen sie doch was sie wollen. Oder sind sie etwa? … nein … (lacht freudlos) … nein das wäre zu komisch …

D.: Was wäre zu komisch?

Sek.: Dass sie eifersüchtig sind. Nein das glaube ich nicht. Eifersucht ist verboten. Wir leben im Vernunft-Zeitalter.

D.: So?

Sek.: Aber, ja ja. Das ist doch klar. Das ist doch ganz klar.

D.: Klar?

Sek.: Aber natürlich! Selbst Märchen erzählt man zweckmäßig. Unser Erziehungsprogramm, sie wissen wie es …

D.: Ja, ich weiß, wie es gehandhabt wird.

Sek.: Kein äffisches verzärteln der Kinder mehr. Das Programm lautet: Ammenheime, Kindergärten, Erzieher, Ausbildner. Alles beruht auf gesundem Menschenverstand. Oder sind sie anderer Meinung? (Nimmt eine Zigarette zwischen die Lippen. D. gibt Feuer.)

D.: Sie weichen aus.

Sek.: Keine Blödheiten mehr. Alle Sentimentalität abgeschafft. (Tränende Handbewegung die sich forsch gibt.) … pfffft weg … (schluchzt)

D.: Das klingt nicht sehr überzeugend.

Sek. Tränen schluckend: Nein?

D.: Nein.

Sek. nimmt Puderdose und Lippenstift aus der rechten Schreibtischlade.

D.: Sie haben sich also schon eingenistet?

Sek. während sie sich schminkt, trotzig: Der Posten ist doch gut … oder? … und Terra ein netter Mensch … oder? … ich meine, er könnte anders sein.

D.: So … Terra … einfach Terra. Offiziell mag unser verehrter Weiser solche Anreden nicht. Auch nicht in seiner Abwesenheit.

Sek.: Ich meine er könnte hässlicher sein.

D.: Ich lausche mit Hingabe weiter?!

Sek. sich im Handspiegel betrachtend: So geht es schon. Finden sie nicht?

D.: Sie wissen genau, dass ich nur ihretwegen alle Erniedrigungen auf mich nehme.

Sek.: Ist meine Frisur in Ordnung?

D.: Das wissen sie!

Sek.: Sie Kindskopf, ist das nicht egal? (Pudert das Gesicht) Sie sind komisch. (öffnet die Cremedose und reibt sich die Hände ein) Sie sind wirklich komisch. (räumt die Schminksachen weg)

D.: Auch wenn sie es komisch finden. Ich liebe sie.

Sek. platzt hysterisch heraus: Ha, ha … ist ihnen das nicht … sie, sie Schnellzünder … (schluchzt, wieder in Lethargie zurückfallend). Das ist ihr Problem. (Hat den Stift aus der Tasche genommen und zieht die Brauen nach) … (während sie sich scheinbar nur auf ihre Tätigkeit konzentriert): Wie sehr? (bricht wieder in Lachen aus, das wie abgeschnitten endet) Verzeihung … ich … (streicht die Wimpern mit dem Bürstchen zurecht) Wie sehr?

D.: Mehr als sie glauben.

Sek. den Stift und das Bürstchen verstauend: Hätte ich bald vergessen. Übrigens, glaube ich überhaupt nichts mehr.

D.: Ich liebe sie!

Sek.: Wie sehr? (Lacht) lassen sie mich, ich muss mich beruhigen … (scharf) Mehr als ihr Leben?

D.: Ja

Sek. hysterisch: Dann beweisen sie es (zeigt nach links) das Bett ist noch offen und ich bin noch warm. Was mir jetzt fehlt kann ihr Vergnügen nur erhöhen.

D.: Sie sind verrückt! … war es wirklich das …

Sek.: Ja, es war das erste Mal. (auflachend) Wundert sie das? Mehr als sein Leben … so schaut das aus … sie sind feig … sie Feigling!

D.: Ich bin nicht übergeschnappt, meine süße Verrückte. Ich verstehe ihren Zustand gut …

Sek.: Meinen Zustand? Was für ein Zustand?

D.: Ich liebe dich, begreifst du? (Nimmt ihre Hand, die sie ihm schlaff überlässt) Begreifst du was das heißt? Was das wirklich bedeutet?

Sek.: Sie kommen ein bisschen spät drauf …

D.: Ich will sie beschützen …

Sek.: Jetzt? (schluckt) etwas spät …

D.: Es ist nie zu spät. Wir haben die Uhr erfunden. Wir zertrümmern sie und mit ihr die Zeit.

Sek.: Sie sind nicht mein Hausdichter.

D.: Ihre Ironie trifft mich …

Sek.: Sie verwirren alles noch mehr …

D.: Ich bin ehrlich …

Sek.: Aber Terra …

D.: Auch das lässt sich machen. Bitte hör zu weinen auf. Da hast du ein Sacktuch. (sie schluchzt) Es ist alles halb so schlimm. Glaub mir. Wir müssen schlauer als Füchse sein, den Schwanz eingezogen, den Bauch nach oben gedreht und totgestellt. Das ist nicht sehr lustig, ich weiß, aber gemeinsam …

Sek.: Gemeinsam … soweit habe ich noch nie gedacht. Wozu? Es kam alles so plötzlich. Etwas ist kaputt … in mir zerbrochen … obwohl ich mir der Ehre bewusst bin ...

D.: Keine Panik. Jammern nützt nichts. Wir müssen zusammenarbeiten. Im Augenblick musst du bei Terra um Sympathie für mich werben, tapferes Mädchen, dann können … das andere wird sich finden.

Sek.: Wie Füchse? Schlau wie Füchse?

D.: Ja.

Sek.: Füchse haben keine Schwänze. Dein Plan ist absurd … wenn man uns …

D.: Wieso haben Füchse keine Schwänze?

Sek.: Sie haben Ruten … Als Rute bezeichnet man die hintere Extremität.

D.: Ach so, ich bin kein Jäger.

Sek.: Du willst ihn loswerden … ich verstehe das, aber … ich weiß nicht so recht … Und wenn? Was ist mit den anderen? Was ist mit den anderen Weisen?

D.: Die Unterweisen haben ihn längst über. Sie trauen sich nur nicht das Maul aufzumachen und sind von schwacher Entschlusskraft. Aber man kann sie dazu bringen … (auf den zweifelnden Blick der Sek.) … ich begreife meine Rolle ist nicht sehr heroisch. Intrigen und Heroismus vertragen sich schlecht. Schlecht wie Feuer und Wasser …

Sek.: Weshalb tust du das?

D.: Deinetwegen, sagte ich das nicht?

Sek.: Es kommt zu schnell.

D.: Wir müssen eine Zeit lang gemein sein. (Durch die zweifelnden Blicke der Sek. in sprudelnde Verteidigung gedrängt.) Glaubst du mir fällt das leicht? Mir fällt das genauso schwer wie dir. Wenn der Chef spuckt reiße ich den Mund auf, bedanke mich und schlucke. Lang halte ich das nichtmehr aus. Und dann kommt noch die Qual so ein bezauberndes Geschöpf wie dich zwischen seinen Pratzen zu sehen.

Sek. mit naiver Koketterie: Bin ich denn bezaubernd?

D.: Mehr als bezaubernd!

Sek.: Schwör mir‘s!

D.: Ich schwöre!

Sek.: Ich finde mich nicht sehr hübsch. Nein.

D.: Du bist für mich eine bezaubernde Frau. Du bist für mich die reizendste Frau der Welt. Ich lüge nicht.

Sek.: Das Wort Welt habe ich befürchtet. Das sind doch Phrasen.

D.: Wie kannst du das unterscheiden? Verliebte wählen die Worte nicht. Echtes klingt oft falscher als Konstruiertes. Der ehrlichste Gefühlsüberschwang kann lächerlich wirken. Aber was rede ich. Terra muss weg. Anders können wir nicht leben. Ich erledige ihn. Wir erledigen ihn.

Sek.: Das sind blutige Blumen … du bringst ein blutiges Bukett zum ersten Rendezvous … meine Hände stinken nach seinem Schweiß … ich fühle mich schmutzig …

D.: Es war Nötigung.

Sek.: Glaubst du das? Macht das was aus?

D.: Nein.

Sek.: Magst du mich tatsächlich? … Mir ist alles egal.

D.: Das warst nicht du (küsst ihre Hände).

Sek.: Lass das, mir ist alles egal.

D. flüsternd: Ich brauche dein Vertrauen, dein absolutes Vertrauen.

Sek.: Sie sind ein Träumer.

D.: Ich bin Realist. Du musst mir sein Vertrauen erschmeicheln. Nein, sag‘ nichts … Er macht zwei grundlegende Fehler.

Sek.: Welche?

D.: Er hält sich für weise …

Sek.: Und zweitens?

D.: Glaubt er sich völlig sicher. Er hat sich mit Größenwahn infiziert. Die Krankheit endet für einen Politiker tödlich.

Sek.: Ich weiß noch nicht … er hat doch nichts Schlechtes getan … er …

Von der linken Seite her Pfeifen. Die beiden fahren auseinander. Terra tritt in einem Anzug und nach Frische duftend herein.

Terra: Fertig?

Sek.: Ja.

Terra: Was steht noch auf dem Programm?

Sek.: Heute … heute … (sieht im Terminkalender nach) Das Fernsehen wartet auf ihre Rede. (kurzer Blick auf die Uhr) Sie sollten längst hier sein.

Terra betätigt eine Klingel; Sekr. tritt ein.

Sekr.: Darf ich mir erlauben sie daran zu erinnern …

Terra: Ich weiß …

Sekr.: Darf ich das Team hereinlassen?

Terra: Sofort. (zum D. und der Sek.) Sie werden im Augenblick nicht gebraucht. Moment … (sucht am Schreibtisch)

Sek.: Erlauben sie … (reicht ihm eine Mappe)

Terra: Das war es "Danke". (Abgang der Beiden) Lassen sie die Herren eintreten!

Sekr. geht zur Tür, öffnet sie: Bitte

Das Team wälzt sich lautstark mit Kameras, Lampen, Kabeln und anderen Requisiten bewaffnet in den Salon. Hervorstechend ist ein Thronsessel mit hoher, schmaler Rückenlehne. (Er soll ernst und würdig wirken; am besten modernisierte, vereinfachte Gotik.) Das Gebilde ist aus Holz. Vier daran befestigte Treppen führen hinauf; umgeben den Sessel wie ein sich verjüngendes Podium. Er wird in der Bühnenmitte aufgestellt. Beleuchter, Kameramänner, Regisseure, Reporter, Bühnenarbeiter. Teils zivil, teils blaue und weiße Arbeitsmäntel. Die Leute arbeiten hastig und verändern binnen weniger Minuten die Symmetrie des Zimmers. Die abgehackten Zurufe sind nicht verständlich.

Regisseur zu Terra: Wir sind gleich so weit.

Terra hinter dem Schreibtisch sitzend: Bitte …

Maskenbildner zu Terra: Würden sie bitte zum Licht kommen Weisester. (Komplimentiert ihn auf einen Lederfauteuil vorm Schreibtisch) Darf ich sie ein bisschen behandeln?

Terra: Walten sie ihres Amtes … es muss ja angeblich sein …

Ma.: Der ungünstige Einfluss des Lichts … sie würden unnatürlich wirke … selbst einen Apoll müsste man schminken … womit ich nichts gesagt haben will …

Terra: Geht es wirklich nicht so?

Ma.: Die Leute würden glauben sie haben die Gelbsucht … bitte setzen sie sich. (Ein Spiegel und eine Kiste werden herbeigebracht. Der Maskenbildner nimmt aus ihr ein weißes Handtuch und bindet es Terra wie eine Serviette um.

Terra zum Sekr.: Welche Rede ist heute dran? Die aufputschende oder die ermutigende, beruhigende …?

Sekr.: Die Hass-Rede.

Terra: Aah …

Ma. zum unterwürfig wartenden Gehilfen: Den Lippenstift! So ein bisschen Rouge … sehr schöne Wimpern … Den Stift! …

Terra: Die Lippen lassen sie so wie sie sind … (wischt sich mit dem Tuch die Lippen ab) … ich mag das nicht.

Ma. Jammernd: Mein Kunstwerk … nein, bitte nur das nicht …

Terra: Machen sie weiter!

Ma.: Zu Befehl … ich sag ja nichts.

Terra: Hauptsächlich die Augenbrauen!

Ma.: Was für ein Instinkt! … und nun noch etwas blau für die Lidschatten … (den Arm starr nach hinten streckend, schrill) Violett! (Der Gehilfe klatscht das Gewünschte in die Hand) Bezaubernd … charakterfeste Züge … klar … herbsüße Linien … bezaubernde Reife … gut, sehr gut.

Terra: Fertig?

Ma.: Gleich, gleich nur noch eine kleine Betonung der Nasenwurzel … so jetzt wirken sie viel despotischer … nein, ausgezeichnet! … manche Menschen haben sich nach meiner Behandlung nicht wiedererkannt … sie suchten ihre Identität und fanden sie nicht … (Betrachtet sein Kunstwerk)

Terra: Fangen wir an!

Regisseur: Den Sessel etwas mehr nach links bitte! Nein, nein. (winkt mit der Rechten) etwas mehr rechts, nein nicht so weit rechts … wir haben das doch schon sooft geübt … wir haben doch immer die gleiche Position … ja … na endlich!

Der Sessel (Thron) steht jetzt auf der linken Seite nicht zu weit entfernt von der Bühnenmitte. Beim Transport wird er von der

Menschentraube der Bühnenarbeiter halb verdeckt. Erst am Bestimmungsort wird der Blick auf ihn frei. Die Beleuchter stellen ihre Lampen auf ihn ein. (Weißgrelles Licht) Auf der übrigen Bühne wird es dämmrig. Das Licht kommt (die Dämmerung abgesehen) ausschließlich von den Scheinwerfern, die sich auf der Bühne befinden.

Terra geht zum Thronsessel und wird vom Licht erfasst: Wo sind die Insignien?

Vier prächtig gekleidete Herolde schälen sich aus dem Dunkel ans Licht. Sie tragen feierlich den roten Zeremonienmantel. Hinter ihnen zwei weitere Herolde mit Zeremonienstab und Krone-Helm. Letzterer ruht auf einem roten Kissen. Sie nähern sich Terra und legen ihm den Mantel um. Er nimmt die Krone vom Polster hält sie einen Augenblick lang hoch und setzt sie dann auf. Die Herolde umdrängen ihn, während er langsam die Stufen hinaufsteigt. Nur sein Oberkörper und die Schultern der Herolde sind in Licht gebadet. Das Zeremoniell muss lautlos vor sich gehen. Terra setzt sich und ergreift den Stab. Das Licht ist seinem Oberkörper gefolgt. Zwei Herolde nehmen rechts und links von ihm Aufstellung. (auf der untersten Stufe des Podiums.)

Die Insignien. Die Krone: Grundform/=Tiara.

I.) Aus der mit einem Knauf (oben) versehenen Tiara wachsen in Kopfhöhe rechts und links sanft geschwungene Golddrahtbündel von etwa je einem halben Meter Länge. (Das ist variabel) Sie streben nach oben und enden in der Waagrechten. Von ihnen hängen (außen) golddurchwirkte, breite Bänder bis auf den Boden. Sie sind mit dicken Goldfransen verziert und können etwas nachschleifen.

1-ste Variante: Mischung aus Tiara und flachgedrückten Napoleonshut. Voller goldener Halbkreis von etwa 1 m Durchmesser (der Breite nach; die Tiefe darf höchstens 3 cm betragen) über dem sich die Spitze der Tiara erhebt. Die beiden Teile des Halbkreises sind seitlich anzusetzen. (zerschnittene Sonnenscheibe) Bänder wie oben.

2-te Variante: Der flache Halbkreis ist durchbrochen oder besteht aus Drahtgeflecht! Rosetten, Kettchen, Glasplättchen. Die Bänder bleiben. Der Stab ist übermannshoch und soll nicht unbedingt an einen Bischofsstab erinnern. Beide Gegenstände sind reich mit Steinen besetzt. Der Mantel: Großflächiges Muster in Form eines (oder zweier) Fabeltiers/re/ Unter Umständen nur Schmucksteine.

Die Aufmachung soll phantastisch und kostbar aussehen.

Kleidung der Herolde: Wämser mit Puffärmeln (vielleicht gezogen) weite Kniehose, hohe Schuhe. Das Gewand ist über und über mit silbernen und goldenen Pailletten bestickt. Dazwischen auch größere Plättchen aus Glas und Silber. Silber soll vorherrschen. Die hohen, sonst schmucklosen Hüte sind mit Federn versehen. Weiße Seidenschleifen. Die Aufmachung darf nicht lächerlich wirken.

Regisseur: Es ist so weit (gedämpft)

Maskenbildner, leise: Ein bisschen Schatten über den Wimpern …

Stimme: Pssst …

Terra: Ist das Manuskript sichtbar?

Regisseur: Nein sie sprechen frei.

In der Dämmerung, die vor Terra liegt, kniet ein Mann mit weißem Arbeitsmantel und hält das Manuskript hoch. Das Licht umfasst jetzt auch Terras Knie. Auf ihnen liegt der Mantel in malerischen Falten. Alles übrige wird in Finsternis getaucht. Auch der Mann im Arbeitsmantel erscheint nur mehr in Schemen.

Regisseur: Eins, zwei, drei – Klappe.

Terra; seine Stimme ist überlaut (Mikrophon): Terra der Oberweise spricht zu euch! Wir sind eine Nation von Weisen, Helden, Soldaten und Arbeitern. Dieser Idealzustand ist nicht von ungefähr gekommen. Nein, wir haben ihn mit Blut und Tränen erkauft und dafür bezahlt! Dank unserer gemeinsamen Bemühungen ist für die Arbeit eines fleißigen, aufrechten Volkes gesorgt. Dazu können wir mit glühendem Herzen und aus voller Kehle nur ein offenes "JA" sagen. (Deutet dem Mann das Manuskript näher zu halten. Das muss sehr diskret geschehen.) Aber ich habe ein Anliegen an euch. (Das Licht wird rötlich und steigert sich zum Rot.)

I. Vorschlag: Das Rot während der Rede andauernd wechseln.

II. Vorschlag: Wellenförmige Bewegungen des Lichts.

III. Vorschlag: Nur Mantel und Insignien in blutigem rot anstrahlen und das Gesicht weiß ausleuchten.

IV. Vorschlag: Kleine rote Glühbirnen sollen über Gewand und Insignien verstreut, abwechselnd aufglühen.

Schwächlicher Individualismus muss für immer ausgelöscht werden! Gesund, hart und immer mit feuchten Schnauzen lautet die Devise! Ich liebe euch Bürger! Solange Hirn, Hand und Fuß noch "Ja" rufen können liebe ich euch. Aber wehe den schmalbrüstigen, angstkeuchenden Individuen. Diesen myrmekophilen Parasiten mit ihren Verbrecherphysiognomien, ihrer ererbten Freiheit und den viehischen Hass gegen unsere Ordnung, die sie zu untergraben suchen! Sie, die unsere Gnade hassen. Das Wort Gnade sei ihnen ins Gesicht geschrieben. Sie die diese Gnade hassen werden um eben diese Gnade noch winseln und geifern. Ja, Volksgenossen, jenes dreckige Imperium meine ich, das die vollen Brüste seiner weißen Molkereien im Blut unseres Volkes badet! Das nur darauf bedacht ist den eigenen Samen großzuziehen und sich nicht um die Mittbürger kümmert, nein, nur den eigenen fetten Leib mästet. Dieser stinkende Mischmasch aus Korruption und Eigennutz den es, freilich ohne Erfolg, hinter der Maske der Humanität zu verbergen sucht. Ich schleudere ihnen tausendmal mein "Nein" entgegen! Diese Giftmischer der Nation, die vergeblich danach trachten eure Meinung durch anarchistisches Gebrüll zu manipulieren. (Winkt umzublättern) Der Umgang mit ihnen löst nur moralische und psychische Schäden aus. Die Heilanstalten sind voll davon. Und auch jetzt trifft mein Zorn die, die unser goldenes Heer Gottesgeißel nennen und außerdem die ruhmreichen Stützen des Staates als Mordbrenner bezeichnen! Und ich werde unbarmherzig sein! So unbarmherzig wie es nur geht! Sagt "Nein"! Ein offenes Nein wird zum fragwürdigen Ja. Drum Nein und wieder Nein! Da können die Bande des Blutes nichts mehr gelten! Da muss Freundschaft aufhören! Da muss der Hass zum Himmel schreien und das Firmament zerbrechen. Da muss die Wunde ausgebrannt, entgiftet und sterilisiert werden! Nein, da gibt es kein Zögern mehr! (Luftschöpfen) Wir sind keine Brandopfer am Altar des Intellekts! Es entspricht ganz ihrem Konzept, dass sie mit gleisnerischer Beredsamkeit immer wieder darauf hinweisen, es handle sich um kein Brandopfer.

(Brüllend) Es ist eins! (schnell) Es können Hunderte kommen und nach dem Tausendsten werde ich ins Gesicht schreien: Es ist ein Brandopfer! (Pause) Wir alle opfern. (schreiend) Aber keine Brandopfer! (ruhiger, sachlicher) Der innere Feind muss geschlagen werden, wo immer er auftaucht. Unter welchem Vorwand er sich auch nähert. Es ist unsere heiligste Pflicht diesem Gesindel das Handwerk zu legen. Das leiseste menschliche Mitgefühl wäre falsch am Platz, denn die Hand, die der aufrichtige Volksgenosse ihnen entgegenstreckt, bringt ihn selbst zu Fall. Aus diesem Grund bringen sie ja Argumente, die für einen Uneingeweihten anfänglich vernünftig klingen. Es ist Gott sei Dank so weit, dass die meisten Mitbürger ihr pseudointellektuelles Geschwafel anwidert. Dass ihre Worte in der Luft verpuffen. Trotzdem gilt es den Kampf weiterzuführen! Immer und ewig. Nur der stete Zustand des Kampfes kann den gesunden Volkskörper von der Milbe des Zweifels befreien! (Pause) Über euch, die ihr treu zur Idee steht, verstreuen wir unbarmherzige Gnade und niemand kann sagen, dass wir nicht zu unserem Wort stehen. (Kopfbewegung. Die Scheinwerfer erlöschen. Zugleich Bühnenlicht, Arbeitslicht, dass sich langsam erhellt.)

Alle applaudieren.

Terra nimmt die Krone ab, steigt herunter, wischt den Schweiß von der Stirn: War ich gut im Bild?

Sekr.: Sie waren großartig!

Terra: Nehmen sie das! (Gibt die Krone dem Regisseur. Der reicht sie an einen Untergebenen weiter.) Puh ist das heiß! (Öffnet den Mantelverschluss. Ein Bühnenarbeiter nimmt ihm den Mantel ab und wirft ihn über einen Sessel, auf dem bereits die Krone liegt.)

Terra: Das ist immer sehr strapaziös. Man müsste da was erfinden. Vielleicht eine Imitation die weniger wiegt …

Bühnenarbeiter zu einem anderen: Nimm den auch weg (zeigt auf den Stab der noch am Thronsessel lehnt) und leg ihn zu den übrigen!

Anderer B.: Ja, sofort …

Regisseur zu Terra: Wissen sie das ist Sprachkunst …

Bühnenarbeiter zum anderen: Dir ins Gesicht gesagt, das schaffst du nie …

Sek.: Die Rede war brillant. Klarer Aufbau, gute Sprachtechnik …

Bühnenarbeiter: Mach das doch nach, du Angeber!

Anderer: Ich sag ja nichts …

Regisseur: Ich bin gerührt …

Bühnenarbeiter: Ins Zentrum getroffen …

Terra, nach dem Handtuch greifend: Verflucht, sah man das?

Ma: Es störte nicht …

Terra, aufgebracht: Unmöglich! (Reißt das Tuch herunter)

Sekr.: Wenn ich mir eine Bemerkung erlauben darf, es störte nicht. Ihr Gesicht kam dadurch stärker ins Spiel.

Regisseur: Reines weiß unterstreicht …

Terra: Ich will auf keinen Fall lächerlich …

Ma.: Ganz im Gegenteil. Der Kopf des Johannes auf dem Tischtuch der Herodia … die Charakteristik ihrer Züge wurde besser ausgeleuchtet.

Terra: Ich will es ihretwegen hoffen!

Ordonanz tritt ein stramm grüßend: Mein Weisester!

Terra: Was gibt's?

Ordonanz: Darf ich sie einen Augenblick (blickt zweifelnd um sich) allein sprechen?

Terra: Selbstverständlich.

Die beiden ziehen sich in die Ecke zurück. Das Fernsehteam hantiert lautstark, rollt Kabel auf, schiebt den Thronsessel, unterhält sich mit den Herolden und betrachtet die Insignien (hebt sie hoch, probiert sie im geheimen, verstohlene Blicke nach Terra werfend und von Ernsthafteren dabei behindert).

Terra und die Ordonanz nähern sich dem Vordergrund.

Ordonanz: Sie gaben mir den Befehl es sofort zu melden.

Terra: Gut. Wo ist denn? Ah, … da! (zum Regisseur) Nicht so eilig ich kann sie noch brauchen.

Regisseur: Stopp, aufhören, stopp …

Terra zum Sekr.: Bitte richten sie meinen weisen Brüdern folgende Bitte aus. Sie sollen sich schnäuzen, kämmen und saubere Anstaltskleidung anziehen. Der Gefangene soll die Orden anlegen. Blödsinn ich meine das natürlich umgekehrt. Wiederholen sie.

Sekr.: Der Gefangene soll in sauberem Zustand erscheinen. Die verehrten Weisen mögen ihre Orden anlegen.

Terra: Machen sie schnell! (Sekr. ab) Terra, zu sich: Das ist die Gelegenheit (zum Team) Meine Herren, ich bitte um einen Augenblick Geduld. Gleich werden sie Zeugen eines historischen Moments sein. (Zum Regisseur) So, den Thronsessel brauche ich noch. Stellen sie ihn dort auf (zeigt auf die rechte Seite) Bühnenarbeiter befolgen den Wunsch.

B.: So?

Terra: Ja, gut. (Zu den Herolden) Bringen sie ihr Gewand in Ordnung.

Herold: Sehr wohl. (Machen sich am Gewand zu schaffen. Gegenseitige Hilfe.)

Terra: Bürsten sie den Mantel aus oder klopfen sie ihn, wie sie wollen …

Kämmerer: Selbstverständlich (beschäftig sich mit dem Mantel)

Ma.: Sollte ich nicht noch einmal …

Terra: Was?

Ma.: Ihr Aussehen retuschieren …

Terra: Unsinn …

Sek. eintretend: Wir sind so weit.

Terra: Ich lasse bitten.

Ordonanz öffnet die rechte Tür. Zwei Wachen führen einen Mann herein. Er trägt saubere blaugraue Kleidung. Sein Haar ist kurz geschoren. Es folgen zwei, Terra ähnlich sehende, Männer. Sie sind in Zivil. Die Brust ist mit Orden bepflastert und um den Hals hängt ein Ordensband. Die Ähnlichkeit mit Terra muss zwar auffallen, darf aber nicht zu stark sein.

Terra: Meine Lieben! Ich begrüße sie, sehr geehrte Brüder. (Gibt ihnen die Hand. Zum Gefangenen) Sauber siehst du aus. Dabei hat man dich in zerzaustem Zustand hergebracht. (zu allen) Weil sich diese Individuen gegen eine gerechte Verhaftung wehren! Da spricht man dann von unserer Brutalität. Wissen sie was für Thesen er verbreitet? Thesen die trotz ihrer Lächerlichkeit sehr gefährlich sind! Er spricht von der Gleichheit der Menschen! (leises Gelächter) Ja, er spricht tatsächlich davon. Können sie mir eine Regierungsform oder ein politisches System nennen, in dem diese absurde Idee verwirklicht wurde? Nennen sie mir einen Staat, egal zu welcher Zeit, in dem es keine sozialen Schichten und keine Führerpersönlichkeit, bzw. Führerpersönlichkeiten gab oder gegeben hat? Nennen sie mir ein einziges Beispiel in der menschlichen Geschichte und ich bin ihnen dankbar! Wer so etwas behauptet muss moralisch das Stadium eines Schweines haben! Steht moralisch auf der Stufe eines Schweines! Aber warte, ich werde dich umkrempeln! (zu den Mitweisen) Was sagen sie zu diesem Menschen, falls man dieses Produkt aus komplexen Ansichten überhaupt noch als Menschen bezeichnen kann.

Erster Weiser: Unglaublich!

2. Weiser: Widerlich!

1. Weiser: Es war höchste Zeit.

2. Weiser: Dieser Gleichmacher!

Terra: Ja, seht euch diesen Gleichmacher an (zeigt auf den Gefangenen) seht ihn euch genau an, es gibt noch mehrere von dieser Sorte.

Erster Weiser: Leider.

Terra: Ich leide auch. In Anbetracht der Aktualität des Vorfalls (nimmt einen der Weisen am Ärmel und zieht ihn zur

Rampe, der Andere folgt ihnen) möchte ich euch bitten, dass ihr persönlich … zieht ihm sanft die Würmer aus der Nase. Wir brauchen alle die sich angesteckt haben! Sämtliche Komplizen! … behandelt ihn wie immer.

Der Regisseur winkt die Fernsehleute zurück. Das Team weicht unter Augenverdrehen und himmelwärts schreienden Handbewegungen in den Hintergrund aus.

Regisseur: Aber bitte, bitte … (zu den Weisen und dem Gefangenen) Bitte hierher meine Herren, darf ich bitten … (zum Team) hopp, hopp … ein wenig schneller … (zu den Weisen) Bitte da meine Herren … Weisheit rücken sie auch ein bisschen näher … so, ja … gut … sehr gut … den Kerl von oben beleuchten … krasser … ein Gangster, soll wie ein Gangster aussehen.

Terra: Die Kamera schwenkt von mir zum Gefangenen und zurück. Verstanden? Einzelheiten überlasse ich ihrem Talent.

Ma.: Wir müssen den Gefangenen und die verehrten Herren schminken. Wissen sie ein wenig zumindest …

Terra: weshalb soll nur ich alles erdulden; freilich, freilich …

Regisseur: Ist etwas?

Terra: Schminkt das Schwein und meine Mitbrüder … (zu ihnen) Ich sehe euch gerne einmal in der Rolle des Opfers.

1.W.: Wie kann man nur so boshaft sein (lacht)

Gefangener: Nein (schreiend) Nein!

Terra: Das werden wir sehen.

Mehrere Wachen stürzen herbei, um den Gefangenen niederzuhalten. Ihr grauer Klotz klebt den Mann am Sessel fest. Es wird versucht ihn zu reinigen und zu schminken. Zwei neu hinzukommende Maskenbildner befassen sich inzwischen mit dem Weisen. Deutlicher Gegensatz in der Behandlung.

Ma. zum Gefangenen: Brav sein Schätzchen. Es geschieht dir nichts. Stillhalten! (zu Terra) so geht das nicht … so kann ich unmöglich arbeiten …

Terra: Eine Spritze!

Der Gefangene wehrt sich verzweifelt. Das Fernsehteam steht abwartend da. Man hört nur das Schnaufen und Ächzen der Ringenden. Eine Wache kommt mit einer Ampulle, schiebt den Ärmel des Gefangenen hinauf und verabreicht ihm die Spritze. Alles geschieht der Situation entsprechend sehr umständlich.

Terra: Na?

Ma.: Er wird schon ruhiger. (macht sich an die Arbeit) Es klappt. Wenn das kein Fortschritt ist … na … so … ja, so … so … jetzt sieht er schon eher wie eine Kanaille aus … (zurücktretend) zufrieden?

Terra: Ja.

Regisseur: Bitte auf die Plätze!

Die Wachen ziehen sich zurück. Die Weisen nehmen rechts und links vom Gefangenen Platz. Terra setzt die Krone auf. Die Herolde hängen ihm den Mantel um der diesmal von gelber Farbe ist. Terra erklettert den Thron. Helles bläuliches Bühnenlicht. Vom Schnürboden herab fallen warme gelbe Strahlen auf Terra und hüllen ihn ein.

Regisseur: Achtung …

Terra: Wir können …

Regisseur: Aufnahme!

Terra: Der Mann mit dessen Anblick ich euch leider belästigen muss ist ein Volksverräter. Ich will weder die Zahl seiner Delikte anführen och ihre Art. Es könnten sich Jugendliche unter den Zusehern befinden die dadurch moralischen Schaden erleiden würden. Also verzichte ich darauf. Freilich könnte ich ihn als armen Verirrten bezeichnen, als verirrtes Schaf, wenn ich das wollte, aber seine Schandtaten sind zu groß. Wir werden versuchen ihn, unter Berücksichtigung seiner zerschundenen Seele, auf den richtigen Weg zu bringen. Es ist für mich immer schrecklich, wenn ich sehe, wie ein Mensch sich selbst vernichtet. (wendet sich an die Weisen) Ich lege ihnen diesen bedauerlichen Fall ans Herz und baue dabei auf ihre Erfahrung. Behandeln sie ihn mit größtmöglicher Rücksicht. Dass ist meine persönliche Bitte an sie. Ich weiß, dass sie unnötig ist, spreche sie aber trotzdem aus. Ich kenne nur zu gut die Qualität ihrer therapeutischen Behandlung und habe deshalb vollstes Vertrauen zu ihnen. Ich weiß, dass sie wie immer mit Rücksicht und Sanftmut vorgehen werden. Er wird bei uns alle Annehmlichkeiten genießen. Daran besteht kein Zweifel. Ich sehe jetzt deutlich eure empörten Gesichter vor mir, eure gereckten Fäuste, ich höre euch schreien: Weg mit diesem Auswurf! Es ist aber nicht unsere Aufgabe Verbrechen mit Verbrechen zu vergelten, nein wir wollen heilen und helfend wirken. Verdrängt deshalb euren Zorn, schließt ihn in die geheimsten Winkel eures Herzens ein, vergesst ihn. Wir werden ihn in die menschliche Gemeinschaft zurückführen. Ich danke euch.

Die Lampen erlöschen. Die Geschminkten werden gereinigt. Aufbruchslärm.

Terra; er hat die Krone abgelegt und schleppt den Mantel nach: Wir müssen seine Kumpel … mit allen Mitteln … so sanft wie … (lauter) sie wissen lieber Herr Kollege, sanft.

1.W: Ich habe begriffen.

2.W: Man kann das nicht dulden. Auf bald. (ab) Auch das Fernsehteam ist im Abgang begriffen.

Ordonanz: Noch Befehle?

Terra: Nein.

Ordonanz geht stramm grüßend hinaus.

Terra: Zwei Hunde bin ich los. (klingelt)

Dichter eintretend: Mein Weisester?

Terra: Das Verhör sofort aufzeichnen! Aber das bleibt unter uns! Verstanden?

Dichter: Ich bin mir …

Terra: Beeilen sie sich! Das ist wichtiger als sich ihr Kleinhirn träumen lässt.

Dichter: Jawohl (ab)

Terra: Das Wort "sanft" konnten alle hören … Eine Folterung! Ein Gruselkabinett! Potentielle Sadisten! Hinter ihrer sauberen Fassade … man hintergeht mich … so eine Teufelei hinter meinem Rücken!

Dichter: Die Sache läuft!

Terra: Gut. Die sind mir … ich stolpere zu oft über sie. Man schleppt sie wie Unrat mit sich … nicht wahr? … sagten sie was?

Dichter: Ein treffender Vergleich.

Terra: Die sind Behinderung sonst nichts.

Dichter: Das ist klar.

Terra: Die verdammte Schminke. Das Zeug klebt. Ich muss mich waschen. Ich schenke ihnen großes Vertrauen. (ab)

Dichter: Arschloch.

Sek. eintretend: Sei vorsichtig!

Dichter: Ich pfeif drauf.

Sek.: Bitte!

Dichter: Deine Zuneigung macht mich stark. Ich könnte brüllen!

Sek.: Im Zwinger?

Dichter: Es müsste ja nicht sehr laut sein.

Sek. lacht.

Dichter: Du lachst wieder! Ich sehe dich gerne lachen. Ja, ich sehe dich gerne lachen. Wusstest du übrigens, dass das der einzige Raum ohne Wanzen ist?

Sek.: Wanzen?

Dichter: Ja, Wanzen.

Sek.: Ach so, Wanzen. Daran hab‘ ich gar nicht gedacht.

Dichter: Könnte ich sonst so reden?

Sek.: Daran hab‘ ich gar nicht gedacht. Wir haben ein wenig Zeit …

Dichter: Ich liebe nicht nur deinen Körper, ich liebe dich!

Sek.: Ruhe, das redet sich so leicht … hast du hingehalten?

Dichter: Das fehlt noch. Aber, deiner Erziehung nach müsste es dich ehren.

Sek.: Zyniker!

Dichter: Wir brauchen erst eine gesunde Basis.

Sek.: Basis.

Dichter sie leicht umarmend: Ruhe, Gelassenheit … lache doch.

Sek.: Wie lieb du das sagst.

Dichter: Kühles Köpfchen bewahren sonst geht der Kopf allein spazieren.

Sek.: Ich werde schon …

Dichter: Zusammenreißen!

Sek.: Ja.

Dichter: Ihr Frauen seid doch Naturtalente. Überhaupt du.

Sek.: Ich? Findest du mich hübsch?

Dichter: Mehr als ich im Moment beweisen kann.

Sek.: Gefällt dir mein Make-up?

Dichter: Könnte dezenter sein.

Sek.: Terra wünscht es so.

Dichter: Das geht vorbei. Ohne Hormonspritzen ist er ein halber Mann. Du bestätigst ihn.

Sek.: Ich?

Dichter: Das ist deine wichtigste Funktion.

Sek.: Ich will nicht mehr …

Dichter: Ich sage doch wir müssen (schneidend) und du wirst ausharren mein armes Opferlämmchen. Ich auf meinem und du auf d. einem Posten.

Sek.: Jeder auf seinem … wir sind eigentlich herrlich verboten.

Dichter: Das sind wir.

Sek.: Aber … er hat doch nichts … außerdem ist Terra ein schöner Name oder findest du ihn nicht gut? Ich meine er hat irgendetwas.

Dichter: Terra. Weißt du wie er tatsächlich heißt? Aloisius Hundsburger. Einfach Aloisius Hundsburger!

Sek.: Das ist sehr ernüchternd. Das ist … aber wird es … nein das habe ich nie gedacht. Eine Frage noch … wird es wirklich gut gehen?

Dichter: Das ist fast hundertprozentig klar.

Sek.: Ich vertraue dir … und hoffe …

Dichter: Ich glaube er kommt.

Terra tritt ein: Dichterchen … ja was wollte ich ihnen sagen? Ach ja, sie werden nicht gebraucht. Machen sie sich eine angenehme Stunde. Es wird ihnen schon etwas einfallen. Nachher … wir werden sehen.

Dichter mit stummer Verneigung ab.

Sek.: In wenigen Minuten müssen die Kinder eintreffen.

Terra: Ja, ja, die Fratzen aus der Provinz wollen mich begucken. Einmal im Leben den Oberweisen sehen. Nett was? Die süßen Bengel mit den winzigen Stupsnäschen und den roten

Apfelwangen … man wird direkt sentimental. (Streicht der Sek. kurz übers Gesicht) Ich hab‘ Kinder gern. Ja das ist eine Schwäche von mir. Außerdem erhöhen sie die Popularität … Ich verbinde gerne das Nützliche mit dem Angenehmen.

Sek.: Immer?

Terra: Fast immer. Setz dich dorthin. (deutet nach links) Ja.

Er nimmt hinter dem Schreibtisch Platz. Drückt eine Klingel. Zirpendes, heiseres Schrillen.

Ordonanz: Ist es so weit Weisester?

Terra: Die Knospen sollen zum Gärtner kommen. … lassen sie die Kinder ein.

Ordonanz: Zu Befehl. (Ab)

Terra zur Sek.: Wie ist der Dichterling eigentlich? Er wirkt nichtssagend, ist er dumm? Oder ist er treu? Oder ist er beides? Das wäre eine gelungene Mischung.

Sek.: Treu!

Terra: Ist er dumm?

Sek.: Ein Löwe …

Terra: Wie bitte?

Sek.: Völlig ergeben. Er hängt … hängt mit einer naiven Liebe an dir.

Terra: Also dumm. Ich mag unvoreingenommene Menschen. Wo bleiben die Kinder?

Sek.: Du bist ungeduldig!

Terra: Du? Ach so, … aber ab jetzt per “Sie” mein Engel … und ich bitte sie, das auch in Zukunft so zu halten … nämlich in der Öffentlichkeit … oder wenn sich andere Personen in der Nähe befinden …

Sek.: Entschuldigen sie Weisester.

Terra: Nicht so förmlich … Mittelmaß bewahren! … Ich brauche Kräfte denen ich vertrauen kann. Der Poet … sind sie sicher, dass er brav ist?

Sek.: Absolut.

Wache eintretend, stramm: Die Kinder bitten empfangen zu werden! (Von Ferne Gesang)

Terra, mit übertriebener Begeisterung: Wo sind sie? (erhebt sich) … wo sind die Knirpse? Streng zur Sek.) Ist alles fertig?

Sek.: Wie? Ach ja, gerade, ja.

Die Kinder marschieren in steifen Zweierreihen herein. Sie haben den Mund mit weißen Tüchern verbunden. Die Tücher spannen sich straff über Lippen und Nasen und sind im Nacken verknotet. Einheitskleidung. Sämtliche Laute der Kinder, auch das Gedicht, werden von einem Lautsprecher ausgestrahlt. (Überdurchschnittlich laut) Sie singen folgende Hymne, die erst beendet wird, nachdem sie vor Terra ein Quadrat gebildet haben. Zwei herbe, trockene Frauen in strenger Tracht kommandieren die Kinder mit nervösen Handbewegungen und buckeln jedes Mal, wenn sie sich in Terras Blickwinkel glauben. Terra nickt während des Ganzen gerührt.

Die Hymne:

Oh, du mein Weisester.

Oh, du Gescheitester.

Oh, oh, oh, oh.

Oh, du mein Allerlei.

Liebliche Kind-Schalmei.

Oh, oh, oh, oh.

Und wir glauben an dich.

Leben und Sterben ist

nur oh, oh, oh …

Knabe mit einem Blumenstrauß in der Hand tritt vor. Monotones Geleier aus einem Lautsprecher (der Ton kann schwanken).

Lass‘ die Strahlen deiner Gnade

nicht an uns vorübergehen.

Lass‘ oh Weisester von allen

Nicht nur uns im Dunkel stehen

lass‘ … lass‘ … (Weinen aus dem Lautsprecher)

Erzieherin nimmt den Blumenstrauß und überreicht ihn Terra.

Giftig zum Kind: Dummkopf!

Terra: Die Aufregung … (Tätschelt den Knaben) Ist schon gut … das ist doch verständlich … (Der Knabe folgt der ausgestreckten Hand der Erzieherin und ordnet sich wieder ein.)

Erzieherin: Ich bitte …

Terra, mit hoheitsvoller Handbewegung: Aber nicht doch … psst … (die Blumen hin und her drehend) … für mich gepflückt? … sehr brav … (zur Sek.) Sind sie nicht putzig? (Gibt der Sek. die Blumen)

Sek.: Sehr!

Terra: Ihr seid bezaubernd Kinder! Wollt ihr Schokolade? (Klatschend) Wo bleibt die Schokolade?

Diener, eintretend: Sehr wohl die Schokolade.

Terra: Und viel (zaghaftes Lachen aus dem Lautsprecher) … für alle muss euer Weisester sorgen. Was hältst du da in der Hand?

Kind, zaghaft (sehr laut): Eine Pfeife …

Terra: Darf ich? Oder erlaubst du es nicht? (Er pfeift) Guter Klang. Klingt sie immer so gut?

Kind, schüchtern (sehr laut): Ja Weisester.

Terra: So ehrfürchtig … aber ich hätte mich an eurer Stelle nicht anders benommen. Nein, gar nicht anders. Ich bin voll Freude … Weshalb? Weil ihr mich liebhabt. Weil wir uns alle liebhaben. Dass muss aber auch so sein. Ich kann aber auch streng werden. Bei so folgsamen Kindern, freilich nicht … befolgt ihr immer die Anweisungen der Erzieherinnen?

Kinder: Wir sind sehr brav.

Kind mit süßer Kinderstimme, entzückend vorlaut: Wir sind die bravsten von allen!

Terra, lachend: So jung und schon so klug. Als ich so groß war (zeigt die Größe) spielte ich mit Zinnsoldaten, piff, paff …

Kinder: Wir wollen gute Soldaten werden.

Terra: Das ist klar … und die Vaterlandsfeinde totschießen, nicht wahr? Bumm … weg mit ihnen. Da lacht ihr was? Die

Sonne geht auf euren Gesichtern auf, würde mein Dichter sagen. Dichter sagen immer so etwas. (Ärgerlich) Wo bleibt die Schokolade? Gleich ihr Lieben, sofort.

Diener tritt ein. Er verteilt aus einem großen Korb Schokolade unter den Kindern, die sich stumm und marionettenhaft verneigen. Sie stehen nach dem Empfang der Nascherei gleich wieder starr da.

Terra: Wie das schmeckt. Nun muss ich mich aber wieder um das Wohl des Staates kümmern. Ab durch die Mitte! In Zweierreihen marsch! (schnalzt mit den Fingern)

Erzieherin: Es war uns eine große Ehre mein Weisester. Sie haben durch den Empfang unsere pädagogischen Bemühungen sehr unterstützt.

Terra: Sie haben mir eine große Freude bereitet.

Alle Kinder bis auf eines gehen die Hymne singend ab. Der Diener folgt ihnen.

Kind, im normalen Ton: Dein Autogramm bitte!

Terra: Ausnahmsweise (schreibt) … aber nur dir allein. (Klatscht das Kind auf den Popo, es läuft den anderen nach, wird auf halbem Weg von der Erzieherin eingefangen und zur Gruppe geschleift. Die Türe wird geschlossen.

Terra zur Sek.: Wie war ich? Gut, wie?

Sek.: Sehr.

Terra: Lieben sie Kinder?

Sek.: Natürlich.

Terra: Gute Show, finden sie nicht?

Sek.: Sie haben sich selbst übertroffen.

Terra: Das ist kaum möglich.

Sek.: Ja.

Terra: Kannst du nicht widersprechen? Du nickst immer nur … Ich bin für Gehorsam aber manchmal könntest du anderer Meinung sein. Das steht dir doch frei.

Sek.: Es ist ein bisschen viel …

Terra: Ich verstehe deine Verwirrung …

Sek.: Es ist etwas …

Terra: Am besten sie spannen ein bisschen aus … schicken sie mir den Phantasten rein!

Sek.: Ist er einer?

Terra: Zeitweise.

Sek. ab.

Terra: Die beiden braten am Spieß meiner Liebe.

Sek. tritt mit Dichter ein.

Dichter: Mein Weiser! Ich habe gehört, dass ihr meine Wenigkeit …

Terra zur Sek.: Sie sollen nicht alles ausplaudern! (Droht scherzhaft) außerdem habe ich noch nichts Konkretes gesagt …

Sek.: Verzeihen sie, ich dachte …

Terra: So, sie dachten. Zufällig haben sie richtig vermutet. (Zum Dichter) Mein lieber Freund, ich schenke ihnen mein Vertrauen in noch unbegrenzterem Maße als ich es bis jetzt getan habe. Sie übernehmen ab sofort die Verantwortung für meinen persönlichen Schutz. Das ist mehr eine Formsache. Außerdem möchte ich sie mit einer Stelle im Staatssicherheitsministerium betrauen, aber das ist noch nicht aktuell, der Posten ist noch besetzt … ferner erhebe ich sie in den Rang eines Stabsoffiziers mit den entsprechenden Privilegien und der zustehenden Dotierung … ja, das wäre alles.

Dichter: Ihre Gnade erschlägt mich. Ich hoffe, dass ich der Aufgabe gewachsen bin.

Terra: Gut. Das wird sich zeigen. (Zur Sek.) Sie können sich frisch machen. (Sek. ab) Sie sind über mein Vertrauen überrascht, aber mit ihnen habe ich keine Komplikationen … sie sind der Idee treu. Man hört nur Gutes über sie. Nicht, dass mir jemand schaden könnte, aber ich brauche Leute, auf die ich mich hundertprozentig verlassen kann.

Dichter: Ich hoffe ihr Vertrauen zu rechtfertigen. Ich bin mir dabei der Verantwortung voll bewusst.

Terra: Was ist mit dem Gefangenen?

Dichter: Er liegt flach.

Terra: So schnell?

Dichter: Er hatte eine zarte Konstitution.

Terra: Traurig. Traurig und gemein. Wo ist die Aufnahme?

Dichter: Zur Stelle (Geht zur Tür, öffnet sie und schleppt eine koffergroße Maschine herein. Sie kann durch wegstehende Drahtbüschel und Antennen ruhig etwas utopisch aussehen) Bitte!

Terra: Sie treue Seele!

Dichter: Ich tue nur meine Pflicht.

Terra: Freilich … sie hören und sehen was ich will …

Dichter: Und liebe was sie lieben.

Terra: Ich möchte sie fast als kleinen Bruder bezeichnen.

Dichter: Soll ich die Stimmen tanzen lassen?

Terra: Rasch, ich möchte die Rüden bellen hören.

Dichter: Ersticken werden sie im eigenen Gift …

Er hantiert am Apparat. Ein den Raum unangenehm durchschleifendes Quietschen. (Es muss für den Zuhörer peinlich sein.) Der Dichter spielt eine Zeit lang, sucht den richtigen Ton, das Geräusch verändert sich dementsprechend ein paar mal. Dann Stimmen, die langsam an Klarheit gewinnen. Diese Stimmen werden lauter und leiser, tönen bald aus dem Rücken des Zuschauerraums, bald von der Seite. Dazwischen überdeutliches Schnaufen.

1.Weiser: Wir sollen dich sanft behandeln. Das heißt das Gegenteil von sanft. In unserer Sprache zumindest. Wir leisten Maßarbeit. Es geht um unsere Existenz. (Klatschen)

Terra: In ihrer Sprache … Existenz.

2.Weiser: Wir pressen dich aus wie eine Zitrone. Der Weise Bruder will, dass du quatschst ... und das wirst du auch, du Kretin. Namen wollen wir, Namen … sonst nichts. Das ist doch ganz einfach. Vornamen und Zunamen. Mehr nicht.

Gef. undeutlich: Ich weiß nichts … nein, nein, nein … (Das Schreien geht in gurgeln über das sehr laut ist aber bald zum undefinierbaren Geräusch abstirbt.)

Terra: Was? Die machen sich über mich lustig!

1.W.: Wir sind nicht kleinlich (sehr lautes Winseln) Druck verstärken! (Summen, beides stirbt ab)

2.W.: Sachte mein Lieber, wir bringen ihn noch um … na Kleiner, kennst du die Folter der hundert Tage? … schau‘ dir das Lager hübscher Spielsachen an … alles zu Diensten … (Metallgeklirr) So spuck aus (man hört das Geräusch eines Bohrers.)

Terra: Eine Gemeinheit.

Dichter: Unglaublich.

1.W.: Reiß die Augen auf! Mittelalter und Neuzeit treffen sich hier. Lauter kitzlige Alpträume. Renaissancemethoden gefällig? Oder etwas Chinesisches? Ein wenig guter Wille und alles wird zum Folterwerkzeug. Mach endlich das Maul auf! (Stöhnen) Na gut? Na? Na? (Gebrüll) Gefällt dir das besser? Ich glaube er hat was gegen Strom. (Geplätscher) Wasser erfrischt mein Engel. Na, komm schon … na komm (Klatschen) Dein Wunsch ist uns Befehl und heute ist Ausverkauf. Einmal quatschst du ja doch. Du quälst dich umsonst ab. Wie er schwitzt!

2.W.: Na? Sollen wir schärfer werden? Es tut uns genauso weh wie dir. Wir sind ja keine Sadisten! Wir sind feinfühlige Menschen. Das alles wäre gar nicht notwendig. Wir könnten uns gemütlich miteinander unterhalten. Eine Plauderei, von Mensch zu Mensch. Es scheint dir gleichgültig zu sein, dass Privilegierte so mit dir reden … ich spreche fast wie ein Gleichgestellter … (surren, Gebrüll) … die armen Finger … aber wir haben gute Ärzte, die renken alles wieder ein … spielst du Klavier? … was?

1.W.: Spielt er? … damit wird's vorbei sein … ach das gehört geölt … überhaupt der Staub … das muss wieder einmal geputzt werden sonst hängt man uns eine Klage wegen mangelnder Hygiene an. (Lachen) … ist der Kerl stur …

2.W.: Dabei erleichtert ein Geständnis … du hast ein Faible für so alte Dinger … mir ist die Methode zu direkt. Elektrizität ist mir lieber …

Der Gefangene, unartikuliert: Nein … ich kann nichts sagen … (langes Heulen)

Terra: Dreh ab mir wird schlecht. Diese Kanaillen! (Dichter schaltet den Apparat ab.) Was taten sie noch?

Dichter: Sie steigerten sich in einen Rausch. Deshalb der letale Ausgang.

Terra: Die Hunde! (Klingelt)

Ordonanz: Sie wünschen?

Terra: Ich möchte sofort die Richter sprechen.

Dichter: Sie warten. Es ist alles vorbereitet. Die Aufnahme ist allen zugänglich gemacht worden.

Terra: Gut. Die Henker!

Ordonanz: Ich gehe und öffne den Weisen, den Richtern, den Henkern die Tür. (Macht die Mitteltür auf.)

In Reihen kommen die Gerufenen herein. Die Richter tragen rote Talare.

Terra: Ich begrüße sie meine Herren.

Alle: Es lebe der Weiseste.

Terra auf die Gefangenen zutretend, schnell: Das werdet ihr büßen! (Die beiden sind nur mit Hemd und Hose bekleidet, einer trägt Reitstiefel. Die Hemdkragen sind offen. Sie sind nicht gefesselt.) Ich gab den ausdrücklichen Befehl den Gefangenen sanft zu behandeln. Vor Zeugen! Das ist ein Skandal! Das ist ungeheuerlich!

1.W, schreiend: Das ist ein Komplott!

Terra: Was dachtest du?

1.W.: Du … sie sagten sanft wie immer.

Terra: Richtig. Sanft wie immer.

2.W.: Eben, wie immer. Wenn sie das in die Öffentlichkeit zerren werden sie selbst am meisten darunter zu leiden ha …

Terra: Frechheit! (Brüllend) das ist eine maßlose Frechheit!

1.W.: Sie kennen die Methoden ganz genau, haben sie selbst …

Terra: Was? Das ist der Höhepunkt! Findet man Worte?

2.W.: Mit ihrer Billigung …

Terra: Du willst mich verspotten? Was wird aus braven Beamten, wenn man ihnen freien Lauf lässt? Mörder werden sie!

1.W.: Aber wir behandeln doch schon seit Langem, und zwar auf gemeinsamen Beschluss die Ge …

Terra: Seit Langem? Seit Langem? … Vielleicht jahrelang? … Und ich bin ahnungslos! … tsss … keine Ahnung … weiß davon nichts …

2.W.: Das ist eine Niederträchtigkeit! Ich erhebe Einspruch! Ich werde Beweise …

Terra: Was erhebst du? Einspruch? (Zu den Wachen) Stopft ihm das Maul!

1.W.: Du verfluchte Sau!

Den beiden wird mit weißen Tüchern der Mund verstopft.

Sie ringen mit den Wachen, ohne Erfolg.

Terra: Welcher Mensch wäre auf diese Idee gekommen. Das widerspricht dem gesunden Menschenverstand! Eine Folterkammer in unserem Keller. Sowas muss man sich einmal plastisch vorstellen! Das ist unbegreiflich! Sicherlich trage ich durch meine Gutgläubigkeit Schuld, aber wussten sie, dass wir Kriminelle unter uns haben? Wussten sie davon? So ein Verbrechen! Wie stehen wir dem Volk gegenüber da? Ich für meinen Teil habe nichts gewusst und kann nur hoffen, dass auch sie ein reines Gewissen haben. (Scharf) Das kann ich nur hoffen! Die von unserer Regierung unterzeichneten Todesurteile sind regulär. Aber Folter, meine Herren, Folter! Unglaublich! Ich kann es nicht fassen! (zum Dichter) Haben sie schon die Schlagzeilen für die Presse?

Dichter: Ja, bitte. (Zieht einen Zettel aus der Rocktasche.) Das Vertrauen des Oberweisen auf schändlichste Art hintergangen! Niemand weiß die Namen aller Beteiligten! Werden weitere Köpfe rollen?

Terra: Das kommt fett gedruckt! Haben sie kapiert, meine Herren?

Dichter: Bitte beruhigen sie sich!

Terra: Ich kann das Schreckliche noch immer nicht fassen! Meine Autorität untergraben! Bin ich von lauter Bestien umgeben?

Dichter: Beruhigen sie sich!

Terra, zu den Richtern: Brauchen sie noch Beweise? Wie lautet ihr Entschluss?

Oberrichter: Der Fall ist klar. Sie sind verurteilt Weisester!

2.Richter: Ihre Schuld wiegt wie ein Strick …

Terra: Das Urteil?

Oberrichter: Tod durch Erhängen.

2.Richter: Sie werden so lange am Hals aufgehängt bis der Tod eintritt.

1.W. reißt sich nach verzweifelten Anstrengungen los, flüchtet in eine Ecke, sinkt in die Knie und schreit: Das ist doch Wahnsinn. Das könnt ihr uns nicht antun … hört mit der Komödie auf! (Zum Publikum) Sie sollen aufhören … bitte … das ist doch … (die Wächter umkreisen ihn) … wagt nicht mich anzufassen … (aufspringend, herrisch brüllend) Sie wissen anscheinend nicht wer ich bin! (Die Wachen fallen auf Terras Wink über ihn her) Loslassen, das ist ein Bef … (sein Mund wird verstopft).

Terra: Ich danke ihnen. Widerlich. Da werden noch strenge Untersuchungen folgen. Hochnotpeinlich. Ich danke ihnen.

Die weisen werden hinausgeschleift. An der Tür verneigen sich die Wachen stumm vor Terra. Die Richter, Weisen und Henker formieren sich in Dreierreihen und folgen würdevoll. Ebenfalls stumme Verbeugung. Die Ordonanz schließt von außen die Tür.

Terra: Zwei weniger und noch immer zu viel.

Dichter: Man könnte das rationalisieren.

Terra: Das könnte man … strengen sie ihre Phantasie an, wir brauchen Verbrechen und Mitwisser … (Auf eine Klingel drückend; trauriges Summen ertönt) Das muss weg (Deutet auf zwei Fotos; zum eintretenden Diener) Räum die Fotos weg! Die, die beiden da.

Diener: Die Herren?

Terra: Ja, die Toten. Ab in die Rumpelkammer.

Dichter: Zu den kommenden Leichen.

Terra: Sie haben mich begriffen.

Diener nimmt die Bilder samt den dazugehörigen Lorbeerkränzen von der Wand und schleicht hinaus.

Dichter: Darf ich sie beglückwünschen?

Terra: Noch nicht, das ist erst …

Dichter: Der Anfang.

Terra: Richtig. Man soll den Tag nicht vor dem Abend loben.

Dichter: Ich bewundere sie.

Terra: Und ich bin hungrig. (sieht auf die Uhr) Essenszeit! Wo bleibt der Koch?

Klopfen; ein appetitlicher Koch tritt ein: Sie …

Terra: Weshalb kommen sie erst jetzt?

Koch: Verzeihung, ich wollte nicht stören. Es war so ein starker Verkehr … Parteienverkehr …

Terra: Ach so …

Koch: … und da wollte ich nicht stören. Was wünschen der Weiseste zu speisen?

Terra: Was ich essen will? Ich habe Lust auf Champignons, Gänseleber, Sauce Tartar … sie wissen ja ungefähr … pikant bitte. Ja und Burgunder. Zur Nachspeise Obst und … na das wissen sie schon.

Koch: Selbstverständlich (knicksend ab).

Terra: Essen sie eigentlich auch?

Dichter: Manchmal … zeitweise …

Terra: Wann?

Dichter: Wenn es meine Zeit erlaubt.

Terra: Ein Philosoph ist zur Audienz gemeldet. Plato heißt er. Kennen sie ihn?

Das Essen wird auf Silbertassen hereingetragen.

Dichter: Ja, das ist auch einer von denen …

Terra: Lassen sie das jetzt. Wenden wir uns Erfreulicherem zu.

Dichter: Bitte.

Terra nervös im Teller stochernd: Wo bleibt der Zeller?

Koch: Pardon, sogleich (ab)

Terra: Zeller … lieben sie Zeller?

Dichter: Ich liebe ihn sehr.

Der Salat wird gebracht.

Terra: Auch so zubereitet?

Dichter: Sehr gustiös.

Terra mit vollem Mund: Hat man Brot, so findet sich schon ein Messer. (kaut) Nicht? (Zum Dichter der etwas entfernt – nicht weit – Platz genommen hat.) Wollen sie auch?

Dichter: Wenn ichbitten darf.

Terra: Da (langt mit der Hand in den Teller und gibt dem Dichter mit Schwung ein großes Stück Leber. Es muss fast geworfen werden und darf sich um kein Requisit handeln. Dichter fängt es mit beiden Händen ab.)

Dichter: Danke.

Terra: Schmeckt's?

Dichter: Ausgezeichnet!

Terra: Ich lege Wert auf gute Küche!

Dichter, schlingend: Ausgezeichnet!

Terra: Was? … ja …

Dichter: Tatsächlich ausgezeichnet!

Terra: Das sagten sie …

Sie sprechen. Man versteht infolge der Schmatz- und Kaugeräusche nichts. Das darf nicht zulange dauern.

Terra: Und das … (wirft wieder)

Dichter: Danke!

Terra: Wie behagt ihnen die Stellung?

Dichter, schluckend: Sehr.

Terra: Wie gefällt ihnen der Posten?

Dichter: Wie?

Terra: Wie ihnen der Posten gefällt?

Dichter: Ein guter Job. Wohl wert, dass sich ein Fürst seiner unterwinde … zwischen dem Kind Phrasendrescherei und dem Mann, Mord … liegt er als geldgieriger Jüngling da …

Terra: Sie Ferkel. Da. (Reicht ihm einen Bissen)

Dichter: Zu gütig.

Terra: Wissen sie mein Lieber … es geht über die … über die regelmäßige Einnahme der Mahlzeit geht nichts. Fast die meisten Beschwerden des modernen Menschen sind auf unregelmäßige Ernährung zurückzuführen. Gastritis, Sodbrennen und andere Magenbeschwerden … da habe sie (jetzt wirft Terra tatsächlich und D. muss auffangen) … haben ihre Wurzel in der unregelmäßigen und falschen Ernährung.

Dichter, kauend: Sicher.

Terra: Nehmen sie das noch (reicht ihm langsam ein Stück).

Dichter: Danke.

Terra: Ein gesunder Geist in einem gesunden Körper. Man darf die Speisen weder schlingen noch zu heiß oder zu kalt essen. Der Organismus leidet darunter.

Dichter: Sicher.

Terra: Eben. Die Sauce ist superb. Die müssen sie unbedingt kosten. Da haben sie den Rest. (Gibt ihm den Teller).

Dichter, schleckend: Sehr delikat …

Terra: Schleck nur. Schmeckt sie ihnen?

Dichter: Mehr als gut.

Terra: Wie war das mit dem Philosophen?

Dichter: Plato ist einer … vielen Dank (stellt den Teller zurück) … von denen, die man bei der Tür hinauswirft und die beim Fenster wieder hereinmarschieren.

Terra, sich den Mund abwischend: Was will er?

Dichter: Seine Ideen verbreiten …

Terra: Was für Ideen?

Dichter: Dieselben auf denen unser System basiert. Nur Macht hat er keine.

Terra: Ohnmächtige Tyrannen sind Witzfiguren. Züchtet er Mäuse?

Dichter: Mäuse?

Terra: Oder Hasen, oder Hunde …

Dichter: Hunde?

Terra: Die könnte er tyrannisieren. Als Hunde oder Mäusekönig.

Dichter: Ich … ich glaube nicht.

Terra: Dann kann man ihm nicht helfen. (Läutet. Sehr wohlklingend und satt.) Das hat gemundet. (Zum eintretenden Koch) Sie übertreffen sich. Mein Kompliment.

Koch: Danke. (Räumt mit Dienern die Tafel ab.)

Terra: Ich lasse Herrn Plato bitten.

Diener: Wie der Weiseste wünscht (ab).

Vom Vorraum her ein aufforderndes “Bitte”. Plato tritt ein. Er trägt ein langes Gewandt. Eine Art griechischen Schlafrock. Sein Benehmen ist nervös.

Plato theatralisch: Ich begrüße dich Weiser. Ich beklatsche das Regime und beuge mich. Oh, mein Schüler (nähert sich Terra). Trotzdem machst du Fehler, ja trotzdem.

Terra: Ist er betrunken? Was wollen sie?

Plato, bitter lachend: Der Schüler verleugnet den Lehrer … so ist die Welt!

Terra: Was hat er?

Dichter: Gekränktes Geltungsbedürfnis.

Terra: Ich kann ihn nicht trösten. Also, was zum Teufel will er?

Plato, säuselnd: Meinen Glückwunsch … meinen eifrigsten Glückwunsch …

Terra, nachäffend: Welche Freude, welche Freude … (scharf) Wozu beglückwünschen sie mich?

Plato, singend: Gesunde Kinder, geregeltes Leben. Das Volk neigt sich vorm Staat und der Staat ist weise.

Terra: Und sie wollen am Kuchen mitnaschen?

Plato: Mitnaschen? Ich verstehe nur Kuchen.

Dichter: Sie begreifen schon. Aber die Masse muss kuschen und für uns gehörst du zur Masse. Da gäbe es viele Bewerber.

Monotone Stimme: Da es aber die besten der Wächter sein sollen müssen es da nicht die wächterlichsten Staatshüter sein?

Terra: Das ist richtig.

Monotone stimme: Alle im Staat seid ihr Brüder, so werden wir erzählen aber der bildende Gott hat all denen von euch, die zu herrschen fähig sind Gold bei ihrer Geburt beigemischt, weshalb es auch die Geehrtesten sind …

Terra: Goldrichtig.

Monotone Stimme: Ja, es ist ganz wie du sagst. Haben wir doch auch in unserem Staat die Helfer wie Hunde den Herrschern als Hirten des Staates unterstellt.

Terra: Gut!

Monotone Stimme: Aber den Staatsgründern kommt es wohl zu, die Formen zu wissen in denen die Dichter Sagen erzählen sollen und gegen die kein Gedicht verstoßen darf, doch brauchen sie nicht selbst Sagen zu dichten.

Terra: Ich bin für Zensur. (zum Dichter) Das geht an ihre Adresse.

Stimme: So müssen wir denn offenbar zuerst die Sagendichter beaufsichtigen und eine schöne sage, die sie dichten, annehmen und eine unschöne ablehnen. Aber die Ammen und Mütter werden wir gewinnen, die angenommenen Sagen den Kindern zu erzählen und deren Seelen durch die Sagen noch mehr zu bilden als die Leiber mit den Händen … Werden wir es also leichthin zulassen, dass die Knaben landläufige und von Landläufigen erdichtete Sagen hören und in ihre Seelen Vorstellungen aufnehmen, die zumeist denen entgegengesetzt sind, die sie nach unserer Meinung haben sollten, wenn sie erwachsen sind? Das werden wir keinesfalls.

Terra zu Plato: Was hast du noch zu sagen?

Plato: Es sind Fehler geschehen …

Terra: Jedes Ideal leidet bei seiner Verwirklichung. Menschliche Schwäche musst du mit einbeziehen.

Dichter: Wir danken dir und spenden dir den Lohn der Weisen. Unsere Langeweile und nichts. Nicht einmal unseren Hass! Danke!

Terra: Geh mit Applaus ab!

Plato: Ich dachte der Edelste …

Terra: Du denkst, wir handeln. Eine (zum Dichter) was? …

Dichter: Ideale Ergänzung.

Terra: Da hast du. Es hat mich sehr gefreut …

Plato: Ich …

Terra: Soll ich die Wachen rufen?

Plato: Nicht die Wachen, nicht die Wachen. Das ist unter meiner Würde. (Buckelt zurück)

Terra: Den wären wir los.

Dichter: Ja, für immer hoffe ich.

Terra: Die Leute sind unglaublich lästig.

Dichter: Ja, das sind sie.

Terra: Ich mache jetzt ein Mittagsschläfchen. Der Vormittag war anstrengend. Am besten sie ruhen sich auch aus. Übrigens, was hat der Philosoph geschrieben?

Dichter: Der Staat.

Terra: So, so …

Dichter: Der Staat oder die ideale Diktatur. Es läuft aufs selbe hinaus.

PAUSE

Die folgende Szene muss von Anfang I. bis Ende I. nicht unbedingt im Stück aufgenommen werden.

I.

Bühne wie zuerst. Dichter sitz sehr nahe gegen die Mitte des Schreibtisches. Terra tritt aus den Privatgemächern. Er macht einen ausgeruhten Eindruck.

Dichter: Habe sie gut geruht Weisester?

Terra: Danke, es ging. (Zieht eine Zigarette aus der Brusttasche) Ich bitte um Feuer.

Dichter: Bitte (Hält ihm ein brennendes Zündholz hin)

Terra: Danke (inhaliert)

An der rechten Tür klopft es.

Terra: Diese ewige Klopferei macht einen verrückt. Herein!

Sekr. tritt ein: Die Zensur hat uns ein Theaterstück hingeworfen …

Terra: Was ist schon wieder?

Sekr.: Pardon. Die Zensur hat uns ein Theaterstück übergeben. Die Frage ist, ob man den Autor verwarnen, ihm die Lizenz entziehen oder gleich festnehmen soll. Die Abteilung hält den Mann für gefährlich, will aber die Entscheidung ihnen überlassen. Ich selbst wage kein Urteil abzugeben und …

Terra zum Dichter: Das fällt in ihre Kompetenz.

Sekr. gibt dem Dichter das Manuskript.

Terra: Meine Entscheidung heißt Ruhe! Die Tage zerfließen in Hast, einer wie der andere. Verstanden?

Sekr.: Ja. (bleibt abwartend stehen)

Dichter: Die Thematik?

Sekr.: Ein altes Ehepaar, das streitet.

Terra: Das kann ja nicht so wild sein.

Sekr.: Das kommt auf den Blickwinkel an.

Dichter: Man müsste es sehen.

Terra: Das ist ein Einfall! Könnte man das nicht engagieren? Wenigstens einen Akt, meine ich.

Sekr.: Ich bin Mitwirkender einer Laienbühne. Mein bescheidenes Hobby. Ich wäre imstande das Zeug zu spielen. Laienhaft natürlich.

Terra: Sie wären imstande? Das ist ja großartig! (zum Dichter) Was sagen sie dazu. Das wäre wenigstens eine Abwechslung. (zum Sekr.) Ich wusste gar nicht, dass sie Künstler sind.

Dichter: Zeit hätten wir genug. Es scheinen für heute keine Termine mehr auf.

Terra: Na also! Aber von wo nehmen wir die Alte her?

Sekr.: Das lässt sich machen.

Dichter: Ja, in der Zensurabteilung gibt es doch die eigene Abteilung für Schauspieler.

Sekr.: Sie prüfen den Text genau wie die anderen Zensoren. Nur geht es dabei um Wortmalerei, beziehungsweise Lautmalerei.

Dichter: Ob Stücke vielleicht Worte oder Passagen enthalten, die man verräterisch betonen könnte. Wie im Kabarett, wissen sie.

Terra: Dann ist das Problem ja gelöst. Wurde das Stück schon gelernt?

Sekr.: Ich kann den Anfang auswendig. Das Negative daran hat mich gefesselt. Die Kollegin könnte das Manus haben.

Terra: Ich bin ein musischer Mensch. Schön, besorgen sie das Nötige. (Sekr. mit Verbeugung ab.)

Terra: So einen spaß hab‘ ich schon lange nicht gebraucht. Außerdem ist es von Zeit zu Zeit notwendig, dass ein Staatsoberhaupt persönlich ins literarische Geistesleben eingreift. Meinen sie nicht?

Dichter: Das ist sehr gut.

Terra: Ich habe in dieser Beziehung ein sicheres Urteil.

Dichter: Davon bin ich überzeugt.

Von rechts Lärm. Ein kleines schäbiges Podium wird hereingeschoben. Es rollt laut in die Bühnenmitte.

Sekr. schreiend: Ich brauche noch einen kleinen Tisch – schäbig bitte – zwei Sessel, auch schäbig, Flasche Wein – halbvoll bitte – ein Wasserglas, Hühnerreste, einen Teller, die ehemalige Aufräumefrau!

Terra: Aufräumefrau!

Sekr.: Im Stück natürlich.

Das Gewünschte wird gebracht. Hinzugekommen ist ein schmutziges Tischtuch. Der Sekr. diktiert alles an seinen Platz.

Terra: Wissen sie, dass man in China zu Ehren gewisser Flussgötter Schauspiele gab?

Dichter: Weshalb?

Terra: Um sie zu erheitern.

Sekr.: Nein, kein Tischtuch!

Terra: Wo bleibt die Alte? Haben wir überhaupt alte Angestellte?

Sekr.: Warten sie ab. Wo ist das Huhn? Hühnerknochen bitte! (Ein Diener ab)

Terra: Das wird ein Volksstück …

Sekr.: Ich wage das zu bezweifeln …

Terra: Ein bisschen derber Humor, was?

Sekr.: Ich fürchte einen …

Terra: Sie machen mich neugierig …

Diener kommt, die arme voll Hühnerresten.

Sekr.: Sie sind verrückt geworden, ein kleines Stück.

Diener: Ein kleines?

Sekr.: Ja, ein kleines. (Der Sekr. reißt dem Diener ein Stück aus den Armen und wirft es auf den Tisch. Der Diener lässt dabei einige Reste fallen, die er ungeschickt aufzuheben versucht. Weitere Teile entgleiten ihm.)

Sekr.: Heben sie das auf und verschwinden sie!

Kollegen helfen dem Diener, gehen einsammelnd ab.

Eine alte Frau tritt ein. Sie gleicht der Bedienerin im ersten Akt.

Bedienerin: Da bin ich. Mich alten Knochen bemühen. Man hat komische Ideen. Aber es ist mir eine Ehre … eine Ehre …

Sekr.: Sie werden ein altes Weib spielen und dabei Primadonna sein.

Be.: Alt bin ich selbst …

Sekr.: Da ist ihr Text (gibt ihr das Manus).

Be.: Ich kann aber (kichert) …

Sekr.: Lesen wirst du wohl noch können … wo Alte steht bist du dran.

Be., fettig knicksend: Ich bin geehrt (kichert).

Sekr.: Sie sind eine geborene Heroine.

Terra: Ist das möglich? Wie tief ein Mensch sinken kann. Gehört das wirklich zum Personal? Sofort entlassen!

Sekr.: Sie sollten sie näher ansehen. (Herzlich lachend zur Bedienerin) sie sind nicht zu schlagen.

Be., zieht eine bewegliche, unglaublich natürliche Gummimaske vom Gesicht und entpuppt sich als junge Frau (hübsch). Mit anmutiger frischer Stimme: Lang lebe der Weiseste. Sie vergeben mir den kleinen Scherz. Ich bitte vielmals (faltet affektiert die Hände) um Verzeihung.

Terra: Das ist ja eine bezaubernde Überraschung! Trotzdem müssten sie bestraft werden.

Sekr.: Das soll sie auch. Sie werden uns zur Strafe eine doppelte Probe ihres Talents geben. Sie werden strafweise eine alte Aufräumefrau spielen, die eine alte Aufräumefrau spielt. Ab jetzt sind sie Laie. Haben sie begriffen?

Schauspielerin: Ich glaube schon und nehme an.

Sekr.: Ich mach mich nur ein bisschen zurecht.

Terra, zur Schauspielerin: Wie sind sie auf diesen bezaubernden Gag gekommen?

Schauspielerin: Ich soll doch möglichst echt wirken. Das war eine Probe aufs Exempel.

Terra: Trotzdem bin ich erleichtert. Schade, dass gerade sie ein altes Weib spielen müssen. Noch dazu in … in quasi einer Doppelrolle.

Schauspielerin: Das dauert nicht lange. Nachher stehe ich ganz zu ihrer Verfügung.

Terra: Ich werde darauf zurückkommen.

Sekr. kommt in den Mittelgrund. Weiße schüttere Perücke durch die rosige Kopfhaut schimmert. Faltiges weißes Gesicht. Ein alter Rock.

Die Anwesenden lachen.

Terra zur Schauspielerin: Ihr liebster Mann!

Schauspielerin: Leider. Moment! (setzt sich die Maske auf) So harmonieren wir schon besser. (zum Sekr.) Bleiben sie bei ihrer Strafe?

Sekr.: Ja.

Bedienerin mit noch junger Stimme: Glauben sie nicht, dass das Stück darunter leidet?

Sekr.: Seid wann sind sie so zimperlich?

Be. noch jugendlich: Gut, wie sie wollen.

Sekr. (alter Mann) nimmt die Bedienerin an der Hand und führt sie aufs Podium: Hier ist ihr Platz. (Be. setzt sich steif hin und starrt)

Sekr.: Schlampiger, verluderter, mehr Echtheit, … aber quittieren sie nicht … in beiden Rollen nicht.

Be.: Nein. (Das letzte jugendliche Wort.) Was ist das für ein Leben … ein saftiges Leben wäre mir lieber gewesen … (stockt) … ein saftiger Braten (stockt) … mit Hochwohlgeboren … was für ein un … unglücklicher Zufall, dass gerade ich, gerade ich hierher geraten bin … (sammelt sich) … bin …

Sekr.: Weiter!

Be.: … und das nicht aus eigener Schuld … nein wirklich nicht … nein niemand kann das behaupten … die E… die Evolution … die … (zum Sekr.) heißt das so? Ich kann das nicht lesen … nein … wirklich so was blödes … Verzeihung (kichert) Die Evolution hat mich übergangen. (zum Sekr.) Richtig? Und ich bin alt ohne alt geworden zu sein. Das ist nur außen … das Alter sitz nur außen. Und ich bin … eigentlich nur jung …

ge … nur jung gealtert. Ich bin (mit der Hand die Zeile entlangfahrend) wie? … nur ein altes Kind … blööd (zum Sekr.) … Verzeihung, ich kann das nicht … ein altes Kind, das die Tatsache nicht einsehen will … Die Oberen, ja die können das … altern … aber es wird ihnen auch … auch leicht gemacht … (die Maske absetzend zum Sekr.) … wie bin ich?

Sekr.: Miserabel!

Terra: Aber ich bitte sie.

Schauspielerin: Er hat schon recht. Aber die Rolle …

Sek.: Als Probe lasse ich das gelten … aber kurz die Szene. Bitte darf ich einen Augenblick (nimmt der Schauspielerin das Manuskript aus der Hand) Ja, da. (zu Terra, dem Dichter und ans Publikum gewandt)

Zimmer, in dessen Mitte ein altersschwacher Tisch, an dem ein älteres Paar sitzt. Es wird von einer billigen, verkommenen Einrichtung eingekreist. Der Mann ist hager, über den trockenen Knochen liegt gedunsene Säuferhaut. Die Frau ist ein schwabbelnder Fettklumpen. Sie hat eigentlich keine weiblichen Formen mehr, sondern ist nur ein rundliches etwas, das nach allen Richtungen hin fett wächst. Zwischen die glänzenden Lippen schiebt sie die Reste eines Huhns. Vor dem Mann steht ein Glas mit Wein. Er stiert trüb vor sich hin. Entweder in das Glas oder daran vorbei. Seine Bewegungen zerfließen taumelnd, nach verschwenden matter Energie. Ist ihr Anfang auch noch so hoffnungsvoll, die Konzentration lässt bald nach, verschwimmt. (In Klammer. Wie Tauben sich paaren, also ohne Ausdauer. Klammer zu.) Grelle Beleuchtung. Aufs Podium fällt grelles Licht.

Terra: Das klingt nicht sehr lustig.

Die übrige Bühne versinkt im Dunkel. Schauspielerin setzt sich die Maske auf.

Sek. zur Bedienerin: Da haben sie (gibt ihr das Manus)

Be.: Danke (knickst, soweit das in sitzender Stellung möglich ist).

Sek. leise: Essen sie!

Be. hält sich die Hühnerknochen vors Gesicht.

Sek. zischend: Essen sie!

Be.: Verzeihung (zum Publikum) ich kann das nicht so spontan, obwohl ich eine gebildete Frau war …

Sekr.: Bleiben sie beim Text!

Be.: Entschuldigung (knickst wieder).

Sekr. ganz in der Rolle des alten Mannes: Wie sie schlingt. Kein Wunder, wenn sie kräftig ist, sie kann ja essen … ja, ja … schlingt nur … (zu ihr) wisch dir den Mund ab! (leise als Sekr.) den Knochen in den Mund! Kiefeln, lutschen!

Be., erschrocken: Sofort … (Mit dem Zeigefinger hinter einer Zeile herfahrend) Frau, … nein (sicherer) gleich, wenn ich fertig bin.

Sekr.: Mein Gott wie sie frisst (trinkt) das ist so ekelhaft, wenn man selbst keinen Bissen mehr hinunterbringt.

Be.: Hmm?

Sekr.: Und ihre fetten Hände, ihre armen fetten Hände, selbst wenn sie schöne Finger hätte … mich würden sie nicht mehr … nein nicht im Geringsten … aber so, die abgenützten Krüppel, auch wenn es die Arbeit war werden sie deshalb schöner? Kein Bisschen! Friss nicht so laut!

Be.: Die Zerfließende zu ihrem Gatten …

Sekr.: Das brauchen sie nicht zu lesen … da capo … ab … friss nicht so laut!

Be., trotzig: Es schmeckt!

Sekr.: Musst du mich deshalb beleidigen? (Trinkt) Entzückende Pfötchen hatte sie damals als die Welt noch grün war … was denke ich immer an entzückende Hände? … ich war einmal ein Mensch. Ja, sogar ein kluger Mensch. Ja, ja ich war tatsächlich ein Mensch. Ich glaube es … dass ich damals so war … kaum zu glauben. Nicht einmal einen alten Hund jagt man in diesen Regen, bei dieser Dunkelheit, in diesen ewig rinnenden Regen. Bevor es so regnete, so grau und unaufhörlich, war der Himmel bezaubernd heiter. Nicht das kleinste Wölkchen sah man … aber was soll sie denn tun außer fressen? Es ist ja nicht ihre schuld, dass alles so gekommen ist. Nein an dieser Dämmerung trägt sie keine Schuld. Dabei war sie scharf wie frischer Krenn damals … aber die Jahre. Die Jahre sind schlechte Kumpel. Sie haben das Luder geschändet. Und die Feuchtigkeit. Die steigende Feuchtigkeit hat sie aufquellen lassen. Ja, reich, stumpf und ewig jung müsste man sein.

Be.: Das wäre eine Mezie …

Sekr.: Sie bringen mich aus dem Konzept!

Be.: Entschuldigung.

Sekr.: Das langsame Sterben ist eine Gemeinheit (trinkt).

Be., kauend: Glaubst du ich sterbe rascher?

Sek. ohne die Bemerkung zu beachten: Eine einmalige Gemeinheit.

Be.: Pass aufs Tischtuch auf!

Sekr.: Wo ist es?

Be, böse: In der Wäsche, wo sonst?

Sekr.: Waschen, waschen, waschen … gewaschen muss alles werden. Der Mond, die Sterne, der Kadaver eines Hundes, die Dächer, die Mauern, die Menschen. Dauernde Reinigung bis zur vollkommenen Abnutzung. Wasch nur! Aber wenn du deine Tonne abschwemmst, gib dich keinen Illusionen hin, sie bleibt fettig.

Be.: Altes Ekel!

Terra, lacht gekünstelt.

Schauspielerin nimmt die Maske hoch und verbeugt sich in seine Richtung.

Sekr.: Die Unvollkommenheit ist vollkommen. Wir wollen in ewiger Vollkommenheit - nach unseren Gesichtspunkten – Vollkommenheit leben. Also, ohne Pest, ohne Beschwerden, ohne Diktatur, ohne Alter, ohne Tod, ohne Hunger, ohne Steuern, ohne Naturkatastrophen, ohne Hässlichkeit. Nur eine Seite ist für uns vollkommen. Wir verneinen die Ergänzung. Die Rückseite.

Be.: Was jammerst du? War ich nicht hübsch?

Sekr.: Davon hab‘ ich nicht gesprochen. Wenn du schon zuhörst so hör besser zu Fette! (zu sich) so ab und zu spielt sie mit …

Be.: Fette, Fette, … einmal (verträumt) warst du sehr lieb.

Sekr.: Ach du …

Be.: Außerdem versteh‘ ich nicht, dass ihr Männer immer den ganzen Kosmos herschleppen müsst, wegen irgendeiner Nichtigkeit, wegen eines Bauchwehs, aus einem lächerlichen Grund, weil ich esse und dir essen zuwider ist. Komisch.

Sekr.: Komisch? Sehr komisch! Und was schleppt ihr daher? Die Mutterschaft, die verhinderte Mutterschaft, die erzwungene Mutterschaft, die belastende Mutterschaft, die Charité, das ewig Weibliche, dann Rosen, Nelken, Lavendel und anderes Unkraut, die Vögel des Himmels, Wolkenfahnen, rosiges Getuschel, Maikäfer, Maden, Menschen, Töchter und Söhne.

Be.: Du warst einmal sehr lieb.

Sekr.: Einmal ist keinmal und bedeutet gar nichts. Weshalb können wir nicht aus unserer Haut? Weshalb liegen wir nicht in einem duftenden Garten, der von einer gelben Sonne umsponnen wird? Diese Dämmerung tötet. Oder sehe ich schon schlecht? Um ehrlich zu sein, meine Augen waren nie besser.

Be.: Du brauchst Brillen. Ja, du brauchst unbedingt Brillen! Dein Leben lang hättest du Brillen gebraucht!

Sekr.: Halts Maul!

Be.: Du wirst nie richtig sehen. Ich wollte dir nicht weh tun, aber es ist die Wahrheit. Ich behaupte ja gar nicht, dass mein Augenlicht besser ist.

Sekr.: Habe ich nicht gesagt, halt‘s Maul!

Be.: Ja, ja beruhige dich … der Alte muss jetzt …

Sekr.: Das ist für mich!

Be.: Entschuldigung.

Sekr., steht auf – Regieanweisung; der Alte muss jetzt ein Buch vom Regal nehmen und zitieren.

Terra, ungeduldig: Machen sie weiter!

Sekr. steht auf, fischt ein imaginäres Buch vom unsichtbaren Regal, bläst den Staub weg und setzt sich: Pass' auf! (liest)

Herbstwinde haben mir den Mund zerrissen

Ich zerbrach und floss ins träge Kloakenmeer

Blei ist die Farbe des Lichts

das erdrosselt den Faltenberg

und der Himmel lacht als hätte er nichts gesehen

… aber sowas ist dir egal. (Knallt das Buch auf den Tisch. Man hört den Knall. Steht auf und ordnet das Buch ins Regal ein. Hustet, bläst den Staub fort.)

Be., träge kauend: Was?

Sekr.: Nicht das kleinste Vergnügen vergönnst du einem … Da (blasend, überall Staub, nichts als Staub, fährt mit der Hand über die Bücher und zeigt sie der Be.) Soll das Ordnung sein?

Be.: Solchen Gedichten fehlt die mildernde Süße … (blättert auf die nächste Seite des Manus) Zuckermäulchen sollen Gedichte sein, schaumbeklebte Lippen. Sie sollen den Nebel versüßen. Diesen Nebel, weißt du?

Sekr., schenkt sich das Glas voll und lacht bitter.

Be.: Sauf nicht so viel!

Sekr.: Schau auf dich!

Be.: Eine Frau muss immer auf sich schaun' … ich war auch einmal im Liebestempel der Helden und hab' … glotz nicht so blöd!

Sekr.: Dirne!

Terra ist aufgesprungen. Vom Schnürboden herabfallend heftet sich ein dünner, weißer Strahl an ihm fest. Er hebt die Hände so als hätte er eine Maschinenpistole und zielt auf den Sekr.

Terra, die Garbe quer durch den Körper des Alten jagend, … Ratatatatat (oder Brakakatatata). Man sieht unter den Rückstößen Terras Schultern zucken. Der Alte taumelt vom Stuhl und schlägt unter der Wucht des Todes lang hin.

Terra: Das hat das Schwein verdient.

Dichter: Bravissimo

Sekr., den Kopf hebend: Ich bin erledigt.

Alle klatschen, beklatschen sich gegenseitig.

Sekr.: Soll ich weitermachen?

Terra: Jetzt will ich mich giften. Tun sie was sie nicht lassen können. (Der Lichtstrahl erblindet mit einem Schlag.)

Sekr., sich elegant verneigend: Danke (setz sich) … das war nicht so … das war so gemeint und war es auch nicht … du bist unschuldig … trotzdem kränkt es mich …

Be.: Das sind alte Sachen …

Sekr.: Wenn man es nicht so einrichten könnte wie man wollte, freilich im Rahmen des Möglichen, wenn nur echte Talente an der Spitze stünden, die Scharlatanerie … zum Arsch der Hölle mit ihr … zum ewig glühenden, Blut furzenden Arsch der Hölle mit ihr … sollen sie an ihrem eigenen Erbrochenen ersticken … diese Bastarde.

Be.: Du bist nur neidig, weil du es zu nichts gebracht hast.

Sekr.: Sagt das was aus? Nicht das geringste sagt das aus. Schwamm drüber … ich habe Beweise, der halbe

Bücherschrank ist voll von meinen Aufzeichnungen. Aber es ist egal. Schau, in Milliarden Jahren sind unsere "Ewigen Werte" völlig belanglos.

Terra: Ich protestiere!

Sekr.: Das ist der Text. Pardon.

Terra: Also weiter (zum Dichter) Morbidezza!

Sekr.: Im Augenblick … es ist nur die Gewohnheit, die uns bindet …

Be.: Natürlich wäre ich für dich als junge Frau interessanter …

Sekr.: Ja, beklag dich. Ich kenne die Litanei …

Be.: Das ist doch die Wahrheit.

Sekr.: Was ändert das an der Tatsache? Schmatz nicht!

Be.: Wie soll man ein Huhn anders essen?

Sekr.: Anders eben oder gar nicht. Verschluck dich nicht am Knochen!

Be., boshaft: Soll ich ihn für dich aufheben?

Sekr.: Ich weiß, dass du ein festes Zahnfleisch hast … du frisst ohne Prothesen … die liegen in der Lade, ich weiß das …

Be., kauend: Na und, warum weinst du?

Sekr., brüllend: Die Knochen!

Be.: Ach so …

Sekr.: Musst du mich immer an mein schwächeres Zahnfleisch erinnern?

Be.: Purer Neid!

Sekr.: Nein, Ekel.

Be.: Wie hast du zuerst so schön theatralisch gesagt? … ach ja … in den Arsch der Hölle mit ihr … in den ewig glühenden, furzenden Arsch der Hölle mit ihr … war da nicht ich gemeint Kleiner? Ja, ja und noch ersticken am eigenen Erbrochenen, mein Gott bist du goldig.

Sekr.: Ich sprach von Scharlatanen.

Be: Wir reiben einander auf. Die Reibung wächst mit der Gleichgültigkeit. Wir reiben einander als hätten wir Sandpapier zwischen uns.

Sekr.: Halts Maul!

Be.: Schlag mich tot! … dir ist … (blättert um) dir fällt meine Existenz zur Last … du vergällst mir das Essen, die Luft, das Leben … du schweigst mich tot, du redest fast nur mehr mit dir …

Sekr.: Wenn du frisst, ja …

Be.: Weil du krank bist und nicht mehr kannst … nicht einmal das kannst du mehr …

Sekr.: Kusch.

Be.: Ebenfalls. (minutenlange Stille)

Terra, flüsternd: Was ist jetzt?

Dichter, flüsternd: Kunstpause.

Terra: Zeitverschwendung.

Sekr.: Wir leben in der besten aller Welten. Weißt du was ich drauf mache? Ich scheiß drauf.

Terra, aufspringend, sein Stuhl fällt um: Empörend!

Auf der Bühne flammt das Licht auf.

Sekr., sich die weiße Perücke abnehmend, mit leichter Verbeugung: Eine gezielte Gemeinheit.

Terra: So sind die Menschen nicht. So trivial und egoistisch sind sie nicht.

Schauspielerin, sich die Maske abnehmend: Das finde ich auch.

Terra, zum Sekr.: Was haben sie mir angetan?

Dichter: Ordinär. Vulgäre Monstrositäten!

Terra: Ich finde keine Worte!

Schauspielerin: Ich auch nicht!

Dichter: Dasselbe wollte ich sagen.

Terra: Nicht wahr? Selbst in der größten Scheiße herrscht kein derartiger Ton. Der Mensch muss Mensch bleiben. Basta!

Schauspielerin: Auf solche Rollen scheiß ich. Ich hab‘ das nur ihnen zuliebe gemacht.

Terra: Sie waren ausgezeichnet, meine Beste, mein Kompliment. (zum Sekr.) Und auch sie mein Lieber.

Sekr.: Danke, es war nur eine bescheidene Leistung.

Dichter zur Schauspielerin: Sie haben uns verwöhnt. Ich schwebe förmlich.

Terra zur Schauspielerin: Haben sie sehr gelitten?

Schauspielerin: Es geht.

Terra: auf bald und nochmals vielen Dank.

Sekr., zu den eintretenden Dienern: Schafft den Plunder weg.

Schauspielerin: Adieu.

Terra: Handkuss Gnädigste. (Sekr. und Schauspielerin ab)

Dichter, zu den Dienern: Etwas schneller bitte!

Terra zum Dichter: Na was sagen sie dazu?

Dichter: Eine Bespeichelung der menschlichen Natur …

Terra: Keine Spur vom Schönen und Edlen. Innere Zustände! Kann ich mir den Luxus leisten? Unsinn!

Dichter: Eben.

Terra: Was für Komplikationen! Ich liebe Klarheit. Solche Leute kann der Staat nicht brauchen. Diese Seelenkitzler und Abdecker können einem zur Verzweiflung treiben! Der Autor gehört weg!

Dichter: Außerdem war der Aufbau vom dramaturgischen her schlecht. Die Darsteller müssen sich bewegen, bewegen, und wieder bewegen. Das ist Tradition. Ob es nun sinnvoll ist oder nicht. Das Publikum muss die Arbeit des Regisseurs sehen. Das ist so üblich.

Terra: Richtig!

Dichter: Im Nachwort, das ich kurz überflogen habe, stand, dass die beiden sich trotzdem lieben.

Terra: Weitere Komplikationen.

Dichter: Wenn ich das Thema behandelt hätte …

Terra: Ja?

Dichter: … würde anfangs ein nettes, gepflegtes Heim gezeigt werden. Von ihm umgeben zwei ältere, wohlgepflegte Menschen, die an einem bescheidenen aber anmutigen Tisch sitzen. Ihr weißes Haar wäre vom Glorienschein der geläuterten Ruhe umgeben.

Terra: Gut!

Dichter: Die Alten schmausen beschaulich und plaudern dabei. Das Mütterchen frägt besorgt: Wie es unserem Gönner wohl geht? Wir sind ja so glücklich aber er … Das Väterchen derweilen: Welchen Gönner? … Diese Ahnungslosigkeit wäre sehr humoristisch.

Terra: So, so.

Dichter: Der Alte sagt also: Welchem Gönner? Die Alte darauf: Na ihm! Der Alte derweil: Welchem ihm? Ich kenne keinen ihm! Die Alte darauf: Na, unserem Weisen! Der Alte dagegen: Was? Welchen Weisen? Die Alte begütigend: Na unserem, welchen sonst?

Terra: Ist das nicht ein bisschen scharf?

Dichter: Momentchen … Der Alte selbstzufrieden: Ah, den meinst du, der sorgt sowieso für uns.

Terra: Gut. Man muss ein Thema nur richtig beleuchten.

Dichter: Darauf kommt es an. Ja, und vom Schnürboden müssen Transparente hängen - sie wissen ein beliebtes Mittel – mit ähnlichen Sinnsprüchen wie: Wir sind im Schein der Weisheit des weisen gealtert, der unseren rastlosen Händen zur Ruhe verholfen hat. Der Arbeit Lohn ist des Alters schönste Kron‘ … oder … die große Zeit erfordert starke Greise.

Terra: Auf der Basis müsste ein gutes Stück gelingen. Ein paar deftige, aber harmlose Scherze … na und so weiter … die den erzieherischen Inhalt überdecken.

Dichter: Ja.

Terra: Nehmen sie für ein paar Stunden meine Lasten an ihr treues Herz. Mein Hirn braucht Entspannung und der Ruhe süßen Stachel. Eine gepolsterte Tür wird mich vom Lärm des Lebens abschließen. Watte in den Ohren lässt mich das Singen der Luft vergessen. Wie war das?

Dichter: Reine Poesie.

Terra: Ich bin oberster Kunstsachverständiger. Vergessen sie das nicht!

Dichter: Ich finde sie …

Terra: Bitte, es war nicht ganz von mir.

Dichter: Trotzdem …

Terra: Wir brauchen Stücke die meine Weisheit, meine absolute Unfehlbarkeit besingen. Ich als riesenhaftes Gehirn, hineingesetzt in diese Welt. Ein Hirn, das alles meistert … Sympathie für den Oberweisen, dessen starke, zerbrechliche Seele, allen Stürmen des Schicksals trotzend, das Ruder des Staates fest in der Hand hält … die gottgewollte Aufgabe versteht sich … und so weiter … können sie das?

Dichter: Nichts lieber als das.

Terra: Dann Polizeiengel, Männer die unser Paradies mit eisernen Fäusten verteidigen. Gegen Nackte, Weiber, Kinder und Greise.

Dichter: An ihnen geht ein Dichter verloren!

Terra: Ja, ich habe Talent … das hab‘ ich …

Dichter: Es drängt sich einem auf …

Terra: Sie werden mir immer sympathischer!

Dichter: Danke.

Terra: Aber bitte nicht so förmlich. Ich möchte auch meine Schwächen mit ihnen teilen. Sie sind doch Dichter. Folglich ein gefühlvoller Mensch. Können sie mir nicht etwas Seelenerquickendes zur Nacht sagen? Etwas das mich einschläfert?

Dichter: Sie haben blaue Augen.

Terra: Und?

Dichter: Sie haben helle Augen, wie in Milch gekochte Vergissmeinnicht.

Terra: Vergissmeinnicht in Milch gekocht? Aber, aber, solche Komplimente macht man einer Frau.

Dichter: Sie sind mein Chef.

Terra: Das ist auch wieder richtig … aber habe ich tatsächlich solche Augen?

Dichter: Das ist doch egal, wenn es sich um ein Kompliment handelt.

Terra: Ja, Ja, selbstredend … klar.

Dichter: Wollen sie noch was hören?

Terra: Nein, das genügt. Ich begebe mich zur Ruhe. Das Arbeitspensum reißt einen um. Regieren ist kein Honiglecken. Ich werde tief schlafen. Die Watte in den Ohren lässt mich das Singen der Luft vergessen. (Gähnt) Guten Abend. (Ab)

Dichter: Ebenfalls. (Lümmelt sich hinter den Schreibtisch). Der passt mir. (Schlägt auf die Tischplatte) Passt zu meinem Teint. Der alte Idiot. Das sentimentale Luder. Die Krähe fliegt hoch hinauf und rastet auf einem Schwein. Der Eine errichtet Pyramiden aus faulenden Schädeln. Der andere schreibt ein geniales Stück und beide gehen in die Geschichte ein. Die Konsequenz? Geschickt stinken muss man. Auf welche Art immer. Ob als Schädelpyramidenerbauer, stinkender Schädelpyramidenerbauer einer stinkenden Schädelpyramide, oder als Dichter, als genialer Dichter. Man kann machen was man will, die Ewigkeit, selbstverständlich die begrenzte Ewigkeit, erreicht man nur, wenn man auffällt. Der Mensch wird durch Verbrechen groß. Das ist doch kinderklar. Und wenn es sich nur um Verbrechen an der Mittelmäßigkeit handelt …

Es klopft an der rechten Tür; Dichter: Herein!

Sekr.: Verzeihen sie … ich wollte …

Dichter: Was wünschen sie?

Sekr.: Eine belanglose Sache, eine Unterschrift … ich …

Dichter: Papier, was noch?

Sekr.: Sonst nichts.

Dichter: Sonst nichts. So. Terra schläft. Hast du schon einen schlafenden Tyrannen gesehen? Hast du schon einen schnarchenden Tyrannen gesehen?

Sekr.: Nein.

Dichter: Es ist aber kein erhebendes Schauspiel.

Sekr.: Nein.

Dichter: Wem dienst du?

Sekr.: Dem Mächtigsten.

Dichter: Den tatsächlich Mächtigsten oder dem als Begriff Mächtigstem?

Sekr.: Dem wirklich Mächtigem.

Dichter: Du gefällst mir Bursche.

Sekr.: Ich küsse ihre Hand.

Dichter: Bald … (scharf) und siehst nur diese Finger vor deinen Augen? (Hebt die Hand und spreizt die Finger)

Sekr.: Man erkennt die Sterne und richtet sich danach … sie wissen … einem Schmeichler darf die Geduld nicht reißen …

Dichter: Logisch gedacht.

Sekr.: Das alte Universum gebiert in Todeswehen neue Sterne.

Dichter: Sie wechseln schnell ihre Meinung.

Sekr.: Ich habe keine.

Dichter, die Hand ausstreckend: Ich unterschreibe!

Sekr.: Eine ausgeprägte Handschrift.

Dichter: So? … Hm … was sagen sie zu meinen Dichtungen?

Sekr.: Ein volles, Ja!

Dichter: Kennen sie welche?

Sekr.: Nicht genau, aber ich stehe ganz auf ihrer Seite.

Dichter: Sehr korrekt …

Sekr.: Es ist mir eine Ehre. Ich bin ihr Mann.

Dichter: Hätte ein Pferd etwas zu sagen würde es schon reden.

Sekr.: Wie … sicher … natürlich …

Dichter: Sie wissen?

Sekr.: Ich erlaube mir …

Dichter: Sie sind stumm. Ihr Mund ist wie …

Sekr.: Verklebt.

Dichter: Ja.

Sekr.: Ja.

Dichter: Komm, wenn es so weit ist!

Sekr.: Ja. (Mit Verneigung ab.)

Dichter. Das läuft. Die Puppen tanzen!

Sek. aus Terras Privatzimmer leise eintretend: Darf ich?

Dichter: Schhhstt!

Sekretärin schließt leise die Tür.: Ich … ist es so weit … Ich fürchte mich. Liebling, ich fürchte mich.

Dichter, würdevoll: Du hast gelauscht!

Sek.: Soweit es mir möglich war.

Dichter: Dein Misstrauen beleidigt mich!

Sek.: Ich bin misstrauisch, weil ich dich … weil ich dich liebe … ich bin nicht misstrauisch … ich liebe dich.

Dichter, sie in die Arme nehmend: Deine Lippen sind feucht wie … wie Morgentau; (streichelt sie).

Sek.: Weiter!

Dichter: Du bist mein Tag. Ohne dich ist Nacht. (löst sich von ihr) Geh, die Nacht bricht an!

Sek.: Du warst schon besser.

Dichter, ungeduldig: Geh schon!

Sek.: Du warst schon viel besser …

Dichter: Kann sein, ich bin nicht in Form.

Sek.: Muss ich?

Dichter, schroff: Du musst.

Sek.: Küss mich!

Dichter: Ja (küsst sie schnell) geh bitte!

Sek.: Wie du willst. Aber du unterschätzt mich. Ich bin kein so kleines, unvernünftiges Luder wie du glaubst. Meine Beweggründe sind andere. Ich liebe dich. Ja … das heißt ich bin trotzdem unvernünftig. Ja, das bin ich.

Dichter: Geh bitte!

Sek.: Wie du willst. Ich … ich … (geht auf den Zehenspitzen zur Tür) … ich kann nicht sagen was ich will …

Dichter: Ich verstehe dich auch so … wir verstehen uns doch?

Sek.: Ja (schließt die Tür)

Dichter: Ein blindes Pferd fällt bald in den Graben. (Wischt sich den Mund mit einem weißen Taschentuch ab.) Na ja. (Geht zur rechten Tür und öffnet sie.) Meine Herren? (Gemurmel) Seid … seid … sind sie da? Kommen sie!

Die Weisen, etwa zehn, quellen ins Zimmer. (Lautlos, wie geschoben)

Dichter: Leise!

I.Weiser: Drängt nicht!

II.Weiser: Psst!

Im Zimmer wird es dämmrig.

Dichter: Also seid ihr bereit?

Schweigen.

Dichter: Dass ihr den Zustand bis jetzt ausgehalten habt.

Schweigen.

Dichter: Bei ihrer Intelligenz wundert mich das.

Schweigen.

Dichter: Sind sie denn nie auf diese einfache Lösung gekommen?

I.W.: Herrgott, das ist nicht so einfach. Das ist ein sehr krasser Entschluss.

Dichter: Das stimmt. Aber wir sind doch alle unzufrieden. Ihr und ich. Was gibt er euch? Sehr wenig. Er ist …

I.W., flüsternd: Sein Größenwahn.

Dichter: Ihr seid ihm doch ebenbürtig. Ja er ist sogar minderwertiger als ihr. Endlich ist der Abgrund zwischen uns mit geflüsterten Versicherungen gefüllt. Wir tanzen auf einer Schwertklinge. Ihr seid darüber gegangen, ohne euch die Sohlen zu zerschneiden. Ich hätte … ihr hättet natürlich auch … das zeigt meine Ehrlichkeit. Wodurch haben wir diese Behandlung verdient? Na? Durch nichts! Und was erhebt den Alten über uns? Nichts! Er frisst, trifft seine Anordnungen, wäscht sich und schläft. Er ist auf dieser Erde ein Gast wie wir. Aber ich möchte nicht philosophieren. Ein Gast ist wie der Regen. Dauert er zu lange so wird er zur Last.

Ab jetzt werden die sprechenden abwechselnd beleuchtet.

I.W.: Wie sollen wir's tun?

Dichter: Wie besprochen.

I.W.: Das erscheint mir unmöglich. Man redet das leicht … aber …

Dichter: Lassen wir die Silbe "un" weg und es wird möglich.

Anderer Weiser flüsternd: Aber das Volk?

Dichter: Kennt ihn kaum. Sie kennen die Puppe auf dem Thronsessel. Ich spiele ihn. Mit ein wenig Schminke geht das schon. Außerdem können selbst Weise eines natürlichen Todes sterben. Na? (Pause) Ihr seid ja ganz verschreckt. Er kann selbstverständlich auch ein Staatsbegräbnis haben.

A.Weiser: Das wäre uns lieber.

Dichter: Ich mache alles was ihr wollt … Ich und er haben Nasen im Gesicht und sind gerade gewachsen. Mein Gebiss ist zwar besser, aber das fällt nicht auf. So fett wie er bin ich bald. Das nur für den Fall, wenn wir ihn verschwinden lassen. Ein Staatsbegräbnis erspart uns die Komödie.

A.Weiser: Das Staatsbegräbnis finde ich günstiger. Mit sechs Rappen vorm Leichenwagen …

A.W.: Sie meinen vor der Kutsche …

A.W.: Selbstverständlich meine ich die Leichenkutsche.

Dichter: Einzelheiten können wir später besprechen.

AW: Das klingt alles sehr verlockend, aber so unkompliziert ist das nicht … vielleicht prüfen sie uns nur, und umgekehrt wir sie, sehr komisch … deshalb sind wir gekommen … des Spaßes wegen.

Dichter: Mein Spaß ist blutiger Ernst.

A.W.: Wir glauben ihnen. Aber vielleicht stellt er sich nur schlafend.

Dichter: Er schläft und fühlt sich sicher. Ein unverzeihlicher Fehler.

AW: Gotte gebe ihm mehr.

AW: Ich bin müde.

AW: Ich habe Sodbrennen.

AW: Es ist wie vor einer Reise.

AW: Sie müssen verzeihen, wir leben seit langem in panischer Angst.

AW: Wir sind vielleicht schon umstellt und miauen wie Hunde im Zwinger.

Dichter: Wie bitte?

AW: Miauen …

Dichter, scharf: Seit wann miauen Hunde?

AW: Natürlich nicht direkt.

Dichter: Aber indirekt miauen sie, was?

AW: Warum bestehen sie auf den Punkt?

Dichter, nervös: Egal, egal, … er ist ahnungslos wie ein Säugling. Je länger ein Blinder lebt desto mehr sieht er.

AW: Das leuchtet ein. Aber wir schrecken vor jeder Brutalität zurück. Wir sind herzensgute Menschen. Das wissen sie.

Dichter: Auch ich verabscheue Gewalt. Deshalb müssen wir seine Gewalt bekämpfen. So selbstherrlich wie er war noch niemand. Seine so genannte "Weisheit" ist eine moralische Krücke, auf die er sich bei Verbrechen stützt. Wir sind Idealisten. Des einen Himmelreich kann des anderen Hölle sein. Stoßt das Tor auf und wir sind im Himmel.

AW: Und er in der Hölle.

Dichter: Oder sonst wo.

AW: Die Wachen? Was ist mit den Wachen?

Dichter: Es gibt keine Wachen. Ich habe sie beurlaubt, oder bestochen. Kraft meines Amtes lässt mich der Alte schalten und walten. Schlafende Diktatoren sind schlechte Diktatoren. Er ist in letzter Zeit sehr müde. Wir werden ihn erlösen.

AW: Jetzt gleich?

Dichter: Jetzt gleich!

AW: Und das Personal?

Dichter: Was soll das Personal schon tun? Es hat nicht das Recht das Zimmer zu betreten. Es besteht aus mundtoten Schafen. Ihr werdet euch doch nicht vor ihnen fürchten?

AW: Natürlich nicht. Wenn das so ist …

AW: Wir sind keine Schlächter … wir sind das nicht gewöhnt.

Dichter: Ihr sollt nicht tranchieren, sondern töten … nur töten.

AW: Wir haben das noch nie gemacht.

Dichter: Mein Gott, dann müsst ihr eben umlernen.

AW: Machen wir schnell … damit es vorüber ist.

Dichter: Habt ihr die Messer?

AW: Ja.

Dichter: Eure Begeisterung hält sich in Grenzen.

AW: Nein, wir sind sehr begeistert.

AW: Ja.

AW: Ich habe eine Frage! Sie sind doch Künstler.

Dichter: Ja.

W.: Eben. Ich liebe ein Bild und weiß nicht von wem es ist. Es stellt folgendes dar: Ein kleiner Raum, rechts ein Fenster durch das Licht fällt. Links befindet sich eine halboffene Holztür. In der Mitte des Zimmers steht vor einem einfachen, roh bearbeiteten Tisch ein Bettler und bricht Brot. Alles Licht sammelt sich auf ihm. Er bricht einfach Brot. Daneben steht andächtig eine Bäuerin und ihr Kind. Sie starren ungläubig, fast lauernd, auf den Mann, der von Glorienschein umflossen ist, … selbstverständlich ist es nur das Licht … der Bettler, er schaut abgerissen aber ernst und edel aus … sehr edel … ich meine … kennen sie das?

Dichter: Nein, das Bild kenne ich nicht. Werfen sie den Kitsch weg.

W: Ich habe es nicht, kann mich aber genau daran erinnern. Als ich ein Kind war …

Dichter: Sind sie besoffen?

Die anderen Weisen lachen leise.

W: Nein. Kindheitserinnerungen, wissen sie.

Dichter: Nur nicht hysterisch werden. Äußerste Konzentration meine Herren! (zum Sprecher) Oder wollen sie nicht mitmachen?

W: Doch, doch, ich meinte nur …

Dichter: Das Bild bekommen sie! Ehrenwort! Und noch was … schneiden sie sich nicht meine Herren!

AW: Können wir ihn nicht garrottieren?

Dichter: Das ist noch grausamer.

AW: Ach so.

Dichter, geht rasch zur Tür, die in die Privatzimmer führt und klopft: Sauhund Terra, du Sauhund wach auf!

Die Weisen ballen sich zu einer dunklen Gruppe.

Dichter, lauter: Terra, deine Herzchen erwarten dich! Sie haben spitze Wünsche mitgebracht. Spitze Geschenke für dich.

Terras verschlafene Stimme. Sie schleppt schwer am Schlaf und erschreckt die Weisen: Was ist denn schon … was schon wieder zum Teufel?

Dichter: Aloisius Hundsburger komm endlich! Wir haben ein Hühnchen zu rupfen! Komm du alte Blutsau!

Terra, kommt barfüßig und mit einem Schlafrock bekleidet herein: Was gibt es so dringendes, dass man meinen Schlaf stört? (Zum Dichter) Wie kannst du das erlauben?

Schweigen.

Terra: Wo ich doch so empfindlich bin! (Reibt sich die Augen)

Dichter: Wir sprachen gerade darüber.

Terra: Über was? (Lähmendes Schweigen, es wird sehr hell.) … worüber denn?

Dichter: Es war sehr interessant.

Schweigen.

Terra, unsicher: Was steht ihr so steif? (Ich höre, hält sich die Hand ans Ohr.) Nichts? Wo sind meine Pantoffel. (Sucht tief gebeugt) Wo sind sie?

Dichter schnalzt mit den Fingern. Die weisen drängen einander gegen Terra. Einer von ihnen sticht auf den Gebückten ein und tritt schnell wieder zurück.

Terra, sich stöhnend aufrichtend und nach der Wunde greifend: Sonderbar, Nierenschmerzen … nass (betrachtet die Hand) Das ist ja Blut? Wo kommt … (schreit) Blut (fassungslos die

Weisen anstarrend) Blut (Er hält ihnen dabei die flache Hand hin.)

Dichter: Los, wartet nicht!

Die Weisen fallen über Terra her und metzgern ihn. Sie bilden ein gärendes Knäuel, nur der Dichter steht abseits.

Terra, erstickt aus der Masse: Waaache … Waaache … Polizei … (stürzt blutend auf den Dichter zu)

Dichter: Die Wände haben keine Ohren.

Die weisen holen Terra ein und stechen ihn nieder.

Terra, zusammenbrechend: Nein … ihr Lieben … ihr Guten … nein … bitte … (Wimmern)

Die Weisen zerstechen ihn.

Dichter: Bravissimo. Ihr habt euren Beruf verfehlt. (Die Weisen beenden die Schlächterei und blicken unsicher um sich.) Ihr seid blutig und stinkt nach Schweiß meine Lieben. Meine Hände sind rein. (Hebt sie) Zum Metzger muss man geboren sein. (Die Weisen betrachten verstört ihre Hände.) Das … das da … weg damit … (tritt gegen Terras Leiche) … na … wird's bald!

W: Wir?

Dichter: Zum Kuckuck wer sonst? Oder wollt ihr warten, bis er von selbst zu laufen beginnt? Soll ich mich schmutzig machen?

AW: Beruhigen sie sich.

Dichter: Mir ist sowieso schlecht. (Geht würgend in die Privatzimmer und übergibt sich.)

W: Das kann passieren.

AW: Die Nerven.

AW: Sensible Menschen sind für solche Sachen sehr empfindlich …

Dichter, eintretend: Es geht schon (wischt sich mit einem Tuch den Mund ab) danke … es geht schon viel besser … die Aufregung …

W: Auch ich (würgt) ich … (Hält sich die Hand vor den Mund und läuft nach links.)

Dichter: Tragt das schon weg … da muss einem empfindsamen Menschen ja das Kotzen kommen.

Sekr. von rechts kommend: Ist es so weit? Schon vorbei? Meinen Glückwunsch. Der Staat ist gerettet. (Die Weisen verstecken die Messer.)

Dichter: Der Herr ist eingeweiht.

Sekr.: Ich habe ihnen gratuliert meine Herren!

Die weisen zögernd: Danke … danke … verbindlichsten Dank … vielen Dank …

Dichter: Warum so verlegen ihr Herrn. Ihr seid Helden!

Sekr.: Es ist eine Heldentat!

Terra, röchelt.

Dichter zum Sekr.: Sagten sie etwas?

Sekr.: Ich? Nein.

Dichter: Dan klopft das Gebell der Passanten gegen den Fußboden.

Terra, röchelnd: Den Gnadenschuss … gebt mir den Fangschuss …

Dichter: Er lebt noch … (tritt zurück)

Sekr.: Bitte. (Zieht eine Pistole aus der Tasche und erschießt Terra.) Mann muss menschlich sein … Mitleid, sonst nichts … (steckt die Pistole ein.)

Dichter: Haben sie die immer bei sich?

Sekr.: Nur bei wichtigen Anlässen … nur für den Notfall, falls etwas nicht klappen sollte …

Dichter: Das ist sehr aufmerksam.

Sekr.: Für sie ist mir nichts zu teuer.

Dichter: sie schlauer Mensch. Geben sie mir die Waffe. Ich möchte sie ansehen. (Streckt die Hand dem Sekr. entgegen. Der legt die Pistole hinein. Der Dichter erschießt ihn.) Zu schlau oder zu dumm … ich kann solche Cowboys nicht brauchen. (Zu den Weisen) Sie haben nichts zu befürchten meine Herren.

Sekretärin hereinstürmend: Endlich! (Mit einem Blick auf Terra) Schön sieht das nicht aus.

Dichter: Was wollen sie?

Sek.: Es ist furchtbar, aber wir sind frei … auch wenn die Begleitumstände nach Schlachthaus riechen.

Dichter zu den Weisen: Seine Mätresse!

Sek: Er ist tot … das zählt …

Dichter: Ich verstehe ihren Schmerz, Fräulein, trotzdem muss ich sie bitten das Zimmer zu verlassen.

Sek: Wie lange haben wir gewartet! Jetzt brauchen wir uns nicht mehr zu verstellen! Umarme mich! (Geht auf den Dichter zu)

Dichter: Halt! (streckt abwehrend den Arm aus, sie bleibt stehen) Was erlauben sie sich? Ich begreife ihre Verwirrung, aber das geht entschieden zu weit!

Sek: Ich werde wieder lachen Schatz … wir werden im Garten unter Fliederbüschen sitzen … wie wir es träumten …

Dichter, zu den Weisen: Sie ist verrückt! Ich habe nicht die Absicht sie zu erben. Ich benütze weder sein Rasierwasser, auch nicht seine Kleider, nicht sein Bettzeug, noch seine Geliebte! (Zur Sek.) Sie haben ausgespielt!

Sek: Das versteh ich nicht … was hast du? Sag mir was du hast!

Dichter: Spielen sie nicht Theater! In Anbetracht der Umstände …

Sek: Das ist doch nicht wahr … nein, nein … lassen sie sich das erklären … es ist nicht so … nein, du verstellst dich … (lacht gequält) du verstellst dich … (blickt im Kreis und lässt die Arme hängen) … Wissen sie er verstellt sich. Das macht die Gewohnheit … nein … vielleicht sehe ich im Licht ungünstig aus … aber das gibt sich (greift nach der Frisur) sicherlich gibt sich das … ich … ich liebe dich doch! Ja, ich habe mit Terra geschlafen ihr Herrn, das ist wahr … (zeigt auf den Dichter) Aber, wenn sein fetter Körper über mich glitt habe ich nur an ihn gedacht. Ich habe die Zähne zusammengebissen und …

Dichter: Sie haben den Mund geöffnet, damit seine Zunge den Weg fand. An mich gedacht? Dass ich nicht lache! Wenn ihnen ein Mann nicht genügt, empfehle ich ihnen ein Bordell! Dort können sie ihre nymphomanischen Gelüste befriedigen.

Die Weisen lachen.

Sek: Nein … so bist du nicht … bitte hör mit der Komödie auf … auch wenn du Dichter bist, bitte hör mit der Komödie auf! … ich, ich bin in letzter Zeit etwas hysterisch … (zu den Weisen) … Er, er spaßt!

Dichter: Hören sie endlich auf mich zu duzen! (zu den Weisen) Wie pervers das Weib ist! Ein Toter Freund scheint ihren Trieb zu steigern.

Sek, schreiend: Das war doch alles für uns!

Dichter, kalt: Ist mir neu. (zu den Weisen in äußerster Verwunderung) Wussten sie davon? (Die Weisen lachen) Sie ist verrückt (deutet auf die Stirn) völlig verrückt.

Zwei Weise halten sie fest.

Sek, schreiend: Warum dann? Warum?

Dichter: Die letzte Gnade, die letzte gnadenvolle Antwort. Ich sah Terra beim Essen zu und da kam mir der Gedanke auch einmal zu essen, zu essen, soviel ich will. (Zu den Weisen) und das wollen wir ja alle nicht? (Gelächter)

W: So rächt sich Leichtsinn, Fräulein.

Sek: Ich glaube an nichts mehr.

Dichter: Bringt sie in Sicherheit.

Sek, während sie hinausgeschleppt wird, schluchzend: Glaub mir … es ist nur das Licht … das ungünstige Licht … es ist nur das ungünstige Licht …

Dichter: Das stört. (Zeigt auf die Leichen) saubermachen meine Herren!

Die Leichen werden hinausgeschleift.

Dichter: Das Happy End ist da. Länder, Kontinente, Jachten, Privatflugzeuge, werde ich essen. Auch Kamele mit Gold und Elfenbein beladen, Sekretärinnen, politische Gefangene, den Staat, das Volk, die Religion, die Dichter, die Menschheitsbeglücker. Alles wird einverleibt. (Halb zu den Weisen, halb zum Publikum, das er schon am Anfang der Rede fixiert hat) Ich danke Ihnen.

ENDE

# “THE CONFUSION”

## Die Verwirrung

# "THE CONFUSION"

**Codeword: "Tower"**
**The legacy of the Babylonian tower.**

The Confusion is a play without a coherent plot. It is rather a collage of different scenes, which do not merge into related action. One scene evolves from soldiers and their captain not recognizing the harlequin, their supreme commander. The harlequin is also the single character having the capacity to not only represent a military commander but also a ballet master as well as a fearless fighter for human rights. Part of this collage are in addition actors searching for a new job, supported on and off by a stagehand; a ballerina wanting to boost here carrier; a nanny having lost the child she should take care of in a pond and being advised thereafter by the actors; an exotic beauty portrayed as a diva in her episodes with the theater director and the artistic director.

All of this takes place vis-à-vis the background of a wobbly bobbly machine at stage supplemented by the worldly innocent conversations of the two gentlemen in tails and top hats, while being repeatedly interrupted by the gentleman in a tropical suit or the scientist. The point in time when the actions of the protagonists reach most coherence is in the aftermath of a noise grenade attack, when the artistic director requests all hands at stage for their support. The story thereafter just ends in a confusing confrontation between the young actor and the theater director over his rude refusal of an engagement.

The play – commencing with the actors coming on stage – ends with them leaving it again, while no story that could be taken home, remains in between.

Persons:

Theatre Director

Director

Two Actors

Two Gentlemen in tails and top hats

Nanny with a stroller

Negress; a blond negress (Editor's note: This play was written in Vienna in the early 1980's, at a time when the word "Negro" was used terminologically but was by no means meant to be derogatory. The character of the "blonde Negress" is this play, consequently, shows at no point any racist traits.)

Three Soldiers. One Captain.

Scientist

Gentleman in tropical suit

Ballerina

Clown; a richly dressed clown, more like a harlequin.

Stagehand

Stage design:

A mixture of different, mismatched objects, some of which are used as a seat, some of which serve as an obstacle. Chairs, blocks, an armchair, a sofa, a broken wheel, car tires, a washbasin, a television set, a refrigerator, crockery, bottles, rags, carpets, cloths, indefinable leftovers. (Don't use a toilet seat or toilet paper.)

Center stage is dominated by a machine. A walk-in podium surrounds them. Its substructure is a richly designed cuboid on which, among other things, there are many levers and other control devices. From the approximately 1.50 m high and approximately 2.50 m long cuboid, a rocket-like shape protrudes obliquely into the air. The structure should only remotely remind the viewer of a rocket. To be even clearer, the structure could also represent a highly abstracted, forward-rushing Olympic torchbearer. It consists of various metal and plastic parts, should be confusing and must be movable. In principle, a cybernetic work of art, which it can be in the best case. Wire bundles, spirals, wheels, antennas, rods, light bulbs, and neon tubes that work but are not intended to create a Tivoli-effect are the main components of the machine.

A note on the appearance of the actors and costumes:

The two gentlemen in tails and top hats should look alike. They are of medium height and may sport short gray beards. The buttoned, originally elegant, black tailcoats are dusty, scuffed and crushed, as are the trousers. Torn boots are covered with Leucoplast tape. It must be clearly visible, i.e., oversized, but must not appear cabaret-like. The shirts that used to be white are crumpled and dirty. Silver-grey ties. Maybe walking sticks too. Round gold-rimmed glasses. One spectacle lens might be blocked. Leucoplast can also stick to the cylinder and shirt collar. The shoes are polished. They wear thick, shiny gold chains around their necks, reminiscent of the chain of the Order of the Golden Fleece.

Negress: Should be tall and slim. Wearing an ankle-length, tight-fitting black dress. It is high closed. Side slits reach past the hips. Hem and collar are edged in white. Fishnet stockings, red garters, high black heels. The blond, curly wig is boyishly short and leaves the neck free.

The nanny must be very elegant. She wears a blouse, skirt, jacket, bonnet, apron and heels.

The soldiers are about the same size. No rank insignia. Uniform made of grey-green fabric, visored cap. The helmets are on the ground and are only put on when crawling commando-style.

The gentleman in the tropical suit wears his tropical helmet most of the time.

The theatre director should be massive. Open frock coat, colorful gilet, Homburg.

Harlequin Clown: White makeup, mask-like face. Eyes rimmed in black. Bright red lips that must not be too wide, bald head. He wears a jerkin with puff sleeves and harem pants reaching to his knees. They shouldn't be too wide. Basic tone of the costume: white and silver. Ballet slippers tied with light blue ribbons. The costume is densely embroidered with silver sequins, using gold only sparingly. Also, light blue and light green mesh, as well as glass plates and red stones are scattered over the robe. The performer may wear a pointed hat at times.

Overall impression: Precious, exquisite. This turns him into a clown-matador.

Ballerina: Her lace skirt stands horizontally away from the hips. Iridescent color, reminiscent of a dancer painted by Degas. Pale pink shoes. She wears her hair pinned up or braided into a tight braid.

The scientist is an elderly, balding man. Can wear glasses. Blossom white work coat.

The director is in everyday clothes.

The stagehand wears blue work clothes.

Position of the actors: The two Gentlemen in tails and top hats are sitting side by side, facing the audience, on the right side of the stage, near the ramp (on the audience's left). A little to the side behind them is the location of the ballerina and the harlequin clown. Scientists, theatre director and director sit on the middle stage. The left side of the stage (to the right of the audience) is mainly reserved for the soldiers. The stagehand and the two actors have their main position by the wall, next to the arcade. The Negress sits on the far right.

This version is intended for a daylight performance.

In the case of a performance in a closed room, the stage design looks like this: To the left (to the viewer's right) a fragment of a reddish-brown brick wall punctuated by arches. It runs at a distance, parallel to the ramp (roughly between the ramp and the middle of the stage). Its depth is a few meters so that the two actors and the stagehand have enough space. A meter high wooden podium slopes forward from the wall and ends to the right (left) of the center of the ramp. It continues behind the wall and is closed off in the background by a compact wooden fence. The wood must not look new. The horizon (round horizon) is light blue in color. The props remain unchanged.

A younger and an older man come through the arcades from the left (on the viewer's right). They wear a very stylized Renaissance dress, a simple brown doublet, white shirts, red tights that are torn and lace-up shoes on their feet. The older one is bearded. His head is covered by a white beret. Clothing may be decorated with colorful ribbons.

Young actor patting the wall: Solidly built. I call that building. Touch it! (*Kicks it with the foot*). I hope rich people live here.

Old Actor: Poor on the wallet, poor... we'd need it badly, my stomach is growling. (*Slips his bundle from his shoulders and drags it behind him. He cracks like an old gramophone.*) Do you still have gum?

Young Actor: Don't give up at the last minute. Here, take … (*Old Actor takes the gum and puts it between his teeth.*) Don't forget, you already owe me one.

Old Actor, chewing: It was your fault that we got the boot last time.

Young Actor: Because the director was after me. The bastard. There's nothing I can do about it.

Old Actor: For my sake, you should have...

Young Actor: Not even for your sake...

Old Actor: You turned him on.

Young Actor: So what? Little dalliances are part of our job.

*They enter the stage on which the other actors, with the exception of the nanny, sit, stand or lie silently*; (*most are seated*).

Young Actor: What kind of entertaining company is that? (*He pushes one of them.*) Nothing, he doesn't move! (*Knocks one of the Gentlemen with a top hat on the forehead. It must sound like he is knocking on wood.*) Nothing either.

(To the Ballerina): And you, my beautiful Lady?

(To the old actor): Stiff as a board. Either they are deaf or they don't want us. I've never been so obviously ignored in my life. That's embarrassing for an actor. (*Tugs the beard of the man in tails.*)

Old Actor: Stop the nonsense! Let's wait for them to wake up. I'm tired, let's sit down in the meantime.

Young Actor: If you believe that we will achieve something with it. (*They sit apart with their backs to the wall.*) Dull guys. I imagined it differently. It's actually very quiet here.

Old Actor: Not remarkable.

Young Actor: I would like to have your phlegm.

*The figures move slowly. Not all at the same time. They come round at different intervals. Some awake from their rigidity suddenly, others gradually and imperceptibly. Some yawn and stretch sleepily.*

Young actor bumping the old actor with the elbow: I think it's starting.

Old Actor: Wait!

First Gentleman with top hat to the other: Well, dear colleague?

Second Gentleman: I haven't thought about that sentence yet. That means I'm tinkering with it every second. A tenet must be unimpeachable. He must be armored and helmeted. I recap. I recap. We had stopped at the further development of Homo sapiens. Did I guess correctly? Or…?

First Gentleman: I tell you, the insects will survive. The insects and the machines.

Second Gentleman: The insects are machines. I have to agree with you on that point. The insect represents a special variety of our artificially bred humans, which in many cases, which I do not want to specify now, are built or modeled after the insect. The insect, dear professor has bred itself over the course of billions of years, which I do not have to emphasize, has always adapted to the circumstances, and has always been capable of evolution without changing significantly on the outside. This does not seem to me to be the case with the human race.

First Gentleman: So with the human species you see ...

Second Gentleman: Right, in the human race, in all mammals. Just think how changes fashion. Do you see how shabby we have gotten?

First Gentleman: I have to ask! In addition, the fact that fashion changes speaks volumes for development.

Second Gentleman: For my sake, but not for spiritual development. In addition, I would not call the change in clothing a development, but rather a change in clothing according to the facts. A change that in most cases depends on climatic conditions. Think of cotton. Also on whether a tribe or several tribes move from a cold area to a warm one or vice versa. Which is proven to be less common.

First Gentleman: So you deny a spiritual development of humankind.

Second Gentleman: Not even our experiences, whether they were experiences of certain crowds, masses, or purely personal insights, which were then disseminated - either orally, through beatings or visually - have brought us any further.

First Gentleman: So you do not see a chance.

Second Gentleman: If I am to be honest – no.

First Gentleman: Then I consulted you in vain, sir.

Second Gentleman: I already told you, nothing significant has changed since the cave paintings of Altamira. Spiritually superior people created these works. It could have been highly talented twentieth-century painters, who you meet tomorrow on the street, in a restaurant, at a lecture.

First Gentleman: So we are quasi cave dwellers.

Second Gentleman: All right, star dwellers, which does not change anything.

Man in tropical suit, approaching them: Excuse me; did you happen to see the trail? The lion must have passed here. A big male, not to be missed. As a hunting companion, I ask you for information.

Second Gentleman: You see, dear colleague, the ancient, animalistic hunting instinct, the ancient courtship display, just see how he raises his tail feathers.

First Gentleman: Courtship?

Second Gentleman: Yes, he combines hunting with social position and would play the hero in front of women. He will boast of his trophies, as I said, courtship and cock his tail.

First Gentleman: Only after, he has shot the lion.

Second Gentleman: Faced death face to face, even if only from the safari bus, camera in hand.

First Gentleman: Or with the telephoto lens. There are thousands of lion pictures.

Second Gentleman: They are already getting on my nerves.

First Gentleman: There are also photos of Negro children and photos of naked Negro women with nipples the size of thermos bottle caps.

Second Gentleman: What they can physically endure. It is touching how they starve.

First Gentleman: And the dying cattle? An ideal breeding ground for plagues.

Second Gentleman: The prostitution in front of tourists...

First Gentleman: They have it everywhere. This is not a typical African phenomenon. All you have to do is look around.

Man in tropical suit listening intently with hunched back: Thank you very much Gentlemen. Therefore, you have not seen my Simba. Very nice of you. Hey Safari! (*Walks up and down among the obstacles, searching, finally disappearing behind the machine.*)

A pristine white nanny quickly pushes a pristine white pram across the stage. (B*e careful when setting up the obstacles, her path must be clear.*)

First Gentleman: The swollen bellies under the thin ribs. The open wounds. They clearly lack hygiene and healthy eating. I would say they are starving.

Second Gentleman: But they get beautiful, big eyes. The face consists only of eyes.

First Gentleman: I know the posters. They bother you sometimes.

The nanny pushes the pram back across the stage. When she reaches the middle of the stage, she takes a colorful rattle out of the car and shakes it.

Nanny: It's okay... guti... guti... calm, just calm, I'm here... I'm with you. (*She continues on the way. This must seem as natural as if a real nanny had entered the scene. The two Gentlemen continue their conversation undeterred.*)

Second Gentleman: They die, as has been proven, of exhaustion.

First Gentleman: That is logical.

Blonde Negress, who has stood up and circles the Gentlemen once: I am wearing an haute couture masterpiece. Unique cut, best fabric quality. People say I move very gracefully, but that is inherent in our breed. A privilege of our race. Black models are all the rage. Not the very last, but black is "in". I have the black skin and soul of a gazelle or a wildcat.

Director who stepped behind her: Or that of a good-natured, fat, black mommy, a mother hen with many children.

*Most actors are moving now. They brush out their robes, run their hands over their hair, speak to each other in a low voice or communicate through gestures. This should look very private and carefree.*

First Gentleman: Despite their cultural shortcomings, they are …

Negress, to the director: Your comment was not very cultivated; I thought it was more charming.

First Gentleman: In fact, very charming.

Director: I protest. I am a director, so I am culturally active. I do not mince my words and call things by their proper name.

Second Gentleman: Even though they have funny names...

Negress: Still, you are a nice guy.

Second Gentleman: And there are big boys among them.

Director: Thanks for the nice guy. Then we understand each other.

First Gentleman: Also, the communication is difficult. The different mentality plays a big role.

Negress: Your brutal mentality does not work on me. The stitch does not pull. You are too direct.

Second Gentleman: I do not want to have anything to do with you directly.

First Gentleman: Unless it is, absolutely, necessary.

Negress puts one foot on the thigh of the first Gentleman and fiddles with her fishnet stockings. Turned to the director: These legs are impressive. Look at my ankles. (*Turning to the ballerina over the heads of the two Gentlemen*): There, you see, hey there (swings a leg).

Ballerina: Leave me alone! Leave me alone with your lower extremities!

First Gentleman, ignoring the Negress: Yes, mobility and slender limbs cannot be denied.

Second Gentleman: Although some tribes call their very short extremities their property.

Ballerina: The director is not your property. Black whore, snake!

Negress: Ballet rat!

First Gentleman: The rats eat three quarters of the relief goods stored at the port.

Director: But, but … Ladies.

Ballerina: I do not need your help. I am not a Lady to them. For them I am Miss Mayer. Leave me alone starting today. Do not bother me anymore. I always come to rehearsals on time; you know that as well as I do. I do my duty. You can't ask for more from me. I don't care about your private interests. You don't belong here. However, I won't put up with anything from that one (*points to the negress*). (*Turns away defiantly.*)

Young Actor: I like the black one.

Old Actor: Psst!

Negress: The young Lady is sulking. The little beast pouts. Oh well. (*Steps up the ramp, in a singing voice*): I couldn't say I don't like it here. Even if the climate is a bit rough. But … I was happiest in my homeland. In my eternally sunny homeland. Where I roamed like a shy gazelle through the green bush. Where I bathed in transparent rivers, and played with the fish. Where on hot evenings I listened to the dark sound of the drums; listened, my hips swaying like palm trees in the monsoon, as we carried the calabashes to the field to refresh the thirsty.

How I miss the distant screeches of the monkeys and the grunts of the Cape buffalo as they laze in muddy pools. All was right with the world until the day the slave traders came, burned our village and, tragic fate … dragged me away in chains. They worked my delicate body with the braided whip. I had to be beautiful and dance for them. Me, a tall child of the wilderness with a predator's need for freedom! Eventually I was sold to an old, lecherous sheik who imprisoned me in his harem.

There I sat like a captive bird, refusing food, staring through the bars, wasting away and getting sicker and sicker. My body no longer wanted to hold the soul. The miserly owner decided to sell me. My value had meanwhile diminished so much that a kind, fatherly European bought me cheaply. He took care of me like a daughter and nursed me back to health. I was soon back in possession of my former beauty.

A talent scout who happened to be passing by my sponsor's house, heard my voice and hired me. That is how I ended up here. Sometimes I can still feel the song of the jungle rushing through my blood. Then I have to drink cold water quickly. I am a fabric of ivory and black velvet. The palms of my hands are rosy roses. However, ask my manager. (*Turns around searchingly*) Unfortunately, he is unable to come. He could tell you the story much more poignantly.

Director: Back to your old ways, are we? If only I could prevent that. You make a fool of yourself. Do not believe a word she says. She has never seen the bush. She was born the daughter of a pawnbroker in the slums of Harlem. Her father, who had a legitimate reputation as an unscrupulous exploiter, enriched himself with his own race. With the poorest of the poor. He was also involved in drugs and prostitution. She has never known the need. She grew up sheltered. In addition, she is an extraordinarily enterprising luxury creature.

Captain to the three soldiers: Line up! (*Soldiers approach.*) Rifle at heel! (*Soldiers do.*) We do not have the luxury of laziness. (*Meanwhile he commands the following*): Turn right, turn left, straight ahead, stop, aim rifle, shoulder rifle...etc. (*May only serve as background noise*).

Negress to the director: Now will you get me the role?

Director: It depends on your vocal condition. I am not responsible for the fee. You have to contact the theatre director. Come! (*The two go to the theatre director who is further back. He looks more like a ringmaster in his martial pose. He could be holding a whip and wearing boots.*)

Director: May I introduce you to this Lady, dear Sir ... she would like...

Theatre Director (*rising beaming*): Madame, I'm glad that you honor us ... however, whether the fee meets your requirements...

First Gentleman: The savages are completely undemanding. A handful of rice...

Second Gentleman: You are confusing something there. I believe the continent.

First Gentleman: It could be my dear colleague. That's what the heat does. Where were we?

Second Gentleman: At the evolution of insects, which cannot be dealt with even with insecticides.

First Gentleman raises his cylinder and wipes the sweat from his forehead with a white sackcloth: Right! In contrast to your valuable and certainly well founded opinion - I do not want to deny that it is well founded - I am of the opinion that people are also capable of further development, that this further development is an absolute must for them.

Second Gentleman: You have just wiped the sweat from your forehead.

First Gentleman: Yes and?

Second Gentleman: The primitive people did the same. The only difference is that they used the arm or the back of the hand while you are using a handkerchief. The only reason and purpose of the movement remains the same. (*Picks up glasses and polishes them.*) Just consider the fact that a few hundred years ago Central Europeans could have had a reputation for universal education, something that is impossible today. What I mean to say is that the knowledge has increased, but not the mind.

First Gentleman: The knowledge of Central Europeans concerning Central Europe, you mean.

Second Gentleman: Please, if you want to limit the area like that … of course educated people had an idea of near and far places, of Africa etc., but just an idea. It was never brought to them. The huge material that a modern person, if he really wanted to educate himself universally, would have to cope with it, which of course is impossible. We are overwhelmed by abundance.

First Gentleman: What - we? You and I? We have our expertise. We are experts in our field.

Second Gentleman: No, my dear, we have only specialized. We have become special specialists. We have limited ourselves to a partial knowledge. The brain has by no means grown with it. We belong to one of the many groups that will divide again as knowledge grows. This leads to a permanent split. We have become hordes of hunters again, with our own hunting grounds and special hunting methods. What can a so-called cosmopolitan grasp of what is happening around him? A tiny bit of all things and events. Moreover, even if they existed for three billion and eight hundred thousand years, dear sir, and could split a thousand times, the individual events would only exist in fragments for them. They would have to be artists, revolutionaries, statesmen, prostitutes, pleasure boys, wives, undertakers, builders, astronauts, entrepreneurs, educators, student assistants...I can't list all human manifestations...they would have to be all of these at the same time, in every country, at every hour and in every place. Like a thousand-headed hydra.

Young Actor: They talk something together. The little one from the ballet is very appetizing.

First Gentleman: A very interesting aspect.

Second Gentleman: But not realizable. That's the tragedy.

Man in tropical suit rejoins them: I shot three lion cubs. I mean, I snapped a shot. They walked right in front of the camera. Weren't shy at all. Look at the cute things. (*Shows the two photos ... they ignore.*) Aren't they lovely? My wife will be happy. She's crazy about baby animals. There, I think that's a success too... how he looks...

First Gentleman (*loudly into the man's speech*): The Negress' dried-up breasts, on which half-dead infants are hanging.

Man in tropical suit: My children will be happy too. There …

First Gentleman: I have seen things that are more appetizing. The whining mouths are an open wound. Why are they starving so provocatively? Does it have to be so conspicuous? You must know, dear colleague, that I am a sensitive person and a great esthete as well. I hate such blatant dying. I hate and loathe it, although I have nothing against the human skeleton. Neither that of adults nor that of infants.

Man in tropical suit handing them picture after picture: Aren't they nice? It was a complete success. Even though I didn't get the shot. I thank you for your kindness. (*Moves to the back.*)

Nanny rushes in from the right. She drags the stroller behind her. Screaming: They stole my baby, they kidnapped it!

Captain: Stand still! (*Soldiers do ... kindly to the nanny*) What happened? Can I help you?

Nanny: My child! Kidnapping! My child was stolen from me.

Director, who stepped forward from behind the machine, yelling to the front: Please come up with a better excuse!

Nanny: Excuse me! Very well, Mr. Director.

(*Curtsy*) to the captain: The baby fell into the water. What should I do? What will my lord- and ladyship say? My god, I'm getting fired.

Captain: Calm down for now. We must take strategic action. Actual action is important. However, the case is not provided for in the regulations.

Nanny: I've always spoiled the little one. I cared for him like a mother - no worse - the softest blankets, the softest diapers, so that the little ass doesn't get sore... When the little one blinked, I trembled for his health... he was so tiny and delicate... and at the same time such a nice, funny guy ... what am I doing ... what can you do ... please help me ... I'm completely desperate ...

Captain: I am at your disposal. I could give you a... I mean, you could then pass it off as a child of your masters.

Nanny: I'm not sure. What if it's not a boy? In addition, it takes too long.

Young actor to the old one (*speaking into the nanny's last sentence*): We can earn a few shillings. (*Stands up.*) Maybe I can help you Miss.

Nanny sobbing: You?

Young Actor: Yes, just a moment (unwraps a baby-sized doll from a bundle and holds it upside down by one leg.) There you take it.

Nanny: But...

Old Actor (*standing up*): It doesn't work that way. First, we need to induce labor.

Young Actor: I really forget everything. (*To the nanny*:) Act on behalf of the mother.

Old Actor: Will you become a mother. Become a mother without the joys of lust but with the pains of childbirth. This is a small punishment for your sloppiness. (*He rotates the nanny so that half of the audience sees her. The following scene must not be obscene. To the young actor*:) I'll leave that to you. You do have safer hands.

Young Actor to the nanny: Spread your legs. A little further - yes, like that. Hold on tight … yes … support yourself.

(The nanny is leaning back, holding her hands beneath her on the cart handlebar. The actor slides the doll under her dress.

She rears up and lets out a groaning, drawn-out scream. The actor pulls the doll out from between her legs and waves it in the air. Some other actors clap. He shakes the puppet expertly, slaps her bottom. (*Listen*) Nothing! (*Shakes it again.*) Nothing!

Old Actor: You forgot to turn on the tape.

Young Actor: Yes, right. (*Opens a flap on the doll's back and fiddles around inside. Loud baby cries are heard.*)

Old Actor: Turn it down a bit.

Young actor obeys the wish and then hands it to the nanny: So young lady...

(*She hugs the doll, thinks about it, takes diapers out of the car and wraps it. She handles the doll like a doll, not as carefully as she would a child.*)

Old Actor: It was quite harmless. Except for a little bit of pain.

Nanny: That can...

Young Actor: The most normal thing in the world. I don't know why women make such a circus.

Nanny: You can...

Old Actor: Of course, I can. I am also sensitive to pain. Make a fuss like that. Because of the blessed body and such. Would like to know where the blessing is. What's blessed about it? Moreover, when the brat has arrived. The deep stirrings of the maternal heart. Of course, these only occur if the mother is not criminal in relation to her child or is considered a criminal. Newborns look like frozen blue, crippled old people. At least I think so. That idiotic smile on everyone's face when the infant gives primitive signs of life, or just belches, farts, babbles to himself or saliva runs down his chin. That understanding, unjustified smile that creeps across everyone's face, like an epidemic, drives me insane. Excuse my aggressive nature. Nevertheless, what makes human beings so endearing, so delightful, in this undignified stage?

Nanny: But... it is my child! (*She yells out loudly.*)

Old Actor: Shut up! You are biased! What is delightful about the sleeping or screaming flesh that does not yet deserve to be called human? The shapeless big head? The barely fit hands? The bent legs?

Nanny: But...

Old Actor: The expressions alone, sweet, delightful, charming and cute, are demeaning for a person. That's what young dogs can be called. What is frightening is the fact that, apart from all the unsavory things, they are really just cute. Is playing with dolls to blame? Is it a repeat of the puppet show? Is the attraction in the consciousness of power? In the unique consciousness of power against vis-à-vis a completely helpless creature? Some mothers no longer know what to do with their children as soon as they grow up and show human emotions. The doll has been taken away from them. The doll has become independent. However, I don't want to generalize.

Nanny to Young Actor: How can I thank you?

Old Actor: First, I'm going to make you aware of the advantages of the puppet. First, you can determine their volume. As you have seen, it is very simple. Second, you can turn them off entirely. Third, it doesn't shit and doesn't cry for the bottle. Fourth, you need not to worry that it will ever get colic or a cold.

Young Actor: If you'd have a few shillings for us?

Nanny: Gladly. (*Dumps in the purse.*)

Old Actor: Plus, you can go home knowing that Madame thinks the child is her own. That might be worth a few shillings to you.

Nanny: There you have it. It was my pleasure. (Goes off quickly, pushing the pram in front of her.)

Young Actor, calling after: Thank you, thank you, thank you very much.

Old Actor: How much?

Young Actor: There. (Holds out his hand.)

Old Actor: It works.

Young Actor: I hope she never visits the department store we stole the doll from.

Old Actor: One looks like the other. A serial product.

Young Actor: You're right.

Old Actor, to the stage hand, who is leaning against the wall nearby, hands in pockets: Hey, you!

Stagehand: Do you mean me?

Old Actor: Yes, you.

Stagehand: What is it?

Young Actor: Get us a bottle of beer.

Stagehand: I'm not your servant.

Young Actor: Did I say that? Please bring us a bottle of beer from the canteen. Better two. We are strangers here. Take one for you too.

Stagehand: That's different. I didn't know you were strangers here. (*Young Actor gives him money in his outstretched hand. He gets what they want. They sit down with their backs to the wall and drink.*)

*During the previous action - since the appearance of the nanny - the Negress sang a barely audible coloratura aria with tall guests. The harlequin clown has freshly made up. The scientist worked on the machine. The ballerina practiced a few dance steps and sat down again. None of this should interfere with the plot.*

Captain to the soldiers: You must be a shining example to the nation. Your duty is to act with manly determination, based on initiative and training. You should carry out the orders without thinking about them. You have to obey blindly. Wehrmacht decomposers and agitators are placed against the wall. Who is the agitator determines the top leadership, which is like a mother to you. Did you understand?

All three: Yes.

The Captain, stepping in front of the 1st soldier: Repeat!

First Soldier pushes out his chest and speaks very quickly and monotonously: We must be murderous role models for the nation. We must learn to kill people and see them as predators, as people learn to kill us and see us as predators. We must close our eyes and blindly carry out every command. Individual action is only permitted in this state. People who think differently will be shot down. Who will be shot determines a handful of medal bearers.

Captain, stepping back: Very good! (*Clears throat and continues in an impassioned voice:*) But also think of the waving flag, the drum roll, the victorious flag, the drum roll, the flaming flag, the drum roll, the silent flag, the muffled drumbeat. (*Stepping back even further. He stands with his back to the audience the whole time. The soldiers are facing the ramp.*)

Oh, sword in my left hand
What's the point of your cheerful blinking?
Look at me so kindly.

I didn't ... step away ... nonsense ... your stupid faces throw me off. The emotion brings me ... so it should be said ...

Look at me so kindly.
Enjoy it, hooray!

You there in the first rank, were you laughing? Don't you dare laugh! No? Fine. (*Clears his throat.*) But also think of the dark-brown girls, the adventurous scent of being abroad, the crackling of the campfire. You can consume all of this for free. If things get bad, you will at most lose your arms, your legs, your head, possibly even your life. (*To*

*Soldier Nr.3*): What was my penultimate word?

Third Soldier: Lose.

Captain: Wrong, that was my last word. (*To the second soldier*): Do you know?

Second Soldier: At your command - live.

Captain to First Soldier: And the last one?

First Soldier: Lose.

Captain: So - (*Points to the Second Soldier*).

Second Soldier: Life.

*(Points to the Third Soldier)*.

Third Soldier: Lose.

*The captain pointing alternately. That has to happen very quickly.*

Second Soldier: Life.

First Soldier: Lose.

Second Soldier: Life.

First Soldier: Lose.

Second Soldier: Life.

First Soldier: Lose.

Second Soldier: Life...

Captain: Stop! That already works perfectly. And now to you. (*Steps in front of the Third Soldier.*) I assure you; you will learn it too. Crawl commando-style around the square twice. But with some speed, if I may ask. (*Soldier throws himself to the ground.*) Do you agree? Do you see the correctness of my decision?

Soldier, shouting up to the captain standing just in front of him: Yes sir!

Captain: Discipline is a must, or do you have a different opinion?

Soldier: No!

Captain: Would you kiss my boots if I ordered it?

Soldier: Yes!

Captain: Licking too?

Soldier: Yes!

Captain: With pleasure?

Soldier: Yes!

Captain: Then lick it. (*Holds out his boots. To the other two*): In the modern army one works without harassment. You've seen your comrade grab it. (*To the lying man*): It is enough.

Soldier: At your command.

Captain: I hope you've learned the lesson; crawl then commando-style.

*The soldier crawls across the stage as the action continues. He is not visible all the time.*

Captain: Let that be a warning. Yes! Of course, we are also needed in times of peace. Our sappers are often deployed in the event of storm disasters or when building bridges. But that's not our real job. This is perverse! Roger that?

Soldier: Yes.

Captain: Good! The craft of war has a long tradition. On the one hand we protect women and children, on the other hand we rape and murder them. This happens reciprocally during course of the war. But you will have so much general education. In summary: The real task of the soldier is war. Otherwise, they would be useless. The real task of the soldier is to protect peace. You must see the logic, gentlemen.

Harlequin Clown Slowly Approaching: May I Join? I volunteer.

Young Actor: Don't be stupid...

Old Actor: Don't interfere!

Captain: Go to hell. We don't need joke figures.

Clown, shy: What you just said got my circus blood pumping. It sounded like a dressage act. I smelled predator stench. You know that typical biting...

Captain: Go to hell!

*The clown quickly places a small podium in front of the captain. He mounts it. The stagehand puts a shiny cloak on him that covers the podium. The clown stands with his back almost to the audience. With violent movements, one side of his face becomes visible.*

Clown (*microphone*) yelling at the captain: What are you allowing yourself? Have you gone insane? Don't you know who you're looking at? This is outrageous!

Captain, saluting: At your command! Sorry I have not ... you ...

Clown: You don't recognize your supreme warlord? You are demoted! You have to recognize your supreme warlord even if he travels incognito! (*To the soldiers*); Arrest this man! (*The soldiers take the captain between them.*) Stand still! (*The three freeze.*)

After this unwelcome incident, I want to get to the point of my visit, which is at the same time an inspection, but above all it is intended to serve and to encourage you. (*Pause. With barking roar:*) You are the pillars of the constitution. Most coup attempts are instigated by the military. Most coup attempts are put down by the military. If there was no army, there would be no war. This is Columbus' egg. My strength lies in the glittering splendor of my epaulettes, in the caressing jingle of my medals, in the rhythm of my boots. (*In contrast to the following text, he continues to yell.*)

Gentleness, what gentleness have I poured out on my enemy. Severity, indeed, what severity for my friends? But that made sense. You have to screen your friends in particular; you have to crack down on them and shape them into usable material. We all need to be tougher. Because our proud, bold people should not be unsettled and spoiled by the presence of the slimy, damned slugs and other vermin; as every loyal, upright citizen must describe these elements. Think of our plump, white-skinned women cheering us with rouged lips and applauding with soft hands. (*Three times, incomprehensible roars of the people come out of the loudspeaker, which the clown accepts in a rigid posture.*) The slogan of the day is – never, but never, screw up! (*Yelling again.*) Personally, I am the guarantor that our people never screw up. (*Yelling, he raises his hands soothingly, the noise dies down.*) And that as long as I (*knocks ecstatically on an imaginary parapet, the knocking is loud*) I stand at the head of the state and our flags are consecrated to God. (*Silence. Clown timid*): Did I say something wrong?

Director: Leave God out of it.

Clown: I was talking about sacred flags. Okay, consider that sentence deleted. The consecration of the flags doesn't exist for me, Mr. Director. There are a few more sentences that I would rather omit.

Director: Keep talking in silence.

Clown: As you wish (*gestures*).

First Gentleman: War also has its good side. Think of the happy years of construction.

Second Gentleman: And of the current economic stagnation. The war casualties were basically...

First Gentleman: Economic sacrifice.

Director: Please be quiet!

*The soldier has now crawled back to where he started.*

*Standing at attention to the captain:* Order carried out (salutes).

*His comrades point to the clown with mute head movements.*

*The soldier turns and gives an even sharper salute*: My supreme warlord!

Clown: That's what I call military training. Recognize, understand and react immediately. Bravo, young man. How do they look? What have you had to eat up? Which regiment?

Third soldier yells something unintelligible.

Clown: What are you accused of?

Third Soldier: The captain gave me the order to crawl around the square.

Clown: That's good. Why?

Third Soldier: I didn't catch the penultimate word of his speech.

Clown: So, so, the captain gives speeches. Was it important?

Third Soldier: I don't think so.

Clown: So, you didn't get the impression that he wanted to compete with me?

Third Soldier: No.

Clown: The captain is under arrest. You are a good soldier. Intelligent and quick learner. I'll put you in charge.

Third Soldier: Please don't punish my former superior harshly.

Clown: A noble attitude. Do with him what you think is necessary.

*While the clown, supported by stagehands, climbs down from the pedestal, he has his coat removed, which is thrown carelessly to the ground. The stagehands then slowly push the pedestal to a corner; the soldiers stand at attention; the newly appointed captain salutes and the ballerina walks a few steps.*

The First Gentleman to the other: A good cause demands its sacrifices.

Second Gentleman: Dear colleague, the dead stank like hell. An old woman lay in front of my house for three weeks, across the street. Imagine that; a whole three weeks and that in the summer! Shrapnel, you know, shrapnel got her. And then the flies. I mean the fat, green ones. They sat down on the dishes. They drowned in the soup. Disgusting!

First Gentleman: Decay is a simple decomposition process ... we have the same process, for example, in fermentation...

Second Gentleman: You want to lecture me?

First Gentleman: But by no means, nothing would be further from my mind... (*gesturing or whispering, whereby their gestures do not correspond to the tone of the whisper*).

Third Soldier to former captain: So, you didn't recognize him. Answer me, you idiot!

Former captain, now Third Soldier: Yes Sir! No.

Captain: Stand still! Stand at attention when you answer!

Third Soldier: At your command!

Captain: You're sleeping. I will take care of your encouragement. Crawl commando-style around the square. Pick up a little speed; if you don't mind me! (*Soldier throws himself to the ground*). Do you see the correctness of my decision?

Soldier from below: Yes sir!

Captain: The army cannot exist without discipline.

Soldier: Yes.

Captain: Would you kiss my boots if I ordered it?

Soldier: Orders are orders, Captain!

Captain: Licking too!

Soldier: With pleasure?

Captain: Then lick it.

Soldier: It's an honor.

Captain: In modern training, you work with a sure instinct. You see what joy I give your comrades. (*Speaking downward*) It's enough.

Soldier: Don't deprive me of my pleasure.

Captain: No, enough. My concessions have limits. Continue belly crawling and chill your passion.

Soldier: Gladly! (*crawls*)

Captain to the two soldiers: Are you assigned to guard duty.

Soldier: Yes Sir! (*They shoulder their rifles and pace up and down the left (right) side of the stage. The captain disappears under the arcades.*)

Young Actor: That's a bigger pig than the other one.

Old Actor: Wolves grow from lambs.

Young Actor: We urgently need something to bite. We need money. I want to get drunk again. I want ... do you think we'll be hired?

Old Actor: Do you like the store?

Young Actor: I'm pleased, I'm pleased - given our situation, we have no choice.

Negress, who has come to the fore with the theatre director: Do you really like me? You are not stingy with compliments.

Old Actor: The theatre director should be complimented a few times. So much for the reputation of this renowned theater and so on. It's best if you talk to him. You are the better reciter. Ever since the bear died, we've been going downhill.

Young Actor: One mouth less to feed.

Old Actor: I'm very attached to him. His death saddens me. Go introduce yourself. Even if it's just a supporting role; maybe two.

Negress: I would never play a supporting role.

Theatre Director: Where are you going, my dear, how could I ask something like that from you?

Old Actor: Go on.

Young Actor: Actually, I would like to kick the pompous guy's ass.

Old Actor: We can't afford emotions.

Theatre director to negress: May I give you a … (*rummage in his pockets*)

Stagehand to the two actors: Cigarette? (*Decidedly casual*)

Theatre director holding out the package: Offer?

Young Actor fishes two out of the stagehand's box: Thank you!

Negress to Theatre Director: Ah, that's the kind you smoke?

Young Actor to the stagehand: It tastes excellent.

Negress to theatre director: Just wonderful.

Old Actor: I've been missing such an herb for a long time... I enjoy it...

Negress: I rarely smoke, but when I do I smoke intensely.

Old Actor: ...and inhale every hit with pleasure.

Negress: Since I'm indisposed today anyway, I can afford it.

Theatre Director: I didn't notice any of that madam.

Negress: Yes, yes, I have a terrible cold. That's what the climate does. I'm used to the tropics.

Young Actor who approached the theatre director: Pardon me if I interrupt you. I don't want to keep you long, Sir. My colleague and I are … I wanted to say we don't have a permanent commitment at moment. At least none that corresponds to our talent. Sure, many stages are vying for us, but we're too good for batch roles, so it would be an honor for us to be part of your excellent ensemble.

Theatre Director: Like that?

Ballerina to the clown who pats her thighs: Stop it now! Hands off! You disturb me in my meditation.

Theatre director to the young actor: Don't you notice that you are disturbing?

Young Actor: Excuse me, but I thought you had a supporting role available; maybe two?

Theatre Director: First of all, you should not address me as 'you', but as dear Mr Director, and that at the beginning of every sentence. A bow is indicated, with the eyes humbly closed. Second, you should submit a written request beforehand. Third, no one interrupts me (*yelling*). Away with you, you louts! Once you have been taught manners, you can come back. I expect iron discipline from my ensemble members. A virtue they have yet to learn

Young Actor: Dear Director...

Theatre Director: What else do you want; I don't have time!

Young Actor: Just one minute...

Theatre Director: Not a second. I'm busy, you can see that. I don't know where my head is. One appointment chases the other. Everyone comes to me with their problems. Lighting technicians, directors, stage designers, actors. The ventilation does not work. It's raining through the roof. Then the technical staff went on strike again. I have to negotiate with the works council. The turntable is stuck. A headlight fails. The rehearsal has to be postponed due to the main actor's illness. The premiere falls through. An aging diva has to be talked out of playing Gretchen. The costumes come too late from the tailor's shop and arouse protests from the actors. The curtain is stuck. The props aren't enough and what else is there in terms of delays and inconveniences. Everything weighs on my back. I sacrifice myself. I do my best. I arrange, arrange, improvise. Of course, I don't get any thanks. But you know how it is. You're from the theater. A layman hasn't the faintest idea about this company. You're not a layman, are you? You are an actor. Then you must understand me. I assume so. What did you actually want?

Young Actor: I just wanted to...

Director: Oh yeah, I remember… you wanted to be a cast member. I don't have a second now. Come back another time.

Young Actor: When?

Director: What... when? Let's say tomorrow, the day after tomorrow, whenever you have time … nice meeting you. (Pulls the negress aside.)

*The young actor returns to his place with the word "damn".*

Old Actor: What was? did you achieve something

Young Actor: Nothing again.

Old Actor: Shit.

Theatre Director to Negress: I'd like to invite you if you are free. I know a nice place. We could discuss anything further there.

Negress: Of course. (*Theater Director offers her the arm. Both exit behind the machine.*)

Young Actor: Snooty Monkey. Snot spoon. I want to break his teeth out one by one. But slowly, so he enjoys it.

*The crawling soldier has arrived with the actors.*

Soldier, tearfully: Look at me. I was only doing my duty. As a supervisor, I was strict but fair. Maybe a bit too strict at times, but that comes with the job. In private, I am the most good-natured person in the world and an exemplary father. I can't hurt a fly. Do you want to see a family photo? (*Dumps in the breast pocket. The search is made more difficult by lying down.*) No? You do not want?

Every weekend I go to the countryside with my family. In the fall we fly kites. Sometimes we have a snack at grandmother's house. I mean with my mother and my children's grandmother who lives in a cottage on the outskirts of town. She also owns a little garden and provides us with fresh fruit. That's very pleasant. I'm a moderate drinker. I do not smoke. I feel most comfortable in my cozy home. Do you want to see the picture? (*Shows them a photograph. The two ignore him. They take turns pointing to the ballerina, who is practicing again, with the young actor and the clown exchanging obscene gestures.*) So, this one (*points*) is my oldest. How old? Seventeen, he'll be seventeen in February. Next year he will take the exam. Yes, a good student. I cannot complain. There, on the right, that's my wife. Next to her my second oldest and next to them the youngest. He's only five. This is Waldi, our dachshund. No, the light is too weak. I thought the sun was enough. This is my mother's house. Yes, this is my mother. (*Puts the photos in his pocket. Of course, his answers have to come after a certain time. He listens intently before each reply. Crawling away.*)

It's a shame with these pictures. I didn't have a flash with me. (*He's already turning his back on the actors.*) No thanks, like I said, I'm a non-smoker. I gave up smoking years ago. (*Huffing*) Since then my health has been much better. But you don't have to take me for a health apostle. Yes, initially I gained weight... but then... (*He ducks into the props. There's only mumbling.*)

Young Actor, stretching out: I'm going to take a nap. The earth keeps rotating. Tomorrow as well and the day after tomorrow. The damn dog. (Yawns) But I'm not giving up. Until I get on his nerves so much that he gives me a role.

Old Actor: We're out of beer. (*Waves the empty bottle.*)

Young Actor: Don't be thirsty. I want to sleep; I want to sleep away the trouble just wrapped in a soft, dreamless sleep. In a cottony void, nothing else.

Old Actor: The earth keeps spinning even when he's asleep. Maybe …

Young Actor, sleepy: What?

Old Actor: Is the universe the monstrous remains of a dead person? Perhaps our galaxy is part of its decaying stomach?

Young actor, sleepy: Maybe a part of his decaying brain? The fantastic reflection of a mad brain.

Old Actor: The fantastical reflection of a decaying brain. You mean we don't even exist?

Young Actor: It could be.

Old Actor kicks him.

Young Actor: Ouch!

Old Actor: You certainly exist.

Young Actor: Unfortunately, my stomach is growling. I can't even sleep.

Old Actor: Then lie there. You burn fewer calories.

Scientist, emerging from behind the machine: I'll be there soon. The development of technology is based on an increasingly complex refinement of the basic ideas. (*Handles the machine.*)

Clown, calling to the back: Who cares? Stay in your box! (*To the ballerina*) Delightful.

Ballerina: Excuse me?

Clown: You have a cute little ass. Please let me reach out just once, just once. Please. I'll tell you … the greatest jokes … for your sake. All you have to do is say 'yes'.

Ballerina: But only once. Word of honor!

Clown: Word of honor!

(*Ballerina rests her hands on a block and stretches out the back. He kneels down and strokes the curves. The ballerina pushes him back with her rear end. He falls over.*)

Ballerina: I said only once. Where is your word of honor?

Clown: I beg your pardon. My hands took to themselves as they slid over the delicious curves. You ran away from me. I couldn't catch you anymore. I'm innocent. (*Hands her a red paper flower.*)

Ballerina, who has turned to him: What am I supposed to do with that? (*Throws it carelessly over the shoulder.*)

Clown: You threw my heart in the trash. (*Loud, whining weeping.*)

Ballerina: I want to see your jokes. Come on! I want to laugh. Let us play the ancient game.

Clown, crying: Does that have to be?

Ballerina: You promised.

Pantomime.

*The clown does somersaults, conjures bouquets of flowers out of his sleeve and strews them over the ballerina. Plays a tiny violin, which he tunes beforehand with grotesque facial expressions. (He often begins to play, but always finds mistakes in the sound. The violin is, of course, mute.) He sits next to the armchair several times, wants to kiss the ballerina's hand and stumbles in the process. Sitting on the floor, he ties his shoelace and only gets up again after a lot of effort. He falls on his back and wriggles like a beetle, pulls his mouth into a laughing grimace with his index fingers and cranes his head.*

*He does all this while crying loudly, which is supposed to be funny at first, later touching and towards the end frighteningly real. His movements become more tragic. He bows to the dancer, puts his right hand on his heart, offers it to her, languidly raises his arms, lets them fall again in resignation, raises them again, this time more hesitantly, lets them fall, makes a third, weak attempt to raise his hands and shakes his head sadly. Stands with hanging head and hanging arms. With a sudden movement, he rips his heart out of his chest and offers it to the dancer in the flat cups of his hands. She shrugs. Holding his heart in his outstretched hands, he kneels towards her. She makes a haughty gesture. He carefully lays the heart, which is invisible but almost tangible through his movements, in front of her feet. (This has to be done incredibly tenderly and gently, almost trembling. His crying turns into ragged sobs. The ballerina leans against the cuboid with her arms crossed during his scarifying his heart. At first, however, the more tragic the clown's gestures become, the more she gets bored she laughs. (Her laughter must be passive and must not drown out the clown's crying.) The clown kneeling close in front of her raises his arms and points to his heart. She crushes it with her heel and tosses the remains aside with the toe. The clown falls on his face and lies lifeless. She delicately places one foot angled downward on his back, thrusting one arm forward in goddess of victory pose, stretching the other back and arching her chest so that the Pose has something victorious, rushing forward. The living image lasts about half a minute. In the second half of the pantomime, soft music can start.*

In the meantime, the scientist has cleaned the machine, turned levers, inspected flaps, bent wires, and replaced lamps. He does all this with calm, unobtrusive movements. His factually spoken text comes:

.1. With the silent, counter play of the clown.

.2. While the clown lies on his back, wriggles like a beetle and sometimes pauses, exhausted.

1st Text: Machines have their harmonies and disharmony, which replace each other. I would call them practical works of art. They can slip away from the Creator just like these. They can become independent and turn against their masters; they can bite. Ah, too loose. Same like a kid. Its first hum hits the ears of the inventors and employees, who understandably feel identical to the inventors, like the tinkling of a thousand children's voices. (Break). The screw still needs to be tightened … (pause) I have to work more meticulously ... for the good of humankind, in the interests of the charity ... well, that is all right now...

2nd text: Man describes himself as the crown of creation. Why shouldn't technical development be the crowning glory of man? A crown of gamma rays, hundreds of thousands of volts, billions of horsepower, concentrated solar energy, the song of rockets and gasoline engines; a happy life with fans, batteries, sensors, rotors. A crown of increasing demands that is satisfied by increasing production, a crown that radiates hygiene, zest for action and health. A crown no longer tainted with sentimental, unpredictable, impractical, sadistic and masochistic germs of the past impregnated with mysticism. Man will see the world upright and clearly, master nature and his feelings, feel comfortable in the environment he has created and strive only for what is possible and beneficial. I see swimming pools, luminous meadows, glass sea cities, happy children, adults staying active in old age, moon farms, bright, tall people in athletic suits, eco-friendly, silent modes of transportation ... orchards that bear fruit three times a year, a temperate climate ... (goes behind the machine cleaning).

All the actors give the dancer a short, thin round of applause. She takes the foot off the back of the lying man.

The clown jumps up and gives the ballerina a resounding slap in the face: You bitch, what are you actually allowing yourself?

Ballerina: Excuse me...I, I (sobbing) didn't recognize you, Master. (Quietly crying). I beg your pardon. Please keep me anyway. From now on, I will always come to rehearsals on time. I faithfully promise that.

Clown: Are you really going to, bitch?

Ballerina: I promise you, master.

The clown, hands on hips, circling the Ballerina: So, will you? Your performance is miserable. You are mediocre. A small, untalented ballet rat. A nothing, a complete nothing.

Ballerina: I know, master.

Clown: Ah - you know it ... and … you dare to face me?

Ballerina: I'll do whatever you want. Really everything.

Clown: So, will you? Only I can make you a dancer. If I wanted a ballerina. However, your meager talent will hardly suffice for that. Are you even worth the trouble? I seriously wonder if you're worth the trouble?

Ballerina: If only you would try.

Clown standing in front of her: Fine, I'll play with you. If you don't parry, you are fired.

Ballerina, curtsy: Thank you master.

Clown: Show your thighs. (*Sensing her with his hands.*) I've held better stuff in my hands.

Ballerina: My thighs, my hips, my chest, my stomach, everything, everything is at your disposal, Master. Mold me don't let me fall!

Clown: So and you think you have the necessary talent?

Ballerina: I hope for your genius.

Clown: Aha, so you're putting all your hopes in me. Alright! We'll see if you're any good. The basic step please! Bad again! Looser, you move like a clumsy oaf. (*He has her practice under the stereotyped commands*). Again, please. Loosen up the basic step. (*His voice is quiet but clearly understandable.*)

Second Soldier, crawling past the actor: The duties of the modern soldier require determination, initiative and a sense of responsibility. Every young person who feels called to a task of responsibility should join the army. You can also train as a truck driver, engineer or technician at the expense of the army. The ideal job for dynamic young people. We offer a secure job and a regular income, but you must never forget that our cozy war-games ... (*He crawls behind the props.*)

Clown louder again: One more time, please. Looser! You move like a hippopotamus. Graceful! One more time, please, loosen up. No, it does not work out this way. (*The ballerina stands in despair, her arms hanging down.*) You've got to make an effort, kid.

Ballerina: I'm trying my best.

Clown: Your best isn't good enough. I'm wasting my time there.

Ballerina: I'm trying.

Clown: So ... basic step. Change your legs, you bumpkin! More graceful, graceful! So, basic step. No, no … look, that's how it's done. (He shows her the basic step. Clown-like, he slips, staggers, flaps his hands.)

Ballerina, admiring: Master!

Clown: What?

Ballerina: Will I ever be able to do it like that, master?

Clown: Not like that, almost maybe. However, you saw what you can do with the basic position.

Ballerina: I admire you.

Clown: I don't care. Being admired by you is not an honor.

Ballerina: Of course not, Master!

Clown: But go on, go on. So, basic position … and … basic position … and … basic position … and … basic position ... and … basic position ... and basic position. You're exhausted, aren't you?

Ballerina: No master, I'm not exhausted.

Clown: You dare contradicting me? (*Faster*) … and … basic position … and … basic position ... and … basic position … and … basic position … and … basic position. Are you still not exhausted, dear child?

Ballerina: A little bit.

Clown: All the better. (*Very quickly*) … and … basic position … and … basic position ... and … basic position ... and … basic position ... and … basic position.

Ballerina: I can't take it anymore.

Clown: Look, like I said, you're no good.

Ballerina: But I'm trying.

Clown: Effort alone is useless if there is no talent. Look at me. It was put into my cradle by a kind fairy and I still worked hard on myself … or … do you think fame falls into your lap? No, no my dear. Behind this is hardest work. Work to the point of self-abandonment. You have exhausted me. Keep practicing on your own.

Ballerina: May I hope?

Clown: That depends on your progress. I can't say anything for sure yet. (*He sits on the stage.*)

*The ballerina clearly moves with grace and suppleness throughout the procedure. She continues to practice but very slowly (slow motion) and with long breaks. Each break lasts a few minutes.*

The captain comes out from under the arcades. He's slightly tipsy. The guards salute briskly.

Captain: Parade rest! Where is the demoted cur?

First Soldier: He crawls commando-style, Sir.

Captain: Good.

Second Soldier: Here he comes, Sir.

*Third Soldier crawls to the captain's feet. He has green branches tied around his helmet.*

Captain: Where? I do not see him …

Second Soldier: Below you, Sir.

Captain: There you are at last! Where are you hanging out?

Third Soldier lying down: Order carried out, Sir!

Captain: One shouldn't exaggerate anything. Stand up. (*Reaching for the branches.*) Are you still a bit infantile? Playing Indians at that age! Which chief are you?

Third Soldier: At your command, Sir. I have disguised myself.

Captain: What you look like! Clean off the dirt. What kind of object do you want to raid? A ranch? Or a fort? A motorcade? Hey?

Third Soldier: At your command! You like to joke, Sir.

Captain: Yes, great chief. (*To all:*) We're going to put on a rest break. We're taking a break. We're... yes... resting. You sit down. I have something pleasant to share with you. There will be war soon.

*The soldiers stare at each other, murmuring, shaking their heads and watching the captain, who has turned his back on them.*

First Gentleman to the 2nd: By the way, Indians are all the rage now. The libraries are full of publications about them since it became public how brutally this breed was exterminated. America beats its chest in repentance.

Second Gentleman: I heard that bacteriological weapons were sometimes used.

First Gentleman: America has always been far ahead of us, dear colleague.

Second Gentleman: Especially when it came to the deportation of women and children.

First Gentleman: Which often amounted to a death sentence.

Second Gentleman: In many cases they didn't bother, but slaughtered them on the spot.

First Gentleman: We still have to be patient with South America, but I assure you that books will soon be on the market.

Second Gentleman: Why?

First Gentleman: The Indians are being decimated there. But wait, in a few years we'll be able to worry about it in peace.

Director, who stepped behind the two, seriously: Many will go down the path of tears.

Second Gentleman: By the way, what is the price for an Indian scalp?

First Gentleman: I haven't read any stock market reports yet. It also depends on whether it is the scalp of a man, a woman or a child.

Second Gentleman: It doesn't matter whether it's a boy or a girl, doesn't it?

*The captain lights a cigarette, pulls a card out of his pocket, unfolds it, and spreads it out on the ground.*

First Gentleman: How do you want that with the little one. Diagnosing bloody bits of skin with hair on it?

Second Gentleman: You have shiny black hair. Like crow wings.

First Gentleman: But you can also place the skeleton of a killed chief in the office. That makes it incredibly attractive. Especially if it's a famous chief.

Second Gentleman: Or exhibit the head at the fair. Ten cents entry. Children half.

Director: I am now speaking the lines of Motavato, chief of the Cheyenne. (*Very serious.*) "Though I have been wronged, I am full of hope. I don't have two hearts ... We came together to make peace. My shame is as great as the earth." (*Retreats.*)

First Gentleman: Because you are talking about deportation and slaughter. Didn't something similar happen in Europe recently?

Second Gentleman: I can't remember anything. I didn't know anything. Put these old stories to rest.

Captain to the soldiers: Aren't you happy? (*Folds the card and puts it in his pocket.*) You look so embarrassed. The dawn of war is at hand. It reddens the windowpanes. It breaks into the parlor and carries the men away with it. Real men of course. In a bath of blood and steel the nation will heal. Yes, comrades, steel on flesh and flesh on steel. This is a real test, comrades! Sing (*roaring*) a song! One two three. The three sing hesitantly: When a boy saw a little rose, he saw it with great joy...

Captain: You assholes! Crazy? A soldier's song, of course! Such a song *(bawls*):

It's nice to be a soldier
So beautiful, so beautiful.
We'll smash everyone's skulls
how beautiful, how beautiful.
And if the enemy's eye breaks,
then we spit in his face,
how beautiful, how beautiful.
And when the enemy's eyes glaze in death,
then we kick his face,
how... nice...

So what? Have you lost your language?

First Soldier: We are not used to killing.

Captain: What? Bastards; and something like that wants to be a soldier! You're an eyesore of the army.

First Soldier: If only there was at least a sip of cognac.

Second Soldier: That strengthens...

Third Soldier: Warms the stomach.

First Soldier: Murder is an ugly word.

Captain, roaring: Who's talking about murder? Should I have you put against the wall for defeatism?

First Soldier: I made a slip of the tongue.

Captain: I hope so! I really do hope so! In addition, the supreme army command took care of everything. (*Pulls a bottle from his pocket and opens it. Loud noise as the stopper is removed. The soldiers flinch.*) There, comrade! (*Hands the bottle to a soldier.*) Drink up, comrade! (*The soldier sniffs.*)

First Soldier: Best kind? Booze, real booze!

Captain: Taste it!

First Soldier tastes and coughs: Stiff drink.

Captain: Did I promise you too much?

Second Soldier: I have a wife and children at home, and I am also an animal lover.

Captain: You should protect women and children in particular. That's your job.

Third Soldier: I've never killed anyone in my life.

Captain: It's high time you'd learn it. Especially if it's for a good cause.

Third Soldier: The enemy claims that too.

Captain: The enemy lies. The enemy always lies. The enemy is cruel, brutal and cowardly. The enemy rapes, impales children, eats human flesh. He destroys valuable cultural assets and acts according to the principle of scorched earth. The enemy is subhuman. A barbarian. An inferior creature.

First Soldier, drinking: Excellent. Burns like fire.

Captain: Pass the bottle on. There are more dry throats.

First Soldier: At your command. Hand it to the second.

Captain: One sip each! Discipline, comrades!

Second Soldier: Brrr (*Gives the bottle to the third one*).

Third Soldier: I needed that! (Clicks with his tongue and hands it to the captain.)

Captain: Thank you comrade. I have already helped myself. During the ... during ... after ... after the briefing, you know ... after the briefing ... in the officers' mess ... in the canteen ...

Third Soldier: Then it's for you! (Hands it over to the first soldier. The bottle rotates during the following conversation. It should contain liquid so that the process looks real.)

First Soldier: So, we are just doing our sacred duty. We only stand by the oath we swore. So, nothing can prevent us from doing our sacred duty, nothing at all.

*You can hear the clanking of tank tracks, which is getting louder and louder. The soldiers first look around anxiously and then jump up. They cry out. You cannot understand their words. They point over the heads of the audience. That should be very compelling. It would be best if there was a loudspeaker at the back of the audience. Their head movements follow the individual tanks. Even the clown has turned around. The stagehand explains the individual types of tanks to the two actors. He answers questions, denies, almost argues with the older one, insists on the correctness of his assertions, denies again and explains again. The noise has reached its peak. The theatre director and the negress appear behind the machine and stare in bewilderment. The dancer interrupts her exercise and covers her ears. The theatre director shakes his head indignantly, says something to the negress and withdraws with her. The director raises his arms and waves his hands in the negative. The noise slowly dies away.*

Captain, into the dying noise: They were ours.

First Soldier: Thank God.

Captain: Did you count?

Second Soldier: As far as it went. The dust cloud was too dense.

Captain: Does that calm you down? Do you now believe in the strength of our weapons?

Second Soldier: Armored primeval behemoths.

Captain: Let's sit down.

First Soldier: I thought so ...

Second Soldier: Oppressive …

First Soldier: We'll run ... like rabbits.

Captain: Of course. We only have the rest.

Second Soldier: They will find it to be a hard nut to crack.

First Soldier, shy: Sure.

Captain: Sit!

*They sit down.*

First Soldier: An impressive spectacle. They roll everyone to a pulp.

Captain: The aggressors deserve nothing better. But kids, the bottle is half full. Keep going! (*They drink.*)

Clown, to the ballerina who has meanwhile resumed her exercises: Now listen to me miss. It's enough for today.

Ballerina: How do you find me?

Clown: Good. You just have to show a little more courage.

Third Soldier: I feel strong as a lion.

Clown: Overall I'm happy with you.

Second Soldier: Yes, I'm feeling better too.

Ballerina: Thank you. (*Curtsies, takes a book and starts leafing through it. Explaining to the clown.*) Because I am still studying.

Clown: You just lack a little courage.

*The ballerina ignores him. She is engrossed in reading.*

Second Soldier: I'll break the skull of the world!

First Soldier: The purest nectar. (*Drinks*) Spirit flavored nectar. I think petroleum is also included.

Clown: Of course, everything takes time and a lot of practice.

Third Soldier: I feel like an old soldier, a skilled fighter.

Clown: Practice, practice and practice again.

Third Soldier, roaring: I'm a skilled fighter!

Clown: Given your talent it's just a matter of practice.

Third Soldier: I'm a fighter!

Clown: And take it easy on your free time.

First Soldier: I know no mercy. Neither for me nor for others.

Clown: Take it easy and avoid alcohol.

First Soldier: I spare no one. I'm drunk!

Second Soldier, dreamily: Me too...

Third Soldier: I feel like God... tipsy...

Captain: The comparison is flawed.

Third Soldier: You are right in principle.

First Soldier: With my cough! When I cough, the universe shatters!

Second Soldier to Captain: He... he used to be an actor (*confidential*) a ... a miserable actor.

Clown: You should also beware of wetness and colds; a rheumatic disease.

First Soldier: Who is always chattering in between? (*Stares at the clown.*) What's my rheumatism to do with you?

*Everyone gapes at the clown.*

Young Actor: Drunk Gang.

Old Actor: Shut up!

Clown, turning to the soldiers, calmly: I didn't speak to you.

Captain: Come here!

Clown to ballerina: The precious instrument you play on is your body. He must not be subjected to unnecessary stress.

Captain: Are you deaf? You should come!

Clown: That's fatherly advice.

Captain: Hey, is it soon? Come on! That's an order!

Clown: You don't have to give me orders. I am a free person

Captain: Shall I send you an invitation? Come on!

(*Waves at the clown nonchalantly. He doesn't respond.*)

Clown: If you want something from me, you have to come here.

Director who has joined the clown: For God's sake don't talk like that! This brings us trouble.

Captain, roaring: Well, it will be soon!

Director: Go and apologize.

Captain: I'm waiting.

Director: Say it's a misunderstanding.

First Soldier, with a heavy tongue: Have a sip with us! (*Lifts the bottle.*) Come!

Second Soldier: My comrade invites you. Did not you hear?

Director: Go there while things can still be settled amicably...

Clown: Thanks, I don't drink.

First Soldier: Come on, you damn civilian!

Third Soldier: Do you want to insult me and my comrades?

Clown to the director: It's about time. (*Picks up a raincoat lying on the ground and puts it on.*)

Second Soldier: Where are you going in such a hurry?

First Soldier: Hey, stay!

Director: Hurry up!

Third Soldier: What's the matter, don't hurry, take it easy, you'll stay there!

Director: Quick!

Captain, jumping up: Arrest him!

Soldiers jumping up, not at the same time: At your command!

Director: I warned you. (Fast off.)

*The soldiers have meanwhile crossed the stage and grab the arms of the clown, who is striving to the right (left).*

Clown: Let go of me!

First Soldier: You're coming with me! You're under arrest!

Clown: Where's the written order? Let me go!

First Soldier: Don't get cheeky ... let him go! (*The soldiers step back and flank him.*)

First Soldier: Forward! (*The clown hesitates. The second soldier grabs his sleeve.*)

Clown: Leave it! I can go alone

Captain: Faster! Get him moving!

*The soldiers grab the clown and drag him across the stage.*

Captain: There you are at last. Too bad you didn't come voluntarily. I'm sorry I had to have you picked up. I hope you were treated with the respect you deserve.

Clown: I'm a free citizen. I protest.

Captain: Of course.

Clown: Let me go! I haven't done anything wrong.

Captain: Gently, gently. (*Approaching.*) Why don't you drink with us? My comrades kindly invited you. Or not? Is our society too inferior for you?

*The scientist starts the machine. Light bulbs flash, rattle, whirr, whistle. First quietly, later the volume increases and ends in a piercing howl of sirens at the end of the scene.*

Clown is silent.

Captain: I've asked you something!

Clown, tormented: I didn't say that.

Captain: Ah, you didn't say that. But probably you have thought it. I thought you were mute. Suddenly fallen silent. A momentary spasm of the vocal cords ... It can happen to the smartest of people... (*Hands him the bottle.*) Drink it!

Clown: No.

Captain: So ... hm ... that's the way things are. Comrades, this individual finds it beneath his dignity to drink with us.

Clown: I never drink.

Captain: You could have made an exception for our sake. You wouldn't have died. Doesn't your behavior strike you as a bit strange? I think you have something against us...

Clown: Not at all...

Captain, without interrupting: Yes, you have something against us. Go ahead, enlighten us. Did we make a mistake? Have we offended you? (*Clown is silent.*)

Captain to the soldiers: We're not sophisticated enough for him. The Gentleman does not wish to be bothered by us. Isn't that so? (*silence*) By the way, are you a pro-war proponent? To be precise, do you love war? I'm asking again. Do you love it?

Clown: As a free person, I don't have to give you...

Captain: What? Go on, go on…

Clown: … give an account.

Captain: Shut up! (*Walks around him.*) Hm. You think we don't know about you? (*Pause.*) You feel safe. (*Pause.*) But you are no stranger to us. (*Stops in front of him.*) You've been under surveillance for a long time. Hm. (*Lights a cigarette.*) You're amazed, aren't you?

Clown: But I...

Captain: Shut up! You have nothing to say at all. We know your development. We know your affairs, your debts, and your friends. Even your childhood illnesses. You have three gold fillings. Two on the right and one on the left side. Last year you were unable to come to work for a fortnight because of a bad cold. Over the past year you have made striking statements about our government. Twice towards your maid, once when you were tipsy, and three times in a public place. Look at this sow! His only goal is to smother the soul of our people in filth. If only he were man enough to go public. But no, he digs in secret and officially presents himself as a good citizen. Just look at the criminal physiognomy! The ignoble attitude of his body. You lousy bastard! You mental cesspool! Your face screams for slaps! Repeat after me ... I am a mental cesspool. Come on, open your mouth!

Clown: I don't know what you want...

Captain: I'm a mental cesspool!

Clown: I...

Captain: Next...

Clown: I won't say anything more.

Captain: Oh right. Up to you. (*Kicks him against the shin.*)

Clown: Ouch...

Captain: And self-pitying too. Whining and cowardly. That's how you all are. (*Kicks him again. Clown screams.*) Hit him!

First Soldier: Me?

Captain: Hit him in the mouth!

*Soldier proposes hesitantly.*

Captain: Harder!

*First Soldier hits again.*

Captain: Beat him to a pulp! He still doesn't believe! He's still laughing! (*The soldier slaps the clown. The other two hold him down with a kind of police hold.*) You'll stop laughing! Firmer, not so timid! (*The punches rain down on the clown's face. He cries softly.*) Good, yes...

The clown breaks loose and rushes towards the ramp: I want... (*He gets a punch that throws him to the ground.*) ... a court hearing ... a ... (*They drag him off the ramp.*)

Captain: What stories? Knock him down! Knock down the bastard!

*The soldiers throw the clown onto the boards. They work him with hands and feet. He shouts.*

First Soldier: I'll give it to you...

Second Soldier: You dog...

Third Soldier: He fights back ... the cowardly dog bites...

*Gasping screams and moans of the clown. Unintelligible sounds from the soldiers. This should look very realistic and be of almost unbearable brutality.*

Captain: Give it to him! Give him the freedom he needs! ... Don't you have any intellectual phrases at hand? … And we were so nice to him!

*The soldiers took the clown in the middle. They kick him back and forth like a ball. He rolls across the floor. The target of their kicks is mainly the head and abdomen. The clown writhes in an embryonic position. He's bleeding and whimpering.*

Captain: Do you have any questions? (*Grinning.*) We are at your service. (*Screaming.*) Finish him off! (*The soldiers have huddled close together. The clown lies in a convulsing bundle under a lump of brutality.*)

Captain: Castrate the pig!

*First soldier pulls the knife from the sheath. The others hold the squirming clown, half kneeling on him. You only see the clown's twitching feet and hear his gurgling screams.*

*The soldier stabs him several times between the legs. The siren sound has reached full volume, drowning out every other sound. The knife is bloody. The wailing of the sirens gets a little quieter.*

Director running up: Stop it! Have you gone insane? (*Due to the howling, he is difficult to understand. The sound suddenly collapses. The soldiers get up, exhausted and breathing heavily.*) Make way! You have gone too far! That was not agreed! (*He picks up the bloody clown, whose gurgling stops when touched, and leads him, no, almost carries him back to his old place. A bloodstain spreads across the clown's abdomen. The director carefully slides him onto the boards. He sits with his back to the audience and looks up at the ballerina, who doesn't see him. The soldiers make embarrassed, perplexed movements.*

Scientist, half hidden by the machine: It works. It works. A few corrections and it will be a blessing to mankind; (*disappears*).

Negress, who has meanwhile sat down at the edge of the stage, dangles her legs and is knitting, to the passing director: Is my performance coming up soon?

Director (*on his way back to the soldiers*): Soon, ma'am. It's going to take a while longer.

Negress: Did you hurt yourself?

Director: Why?

Negress: Your right hand is bleeding. Did you have an accident?

Director: Oh, that's nothing. I cut myself a bit with a can opener, actually on the can itself.

Negress: Show me.

Director: Not worth mentioning. (*Grabs a handkerchief in her left hand and wraps it around his right hand.*)

Negress: Just a moment. I wanted you... (*The director leans down to her. The two are whispering.*)

*The captain gestures for the soldiers to sit down. They back away from the pool of blood and flop apathetically to the ground. First soldier offers the third the bottle. He says no. The first throws the bottle away.*

Clown, his text begins when the negress whispers: Practice, practice and practice again. (*He speaks slowly.*) Practice! All you lack is a little courage. But overall, I'm happy with you. Of course, everything takes time and, above all, a lot of practice. With your talent, all that matters is confidence. Take care of yourself in your free time. Take it easy and avoid alcohol. You should also be careful not to get wet or catch a cold. (*Very softly, but clearly.*) The basic step, please... (*His words fade to unintelligible whispers that fade away.*)

The director has meanwhile left the negress and is standing in front of the soldiers: What did you think of gentlemen?

First Soldier: It came over us like this.

Second Soldier: He was cheeky.

Third Soldier: He provoked us. It's not our fault.

Director: That will bring you a disciplinary action. I hope you know that.

Second Soldier: We only carried out an order.

First Soldier: Nothing else.

Director to Captain: You're under arrest. I know that doesn't change anything. Others will come and take your place, but for now it gives me satisfaction. I would like to say: Crawl commando-style! Crawl until I remember you again; unless I forget you altogether and let you die of exhaustion. Of course, I would give you an observer to keep you from cheating.

Captain: At your command! (*Salutes.*) I have no blood on my hands.

Director: Yes, you didn't get dirty. You stayed clean while the dirty work got done. Would you have the kindness to follow me? You get a clean cell with air conditioning. You can put your hopes into a proper court hearing. We know what we owe to captured officers. (*To the soldiers.*) You are criminals. Hand over the guns! The big end is yet to come. (*To the stagehand.*) Take the junk!

Stagehand: Where to put it? The arsenals are already full.

Director: Eventually they destroy the crap.

Stagehand: How come I need to do this? (*Gathers up the guns and carries them backstage. Their thud is heard.*)

Director to the soldiers: You can sit down. I don't want to be in your skin. (*To the captain.*) Come on! (*Walks behind the arcades with him.*)

First Soldier: I don't even know what he wants. I'm a decent person.

Second Soldier: Ah, and I'm not? You were there too.

First Soldier: There… so what? We were all there.

Second Soldier: You thrashed quite a bit. If anyone knew. If this gets out to the public, you're screwed!

First Soldier: Leave my family out of it. War is war.

Second Soldier: Who is talking about your family? Why should I give a shit about your family?

Young Actor to the Old Actor: Look at the twilight!

First Soldier: I don't want to hear anything anymore. Do you have to humiliate me? What is done, is done. (Shrugs.) Basta!

Third Soldier: Stop it. That doesn't make anything better. We small fish always pay extra. (*They sit with their heads bowed.*)

Young Actor: When the sun, the light of my life, goes down, I always get a little sentimental. I feel sorry for myself and blame others for my failures.

Old Actor: Everybody does. How else could we endure life? But, you're not entirely wrong. We are victims of circumstances.

Young Actor: We could be happy if I could direct the world... don't laugh! So, before rehearsals begin, I would say to the participants: Ladies and gentlemen! I imagine a world in which one helps the other - not to say loves - and money becomes what it actually is, namely a necessary, practical evil.

Old Actor: An ideal world.

Young Actor: The most selfish world of all worlds. People would love each other out of selfishness. They would give what they expect of others and others in turn expect of them. Helping each other would be the dictate of reason. Second, the individual can only consume to a limited extent. The abundance would benefit those in need who disappear as development progresses. I should be able to go to the next millionaire and say, “I’m dead broke. I need money, brother.” (*In a different voice*:) “Sit down first, dear friend! Take a break! Do you want a refreshment? Please help yourself! How much should it be?” (*With a different voice:*) “So and so much, dear brother.” (*With a different voice*:) “What? Just such a small amount? You are too humble, I beg you, ask for more! If you don’t, I feel guilty.” (*In a changed voice*:) “If I have to. You know I don’t need you.” (*In a different voice:*) “I’m asking you to. It’s rude but I’m asking you. My reputation is at stake. (*In a natural voice*:) All right, before I get hit...etc.

Old Actor: A hungry man’s pipe dream. You made mistakes in your reasoning. First, all people would have to be industrious and there shouldn’t be any parasites. Secondly, a millionaire in this society is unthinkable to me. Third, I would like … I really like the millionaire.

Young Actor: I expressed myself badly ... it’s the longing.

Old Actor: … after an ideal world.

Stagehand, who came up: What you're talking about is complete nonsense! I don't need help or charity! I just want to be treated the way I deserve to be treated. How many do you think I would outclass. Everyone should be treated according to his ability and take his place. I just want justice, nothing else.

Young Actor: That is completely absurd!

Old Actor: Who is supposed to be the incorruptible referee? Ha?

Stagehand: I...I mean… that would be correct.

Young Actor: Unworldly ideas. How long have you been in the theatre?

Old Actor: Don't argue! We are victims of circumstances. For example, you feel humiliated and insulted. I suffer too (yawns). I suffer so tremendously that I get tired of it. We will not impose any other laws on the world.

Young Actor: Laws! Just because people are beasts, you have to put them in the cage of the law. Woe to you, if you take away the bars! Smack, you're already dead. Life could be heavenly. According to my theory, I mean.

Old Actor: Exceptions prove the rule.

Young Actor: I'm not talking about saints. I'm talking about people!

Old Actor: Let's leave that; (*signals refusal*).

First Soldier: But it was nice! Of course, there were situations that I don't like to mention, but that was the style of the time.

Second Soldier: And how we drank back then! Do you remember the little wine cellar? The entire platoon was drunk as a skunk. My youngest is just like his father.

Third Soldier: I own a cactus farm. You have to take a look at them. One hundred and thirty thousand varieties. A thousand are blooming right now. There is nothing more beautiful than flowering cacti. I love them. You have to have a lot of empathy. You should never give them too much water. The soil must of course be sandy and dry.

Scientist: And someone should deny progress. I have the compulsion to invent. I must invent. The bomb is an ingenious invention. Also, the biological and chemical weapons. It's about the great exploitation of the possibilities. I would give half of humanity for a phenomenal ... Humanity, the word sounds distant and abstract. Humanity, crowd, mass. That's a deformed face. A face that flows together from many faces, flows apart and never takes on a fixed form. I am experimenting. I research purposefully. My logical mind focused on the goal that grows to infinity. I cannot stop. When I discover something, I must move on. Uncover, dissect, analyze, and find new variations. Of course, the work is well endowed. I have my country house, my airplane and ... well, but ... and if the government abuses my inventions or I allow myself to be abused, what should I do in my predicament? Only they can provide me with this well paid job. I am not morally bound. I don't have time for that. I absorb ideas like others absorb oxygen. I'm a bit megalomaniac and a nondescript titan as well. I am the bomb. I enlighten your stables, which you call houses. Granted, it's electricity after all, but I tamed it ... and...

Young Actor: Also, an asshole.

Scientist: Put to good use. I am the neon light. I am the neon sign on your streets. I have a thousand horsepower and more.

I am the satellite, the rocket, the television set, a car, a train, a submarine, the wheel, the shovel. I agree, you can run over someone with a bike and hit someone with a shovel. But that's not my fault. (Walks gracefully behind the machine.)

*Nanny, rushing excitedly out of the arcades*: I've lost the child! It fell in the water! Is nobody helping me? What will lord- and ladyship say? My god, I'm getting fired!

*Old actor bumps the young actor with the elbow.*

Young Actor: Don't take it so tragically.

Nanny: It's easy for you to talk!

Young Actor: I'll help you. I've helped you before.

Nanny: Maybe, but I don't remember.

Old Actor: Where did it happen? How did the child go missing?

Nanny: Wait; (*thinks*).

Young Actor: You must know the place.

Nanny, as if telling a dream: I don't know exactly. It was a beautiful spring day. The air was all blue and the leaves green. The sun was above my crown. Not the slightest breeze stirred. The park was almost empty. The gravel crunched under my feet. Pigeons cooed. Despite the burgeoning shoots, a deadly peace reigned. Not the slightest breeze ... It was like I was dead. But I couldn't fall. The warm air was thick as aspic, holding me.

Old Actor: Next!

Nanny: The pigeons ... I've been there ... I went and am walked, rather I swam ... was pushed.

Old Actor: Continue...

Nanny: The pigeons cooed and danced around the females. There was nothing intrusive about their cooing, it reinforced the silence ... made it even more tangible...

Young Actor: And what happened to the child?

Nanny: Which child? What kid are you talking about?

Old Actor: About your alum.

Nanny: Oh right, I almost forgot about that. You know the sluggish twinkling air of spring. The eye is not yet used to the bright sun. The trees are still half bare, and the shade is cold. The outlines of the objects are sharper than usual. One is dazzled. And suddenly the child was gone. It was there and suddenly it was gone. I didn't miss it. That would be a lie. I could hardly remember it. I was looking for it, of course. More specifically, I was looking for something without actually wanting it. Isn't that weird? Then I remembered lord- and ladyship and got scared.

Old Actor: You are a sloppy person. I don't want to trust you with a child.

Nanny: There was something there. It was like lightning ... sort of like lightning ... and the whole world was empty, the leaves were still, and the statues were remarkably still. Even the sun didn't move. I was completely alone.

Old Actor: You're in shock. You have isolated yourself. I want to help you. (*To the young actor*:) Lucky that we bumped into the two dolls in the department store yesterday …

Young Actor: Bought them.

Old Actor: Yes! (*Unlaces the other bundle. To the nanny:*) Wait!

Second Gentleman to the first: We are exploiters. We exploit the earth until it gives no more milk. There are too many people living on the globe. I'm happy about every catastrophe. I have a notion … again less, again more space for me.

First Gentleman: You are right. We explode …

*Old Actor pulls an approximately five-year-old doll out of the bundle. She is dressed in the latest children's fashion. It's a girl*: There, take it!

Nanny: Thank you very much...(*hesitant*)...but mine was a boy.

Old Actor: It doesn't matter. Or are you still burdened with prejudices?

Young Actor: An excellent doll. The latest model. It can walk and speak. You can also feed it.

Nanny: You convinced me. How can I thank you?

Young Actor: But please. Not worth talking about. It goes without saying.

Nanny: You are too kind.

Young Actor: Compared to living grimaces, the puppet has the advantage that it only makes the pre-programmed movements and speaks the recorded text. This means there are no glitches. It does not hide unpleasant surprises. It works the way you want it to. A very good child.

Old Actor: Put it up once.

Young Actor: The mechanism is extremely simple. You record a tape and let it run when the opportunity arises.

Nanny: Lord- and ladyship will be happy about that. Especially your ladyship. She was always agitated when the boy said something inappropriate.

Young Actor: Go back a few steps!

Nanny: Like that?

Young Actor: Even further! (*He turns the doll towards the nanny.*) Let's go, little one!

The doll, wriggling very slowly towards the nanny, with a loud, sweet Hollywood child's voice, very penetrative: I'll always be good. A child who is good and diligent, washes properly, brushes the teeth, doesn't get the clothes dirty, comes home from school on time, sits well at lunch, does the homework and goes properly to bed in the evening, while it is praised by parents and teachers. In addition, I should always be in a good mood and clean. If I obey the law and cross the street with a green light, I never get in trouble with the law. Always be polite and say please and thank you. Thank you, dear grandma, thank you, dear grandpa, thank you, dear aunt, thank you, dear uncle. Thank you, dear aunt, thank you dear grandma, dear grandpa. Don't forget the handkerchief. It is used for waving and blowing one's nose. Efficiency, decency, and diligence are the way to success. If I go through life well and have learned something decent, nothing can happen to me anymore. I should always be friendly.

*The doll is caught by the nanny; it falls silent.*

Nanny: Adorable. How could I ever make amends?

Young Actor: If you had a few shillings left ... I think it should be worth it to you.

Old Actor: We haven't eaten for a long time...

Nanny: You can't pay for that. What you have done for me is priceless. Believe me, I appreciate it and am eternally grateful to you. I am your debtor forever.

Young Actor: But we...

Nanny: I totally appreciate it...

Young Actor: If you...

Nanny: No, don't say anything more. Every word would destroy everything. (*Exits with the doll.*)

Young Actor: To hell!

Old Actor, smiling: She cheated on you. We are the fools. I can tell you're a lousy comedian.

Young Actor: Kiss me in Kraków!

Old Actor, laughing hard: Thank you. You did really splendidly. The born businessman! The retailer par excellence!

Young Actor: You wouldn't have done it any better. I will have nothing left. I'll speak to the director again.

Old Actor: Do that!

*The machine moves intermittently. It is shaking. Howl of sirens that grows louder and louder. In between aircraft engines. Their noise is getting closer, filling the square. The sirens stop screaming. Only the aircraft noise remains. The performers flee the stage and press against the wall or disappear behind the arcades.*

Ballerina screaming: Now they're coming in broad daylight.

First Gentleman: Quick, quick, do it...

*The sound of impacts. The actors press themselves deeper into the wall, crouching down with their hands protectively over their heads. The clown, slower than the others, staggers, falls onto his back and remains motionless with his arms spread wide. The actors wince at every impact. The planes move away. All clear. The actors slowly stream onto the stage, cleaning their clothes, adjusting props and chatting.*

Negress: In broad daylight! An impudence.

Theatre Director: Did something happen to you?

Negress: No.

Man in Tropical Suit: I lost my topee. Has any of the gentlemen seen it? That's what comes of arming the savages.

Theatre Director: No, I haven't seen one.

*The ballerina puts her hands in front of her face and starts crying. You can hear the crackling of the fire.*

Negress, lovingly embracing the ballerina: Calm down, little one. It's all over. Nothing happened. Calm, calm, calm down. (*She keeps whispering to her. The screaming gives way to sobbing, which gets quieter.*)

Ballerina, sobbing: Thank you.

Negress: Well, you see, it's alright. (*The ballerina wipes away her tears and blows her nose.*)

Negress: Are you all right, little one?

Ballerina: Yes...

First Gentleman to the other: Are you hurt my colleague?

Second Gentleman: You?

First Gentleman: No, but I find it outrageous.

Young Actor: What a shit. Throwing their dirt at living people.

Negress: They call themselves civilized people.

First Soldier, discovering the clown: There's someone lying here. (*Screaming*) First aid!

Negress: Yes, really, there is someone.

*Those present surround the clown.*

Scientist: Let me through, I'm a doctor!

Stagehand: Let him through, he's a doctor!

Young Actor to the man in the tropical suit: Step aside so that the doctor has room!

The actors back off. The scientist kneels next to the *clown:* He has passed out. Pulse normal. Lost a lot of blood.

First Soldier, Second Soldier, ballerina, First Gentleman in tails, director, confused: What is it? What is? What did he say?

Gentleman in tropical suit, backwards: He's lost a lot of blood.

Scientist: He needs a transfusion right away. Who volunteers to be a blood donor?

First Soldier: Me!

Second Soldier Me too.

Man in Tropical Suit: Me too, of course.

Negress: Me!

Ballerina: I'd like to volunteer.

Stagehand: Certainly.

Director: Can I help you as an assistant?

Scientist: Do you know anything about it?

Director: I have a few semesters of medicine...

Scientist: Good. Let's carry him to there. (*Points to the machine*.) I hope the attack didn't damage the instruments.

*The man in the tropical suit, the stagehand, the ballerina and the young actor carry the clown behind the machine, his hands dragging on the floor. First Soldier, Second Soldier and the Negress follow them.*

Scientist: Careful, please.

Director: Meanwhile, I will prepare a nutrient solution.

Scientist: Please, sir!

*The doctor, assistant and porters are obscured by the machine. The two soldiers and the negress are waiting in front of it.*

Scientist's voice: Please wait outside!

(*The porters join the blood donors*.)

Director, shows up: Please the first one!

*Man in a tropical suit goes behind the machine.*

*The two gentlemen have sat down. The old actor and the director have also returned to their places. The latter sits with his back to the donors and ignores them. The man in the tropical suit comes out from behind the machine, which is now humming softly.*

Man in tropical suit … Director, calling after him: Well, did it hurt?

Man in Tropical Suit: What are you thinking? This is not the first time.

Director: Next one please. (He repeats this for each donor.)

*After the blood draw, the actors go back to their places with their arms bare and bent and sit down.*

Meanwhile the First Gentleman to the Second Gentleman: I find that scandalous. That the government does nothing. Where is the army? We have enough weapons to depopulate half the universe. Why don't we use them. I'm sick of this sentimentality.

First Gentleman: Me too. You can't help but show them who's master. The better breed survives. It's the law of nature.

Second Gentleman: Which I would like to doubt, Sir. For there is a difference between a better race and a stronger race. Every well-trained half-idiot is stronger than you - forgive me, dear colleague - without being able to reach your mental potency.

Young Actor, who goes to his place: Your mental potency can remain stolen to me. (*Screaming*) Snooty monkeys! Boneheads! (*He bends down to them. His face rests between their faces.*)

First Gentleman: That throws my theory into disarray. No, no, you're wrong. I have guns. Weapons that I will use if necessary. Technical weapons that have sprung from my intelligence.

Young actor, yelling: Then put yourself on the same level as the half-idiots. I hate your cold ignorance of the facts. You are calcified theorists, whitewashed graves...

Second Gentleman: Yes, that is correct. I give up. I congratulate you on your success. Their machines can destroy more than animal power.

Young Actor: Don't you see what you've done? (*Pulls his head back.*) Completely pointless. (*Goes to his place.*)

*Of course, the two of them ignored him.*

First Gentleman: Where are you spending your vacation this year?

Second Gentleman: I don't really know yet, dear colleague. I am currently working on a paper on whether the transfusion of Jewish or Negro blood has dangerous consequences for the patient.

*The negress sits down on the ramp with her arm bent.*

First Gentleman: Your conclusion?

Second Gentleman: I'd certainly advise to be cautious.

*All donors have taken their places. The director steps forward, takes off his white, bloodstained work coat and throws it over the machine.*

Scientist: But sir!

Director: Excuse me, medical officer of health. The exertions of the last few days, the many wounded... you must forgive me.

Scientist: I can understand that... please take a rest.

Director: You need sleep more than I do.

Scientist: I am an old man. Old men don't need much sleep anymore. (*Takes the work coat from the machine.*)

Director: But if I...

Scientist: Go ahead, I can manage on my own.

Second Gentleman: Despite the great strain, I am drawn to the sunny south. I need to finally relax.

First Gentleman: I have been planning to do this for a long time.

Young Actor: I'm trying.

Old Actor: You want?

Young Actor: I'm trying.

Old Actor: You have my blessing.

Young Actor; moves to the middle stage. To the director who is on his way to see the negress: Could I speak to the theatre director?

Director: Who can I report?

Young Actor: My name doesn't matter. I'm a character actor.

Director delighted: Oh, it's you. Sorry I didn't recognize you right away. That's what twilight does. I'm honored. I've dreamed of meeting you for a long time. I am among your most ardent admirers. Especially your elocution ... but, what am I talking about ... didn't you have a bear?

Young Actor: He perished.

Director: How unfortunate. I am all the more pleased that you found your way to us.

One moment please. (*Calling to the back*) Mr. Theatre Director!

Theatre Director, without turning to them: Yes!

Director gestures in his direction. To the actor: He's coming right away. Please be patient. (*Goes to the negress*.)

Director, calling to himself: I'll be right there! (*He leafs through imaginary books*.)

*The clown comes out quietly from behind the machine and sits down at the ballerina's feet, his back to the audience. She gets up, adjusts her dress, sits down again and reads on. The young actor moves forth and back, picking up props from the floor, looking at them, dropping them, pulling the book out of the ballerina's hand and leafing through it. The ballerina reads on without a book. He gives it back to her.*

Director to Negress: I have a task for you.

Negress, getting up: Finally!

Director: Sorry it took so long.

Negress, pouting: I'll think about it carefully. I'm used to preferential treatment.

Director: Unfortunately, there was no other way, madam. The many wounded. You should have heard the screams. And there wasn't enough morphine ... not even enough bandages.

Negress: What are you talking about, young man?

Director, more intense: I'm not to blame for your treatment, ma'am. You have to complain to someone else.

Negress: I know you want my best.

Director, softly: I consider that my duty.

Negress: What is it about?

Director: Immediately! (*To the young actor*) Please come here! (*To the clown*) You too.

The clown only reacts as the young actor pats him on the shoulder and whispers something in his ear. The two go to the ramp. The clown's pants are red over the privates.

Negress, meanwhile: You're creating excitement, young man.

Director: It's an advertisement.

Negress: All right, if it is paid well. I know my things are tutu tata... I'm so happy since tutu tata works infallibly. A real relief. I can no longer live without tutu tata. Some idiots are a sucker for tutu tata. The blah blah blah blah blah blah.

Old Actor, into the mockery of the negress: The blabla, bla, bla-bla, bla. I feel lonely. I'm locked in a petrified second, like an insect in amber. Time does not pass, no, times run parallel to each other. Sometimes someone breaks through the wall over there and disappears. Sometimes we get visitors from over there. Sometimes we break through the walls ourselves and experience what we have experienced. I long for the boy. I miss him. Maybe he's dead. No, that's all nonsense, cheap consolation. I won't see my bears again either. I can't do the punches undone anymore. If the dead at least suspected that we repent.

Director, aligning the three candidates side by side: So. Closer! Yes. That's too tight. (*His instructions must not disturb the old actor's speech.*) Yes, like that. Well! Good this way. (*The old actor has finished the monologue.*) So, as I said, it's an advertisement. It depends on who speaks his text faster. (*Applicants now face the audience.*) The winner (*slight bow to the negress*) is hired.

Negress: What is the first commandment of advertising? What's that called; fast? (*Impatient to the clown.*) Please help me!

Man in a tropical suit, who has approached in search of his helmet (*he moves very unobtrusively*): Elevating or increasing the need to a need, madam. Small doses of opium are administered to the victims until they become addicted and life without opium no longer seems desirable to them. I am a connoisseur of exotic customs. (*The negress ignores him.*) Of course, the victim can laugh at a stupid advertising slogan. The poison must appeal to the subconscious and lead to the compulsion to buy. It is not for nothing that large corporations employ their psychologists.

Negress to the clown: Think about it! It's on the tip of my tongue.

Man in a Tropical Suit: The ideal end-product is a creature that is perpetually under a pathological buying pressure.

Director: Don't interrupt the rehearsal!

Man in Tropical Suit: Sorry! (*Stands still.*)

Director, who has turned to the candidates, turns around abruptly: What else do you want?

Negress to the clown: Well, do you remember?

Man in Tropical Suit: Did you happen to see my hat?

Clown: No.

Man in a tropical suit: Due to the extremely strong radiation in this area, staying in the sun without covering your head can result in sunstroke

Negress to clown: That annoys me.

Director to man in tropical suit: I believe you; it's annoying but I didn't see your helmet. Please leave now, but quickly.

Man in tropical suit: Thank you very much! (*Bows, automatically raises his right hand to his forehead, shrugs regretfully and walks away towards the backstage.*)

Director: I'll read the lines for you...

Negress: Should we all at once...

Director: No. I would miss the overview. Besides, you would hinder each other. So - it depends on the speed and clear diction. I stop the time.

Young Actor: If I understood correctly, it is an acrobatic performance?

Director: You got it.

Clown: I run out of competition.

Director: As you wish.

Negress: The text, please.

Director, slowly: The world is so beautiful that one could cry about it. This is nothing of importance and therefore not a crime.

Negress: Is that all?

Director: Yes

Negress: Let's start.

Director: It's best if you start right away. (*The actors speak normally.*)

Negress: The world is so beautiful that one could laugh about it. This is something important and therefore not a crime.

Director: Excellent! One minute three hundredths of a second! That's a good time! This is the best time so far! Let's wait and see how fast the second candidate speaks. (*To the actor*) Please!

Young Actor: The world is so sad and dead that one could cry about it. We're in a bottomless boat, heading for the sky.

Director: One minute two hundredths of a second. This is first place! This is a best time that can hardly be surpassed! You were a hundredth of a second faster than the lady!

Negress: Damn shit!

Director to Clown: And now to you!

Clown slow: The world is a tear. We are the vermin of a tear. (*Pause. In a different voice, fast.*) Also, I'd like to introduce you to our new skin cream. She is my only consolation.

Director: That was a slightly weaker performance. That was the slowest time so far. But you speak out of competition.

Negress: I don't know what that's supposed to mean. I do not see any sense. First, it doesn't sound particularly nice, second, it's dangerous, and third, there's always a risk of tongue breakage.

Young Actor: I admit, the hundredth of a second is irrelevant.

Negress: Almost ridiculous!

Clown: Am I among adults or in the kindergarten? What are these strange values?

Director to the young actor: Do you also think it's childish?

Young Actor: I can't say that as a winner. I hope for a plentiful fee.

Director: Did you already feel at the beginning of the speech that you are having a good day today? Were you nervous?

Young Actor: No, not really.

Director: The decision has been made. I congratulate you.

Young Actor: Where is the theatre director?

Theatre Director who has approached: You're disqualified, you louts! It must read: "Where is the dear Mr. Theatre Director?" This salutation must be used in every sentence! Your text should have read as follows: "The world is so sad that one could cry about it, dear Mr. Theatre Director...". On top of that, you stumbled across the word "sad". (*To the director*): Of course, you didn't hear it!

Young Actor: I make you...

Theatre Director, roaring: I would like to be addressed as "Dear Mr. Theatre Director"! How many times do I have to repeat that! Your lack of discipline has struck me for a long time. Also, you're a lousy actor. Just listen to the sentence: "The world is so sad and dead that one could weep over it"... and compare it to the result you have babbled. This is crap! Bungling! And you dare come face to face with me and ask for a role? Not even if you were on your knees here in front of me would I'd have given you one. I don't need such losers in our theater. And then your cheeky demeanor. Your unjustified arrogance! You're done in my eyes. A zero. A double zero!

Young Actor accentuating: You are the biggest idiot I know.

Theatre Director: Wha... what? (*Roaring*) you've gone insane ... you're insane! (*Grabs his chest.*) My heart.

Director: But... but there must be a misunderstanding here...

Theatre Director: Air... my heart...

Director to actor: I don't understand you ... are you drunk?

Theatre Director: My heart. Nothing like this has ever happened to me. I do not get air. I'm dying. (*Breathing convulsively.*)

Young Actor: Then you can at least be used as props.

Theatre Director, groaning: Go, but now!

Director, demanding: Go! Get out of here and don't see me again!

Young Actor: You can all... go and get... stuffed... (*walks slowly to the old actor*).

Stagehand approaching the Theatre Director: I have a request.

Theatre Director pleased, putting an arm around his shoulders: Will be fulfilled. Finally, you're asking me something. If we had waited longer ... if you'd have come earlier … Let's talk! (*Removes the arm from his shoulder and pushes him towards the ramp.*)

Stagehand, facing the audience, humble: I once had a little dog. It wasn't an unusual dog, but it had an unusually soft fur. That makes me sad.

Theatre Director, enthusiastic: Just listen!

Stagehand: He had cute, long ears. Sometimes he moved them, sometimes not. Then they just hung limp. He also had large eyes expressing his soul.

Theatre Director: Just listen!

Stagehand: They were as beautiful as a cow's. Do not laugh! In ancient Rome, women with particularly beautifully cut brown eyes were called cow eyed. Have you observed cow eyes yet? (*More aggressively*) Or do you only love cattle when they are cut up and prepared on the plate in front of you? I know you are carnivores, omnivores. People only become good when they stop eating. Even plants are said to feel pain. So, don't eat anymore. Then all aggression will stop. You will feel better. It is the path to immortality. (*Again, very humble and sad.*) Coming back to my little dog. He had a wet muzzle; it was always wet. His tongue was long, rose red and rough. Sometimes he scratched, but rarely... that's all I really wanted to say...

Theatre Director: You were great, as always; (shakes his hand).

Stagehand: Thank you. (*Takes his place next to the actors and whispers to them.*)

Theatre Director: We have a great staff! All dear, helpful, young people! (*To the negress*:) Of course you get the part. I'll stand by our agreement.

Negress: What if I don't want it anymore?

Theatre Director: But sweat heart, you're not going to do that to me, are you? I ask you on my knees to accept the role!

Negress: That's something else.

Theatre Director pleased: I knew right away that we would come to an agreement.

In the meantime, the following fragments emerge from the whispering of the stagehand: He has … but I laid him out good ... I didn't put up with that... he almost wet himself ... but I ... cold and warm... I ... there is nothing... you don't know me well.

Clown: Do you still need me?

Director: No.

*The clown sits down again in front of the ballerina, the whispering of the three falls silent.*

Negress: I'm getting ready. (*Goes to her chair and puts on makeup.*)

Theatre Director to the Director: This young actor must have mistaken himself for Orpheus.

Director: It was Orpheus himself.

Theatre Director: Well, and if so, what does it matter? We'll get enough other talented actors. I just can't stand indiscipline!

Director: I totally agree with you.

*The old and the young actor discuss silently. The scientist starts the machine. It lights up, buzzes and rings softly. Individual parts move. The ballerina gets up, takes a few steps and sits down again.*

Clown, slowly, to himself: I remember once talking about some exercises. That must have been a long time ago. It's actually not a tangible memory, just a touch that touches me.

Ballerina: I passed the exam. When I was a kid, I wanted to be a dancer.

Theatre Director: I cried that night. I hadn't done my schoolwork. I just sat there and didn't do them. Got bad grades. In all subjects. So, one thousand five hundred and fifty five in total. I feel empty inside. It's a strange state. I'm as strong as ever. I stand beside myself and watch myself indifferently.

Man in tropical suit: My suit has suffered from the tropical weather. I will go to my family and dine with loved ones.

Negress: Everything pisses me off. (*Throws away the blond wig.*) I don't know where I belong anymore.

*The actors assume their original posture, as at the beginning of the play. This should be done slowly. Their movements become stiffer, more sluggish. There is great tiredness. Excluded from this are the two actors.*

Negress: I want to bathe naked on a sunny night. I would like to bath naked in a black night that is full of sun.

Nanny, half visible under the arcades: You're a good child. You will achieve a lot. You are on the right path. Accidents should be an incentive.

Captain: It's getting cold. Where are the victories that warmed me? My sleeves are scuffed. The boots with holes. The medals would have to be cleaned again.

First Gentleman: I assure you, dear colleague, that insects have a better chance of survival.

Second Gentleman: Yes, the moon is very blue.

Director: Everything is perfectly arranged. If you want to make a fool of yourself, you can play along.

First Gentleman to himself: You are right, we will also get the plague of rats under control. They crawl out of their holes on all sides. They are such intelligent animals. Unfortunately, parasites and plague carriers. But I assure you we will...

Stagehand: I once had a little dog. Now he's dead. Maybe he's not dead, just gone. I am very sad. But that's not what I wanted to say. I can't find the words anymore.

*Those present are frozen.*

Young Actor to the stagehand: … are you one of them too? I would not have thought that. (*He goes from one to the other.*) What entertaining company! … stiff, disinterested. (*Kicks the clown in the shin with his foot; loud hollow sound.*) Nothing. He doesn't move anymore. (*Knocks the First Gentleman on the forehead ... loud, hollow noise. It sounds like someone is knocking on a wooden door or a coffin lid.*) Nothing either. (*Goes to the ballerina.*) The little one would be pretty if she weren't so motionless. (*He raises an arm to examine it. It falls limp.*)

Old Actor, who has shouldered his bundle: We want to go.

Young Actor, to the theatre director: Buuu … (*tries the Homburg.*)

Old Actor: Come on!

Young Actor: You are right. There is nothing that can be done.

Old Actor: I'm not a hunger artist! I'm hungry! We need a job. We are actors. Our profession calls for the game. We must play while we live. Life and activity are the same for us. And if it were nothing but staring at the moon. After all, sometimes you must close your eyes. Come!

Young Actor: Yes, immediately! (*Takes the paper flower discarded by the ballerina and smells it.*) Still, it's a pity. (*Throws away the flower.*)

Old Actor: Come on! (*They go off through the arcades.*)

End.

# “Die Verwirrung”

Kennwort: “Turm“

“Die Verwirrung“

Das Erbe des babylonischen Turmes.

Personen:

Theaterdirektor

Regisseur

Zwei Schauspieler

Zwei Herren mit Frack und Zylinder

Ein Kindermädchen mit Kinderwagen

Eine blonde Negerin (Anmerkung des Herausgebers: Dieses Theaterstück wurde in den frühen 1980-iger Jahren in Wien geschrieben. Zu einer Zeit als das Wort “Neger“ begriffsbezeichnend verwendet wurde aber nicht herabsetzend gemeint war. Die Figur der “blonden Negerin“ trägt auch in Folge keinerlei rassistische Züge.)

Drei Soldaten, ein Hauptmann

Wissenschaftler

Herr im Tropenanzug

Balletteuse

Ein kostbar gekleideter Clown, der eher einem Harlekin gleicht.

Ein Bühnenarbeiter.

Bühnenbild:

Ein Gemisch aus verschiedensten, nicht zueinander passenden Gegenständen, die teilweise als Sitzgelegenheit benutzt werden, teilweise als Hindernis dienen. Sesseln, Quader, ein Fauteuil, ein Sofa, ein kaputtes Rad, Autoreifen, eine Waschmuschel, ein Fernsehapparat, ein Kühlschrank, Geschirr, Flaschen, Fetzen, Teppiche, Tücher, undefinierbare Reste. (Keine Klomuschel, kein Toilettenpapier verwenden.) Die Bühnenmitte beherrscht eine Maschine. Ein begehbares Podium umgibt sie. Ihren Unterbau bildet ein reich gestalteter Quader, an dem sich, unter anderem, viele Hebel und andere Steuerungsvorrichtungen befinden. Aus dem ungefähr 1,50 m hohen und etwa 2,50 m langen Quader ragt eine raketenähnliche Form schräg in die Luft. Das Gebilde darf den Zuschauer nur entfernt an eine Rakete erinnern. Um noch deutlicher zu werden, das Gebilde könnte auch einen stark abstrahierten, vorwärtsstürmenden, olympischen Fackelträger darstellen. Es besteht aus verschiedenen Metall- und Plastikteilen, soll verwirrend wirken und muss in sich beweglich sein. Im Prinzip ein kybernetisches Kunstwerk, um das es sich im günstigsten Fall handeln kann. Drahtbündel, Spiralen, Räder, Antennen, Gestänge, Glühlampen und Neonröhren, die funktionieren aber keinen Pratereffekt erzeugen sollen, sind Hauptbestandteile der Maschine.

Anmerkung zum Aussehen der Schauspieler und Kostüme:

Der beiden Herren mit Frack und Zylinder sollen einander gleichen. Sie sind mittelgroß und können kurze, graue, Bärte tragen. Die zugeknöpften, ursprünglich eleganten, schwarzen Fräcke sind staubig, abgewetzt und zerdrückt, ebenso die Hosen. Zerrissene Stiefel sind mit Leukoplast überpickt. Das muss gut sichtbar, also übergroß sein, darf aber nicht kabarettistisch wirken. Die ehemals weißen Hemden sind zerknautscht und schmutzig. Silbergraue Krawatten. Vielleicht auch Spazierstöcke. Runde goldgefasste Brillen. Ein Brillenglas kann verklebt sein, auch am Zylinder und am Hemdkragen kann Leukoplast kleben. Die Schuhe sind blank geputzt. Um den Hals tragen sie dicke, glänzende Goldketten, die an die Ordenskette vom goldenen Vlies erinnern.

Negerin: Soll groß und schlank sein. Trägt ein knöchellanges, enganliegendes, schwarzes Kleid. Es ist hoch geschlossen. Seitenschlitze reichen bis über die Hüften. Saum und Kragen sind weiß eingefasst. Netzstrümpfe, rote Strumpfbänder, hohe schwarze Stöckelschuhe. Die blondlockige Perücke ist knabenhaft kurz und lässt den Nacken frei.

Das Kindermädchen muss sehr elegant sein. Es trägt Bluse, Rock, Jacke, Häubchen, Schürzchen und Stöckelschuhe.

Die Soldaten sind ungefähr gleich groß. Keine Rangabzeichen. Uniform aus graugrünem Stoff, Schifferkäppchen.

Die Helme liegen am Boden und werden nur beim Robben aufgesetzt.

Der Herr im Tropenanzug trägt fast die ganze Zeit über seinen Tropenhelm.

Der Direktor sollte massig sein. Offener Gehrock, buntes Gilet, Homburg.

Harlekin-Clown: Weiß geschminktes, maskenhaftes Gesicht. Schwarz eingefasste Augen. Grellrote Lippen, die nicht zur breit sein dürfen, Glatze. Er trägt ein Wams mit Puffärmel, bis zu dem Knieen reichende Pluderhose. Sie sollen nicht zu übertrieben weit sein. Grundton des Kostüms: Weiß und Silber. Mit hellblauen Bändern gebundene Ballettschuhe. Das Kostüm ist dicht mit silbernen Pailletten bestickt, goldene nur sparsam verwenden. Auch hellblaue und lichtgrüne Maschen, sowie Glasplättchen und rote Steine sind über das Gewand verstreut. Der Darsteller kann zeitweise einen spitzen Hut aufsetzen. Gesamteindruck: Kostbar, erlesen. Er wird dadurch zum Clown-Matador.

Balletteuse: Ihr Spitzenröckchen steht waagrecht von den Hüften weg. Farbe schillernd, an eine Tänzerin von Degas erinnernd. Blassrosa Schuhe. Sie trägt das Haar aufgesteckt oder zu einem dichten Zopf geflochten.

Der Wissenschaftler ist ein älterer Herr mit Halbglatze. Kann Brillenträger sein. Blütenweißer Arbeitsmantel.

Der Regisseur ist in Alltagskleidung.

Der Bühnenarbeiter trägt blaue Arbeitskleidung.

Position der Schauspieler: Der beiden Herren in Frack und Zylinder sitzen nebeneinander, das Gesicht dem Publikum zugedreht, auf der rechten Bühnenseite, nahe der Rampe, (vom Publikum aus gesehen links). Etwas seitlich hinter ihnen befindet sich der Standort der Balletteuse und des Harlekin-Clowns. Auf der Mittelbühne sitzen Wissenschaftler, Direktor und Regisseur. Die linke Bühnenseite (vom Publikum rechts) ist hauptsächlich den Soldaten vorbehalten. Der Bühnenarbeiter und die beiden Schauspieler haben ihre Hauptposition bei der Mauer, neben dem Arkadengang. Die Negerin sitz ganz rechts.

Die vorliegende Fassung ist für eine Aufführung bei Tageslicht gedacht.

Bei einer Aufführung im geschlossenen Raum sieht das Bühnenbild folgendermaßen aus: Links (rechts vom Zuschauer) das Fragment einer rotbraunen, von Bögen durchbrochenen Ziegelmauer. Sie läuft in einigem Abstand, parallel mit der Rampe (etwa zwischen Rampe und Bühnenmitte). Ihre Tiefe beträgt ein paar Meter, damit die beiden Schauspieler und der Bühnenarbeiter genug Platz haben. Von der Mauer weg geht ein meterhohes, hölzernes Podium schräg nach vorne und endet rechts (links) von der Rampenmitte. Es setzt sich hinter der Mauer fort und wird im Hintergrund durch einen kompakten Bretterzaun abgeschlossen. Das Holz darf nicht neu wirken. Der Horizont (Rundhorizont) ist von hellblauer Farbe. Die Requisiten bleiben unverändert.

Ein jüngerer und ein älterer Mann kommen von links (vom Zuschauer aus gesehen rechts) durch die Arkaden. Sie tragen eine sehr stilisierte Renaissancekleidung, ein einfaches braunes Wams, weiße Hemden, rote Strumpfhose, die zerrissen sind und an den Füßen Schnürschuhe. Der Ältere ist bärtig. Sein Kopf wird von einem weißen Barett bedeckt. Die Kleidung kann mit bunten Bändern geschmückt sein.

Junger Schauspieler, die Mauer tätschelnd: Fest gebaut. Das nenne ich bauen. Greif einmal (stößt mit dem Fuß dagegen). Hoffentlich wohnen hier reiche Leute.

Alter Schauspieler: Arm am Beutel, arm … wir hätten das bitter nötig, mein Magen knurrt. (Lässt sein Bündel von den Schultern gleiten und schleppt es hinter sich her. Er kracht wie ein altes Grammophon. Hast du noch einen Kaugummi?

Jung.Schausp.: Mach‘ nicht in letzter Minute schlapp. Da nimm. (Alt.Schausp. nimmt den Kaugummi und steckt ihn zwischen die Zähne.) Vergiss‘ nicht, du schuldest mir schon einen.

Alt.Schausp., kauend: Durch deine Schuld sind wir von der Bühne geflogen.

Jung.Schausp.: Weil der Spielleiter hinter mir her war. Der Schweinehund. Da ist bei mir nichts zu machen.

Alt.Schausp.: Mir zuliebe hättest du doch …

Jung.Schausp.: Nicht einmal dir zuliebe …

Alt.Schausp.: Du hast ihn scharfgemacht.

Jung.Schausp.: Na, und? Kleine Tändeleien gehören zu unserem Beruf.

Sie betreten die Bühne auf der die übrigen Schauspieler, ausgenommen das Kindermädchen, stumm sitzen, stehen oder liegen; (der Großteil sitzt).

Jung.Schausp.: Was ist denn das für eine unterhaltsame Gesellschaft? (Er stößt einen.) Nichts, er rührt sich nicht! (Klopft einem der Herren mit Zylinder gegen die Stirn. Es muss klingen, wie wenn er auf Holz klopfen würde.) Auch nichts. (Zur Balletteuse): Und sie, meine schöne Dame? (Zum alt. Schausp.): Steif wie ein Brett. Entweder sind sie taub oder sie wollen uns nicht. So offensichtlich bin ich im Leben noch nie ignoriert worden. Sowas ist peinlich für einen Schauspieler. (Zupft dem im Frack am Bart.)

Alt.Schausp.: Lass den Unsinn! Warten wir bis sie aufwachen. Ich bin müde, setzen wir uns inzwischen.

Jung.Schausp.: Wenn du glaubst, dass wir dadurch etwas erreichen. (Sie setzen sich abseits, mit dem Rücken zur Mauer.) Fade Typen. Ich hab‘ mir das anders vorgestellt. Es ist überhaupt sehr ruhig hier.

Alt.Schausp.: Nicht auffallend.

Jung.Schausp.: Dein Phlegma möchte ich haben.

Die Figuren bewegen sich langsam. Nicht alle gleichzeitig. Sie kommen in verschiedenen Abständen zu sich. Manche erwachen plötzlich aus ihrer Starre, andere allmählich und kaum merklich. Einige gähnen und strecken sich verschlafen.

Jung.Schausp. den alt.Schausp. mit dem Ellbogen stoßend: Ich glaube es geht los.

Alt.Schausp.: Warte ab.

1.Herr mit Zylinder zum anderen: Na, verehrter Herr Kollege?

2.Herr: Ich habe über den Satz noch nicht nachgedacht. Das heißt ich tüftle jede Sekunde daran. Ein Lehrsatz muss unanfechtbar sein. Er muss gepanzert und behelmt sein. Ich rekapituliere. Ich rekapituliere. Wir waren bei der Weiterentwicklung des Homo Sapiens stehen geblieben. Habe ich richtig vermutet? Oder?

1.Herr: Ich sage ihnen, die Insekten werden überleben. Die Insekten und die Maschinen.

2.Herr: Die Insekten sind Maschinen. Ich muss ihnen in dem Punkt beipflichten. Das Insekt stellt eine spezielle Abart unserer künstlich gezüchteten Menschen dar, die in vielen Fällen, die ich jetzt nicht präzisieren will, dem Insekt nachgebaut bzw. nachempfunden sind. Das Insekt, sehr verehrter Herr Professor, hat sich im Lauf von Milliarden-Jahren selbst gezüchtet, was ich ja nicht extra betonen muss, hat sich immer den Umständen angepasst, war immer evolutionsfähig, ohne sich äußerlich wesentlich zu verändern. Bei der menschlichen Rasse scheint mir das nicht gewährleistet.

1.Herr: Bei der menschlichen Spezies sehen sie also …

2.Herr: Richtig, bei der menschlichen Rasse, bei allen Säugern. Bedenken sie nur wie sich die Mode ändert. Sehen sie wie schäbig wir geworden sind?

1.Herr: Ich muss schon bitten! Außerdem spricht die Tatsache, dass sich die Mode ändert für die Entwicklung.

2.Herr: Meinetwegen, aber nicht für eine Entwicklung in geistiger Hinsicht. Ich würde auch die Veränderung der Kleidung nicht als Entwicklung, sondern den Tatsachen gemäß, als Veränderung der Kleidung bezeichnen. Eine Veränderung, die in den meisten Fällen abhängig von klimatischen Bedingungen ist. Denken sie an Baumwolle. Auch daran ob ein Volksstamm oder mehrere Volksstämme von einer kalten Gegend in eine warme wechseln oder umgekehrt. Was erwiesenermaßen seltener vorkommt.

1.Herr: Sie leugnen also eine geistige Entwicklung der Menschheit?

2.Herr: Nicht einmal unsere Erfahrungen, ob es nun Erfahrungen von gewissen Menschenmengen oder Massen bzw. rein persönliche Erkenntnisse waren, die dann weiterverbreitet wurden, ob mündlich, durch Schläge oder visuell, haben uns weitergebracht.

1.Herr: Sie sehen also keine Chance?

2.Herr: Wenn ich ehrlich sein soll – nein.

1.Herr: Dann habe ich sie umsonst konsultiert, Herr Kollege.

2.Herr: Ich habe ihnen doch schon gesagt, seit der Höhlenmalerei von Altamira hat sich nichts Bedeutsames geändert. Diese Arbeiten wurden von geistig hochstehenden Menschen geschaffen. Es hätten hoch talentierte Maler des Zwanzigsten Jahrhunderts sein können, denen sie morgen auf der Straße, im Restaurant, bei einer Vorlesung begegnen.

1.Herr: Dann sind wir also quasi Höhlenbewohner?

2.Herr: Meinetwegen Sternenbewohner, das ändert nichts.

Herr im Tropenanzug, auf sie zutretend: Entschuldigen sie, haben sie vielleicht zufällig die Spur gesehen? Der Löwe müsste hier vorbeigekommen sein. Ein großes Männchen, nicht zu übersehen. Als Jagdkamerad bitte ich sie um Auskunft.

2.Herr: Sehen sie, verehrter Herr Kollege, der uralte, animalische Jagdinstinkt, das uralte Balzen, sehen sie nur, wie er seine Schwanzfedern aufstellt.

1.Herr: Balzen?

2.Herr: Ja, er verbindet Jagd mit gesellschaftlicher Stellung und wird außerdem vor Frauen den Helden spielen. Er wird sich mit seinen Trophäen brüsten, wie gesagt, balzen und den Schwanz aufstellen.

1.Herr: Erst wenn er den Löwen geschossen hat.

2.Herr: Dem Tod Aug in Aug gestanden ist, wenn auch nur vom Safaribus aus, mit der Kamera in der Hand.

1.Herr: Oder mit dem Teleobjektiv. Dabei gibt es Löwenbilder zu tausenden.

2.Herr: Mir gehen sie bereits auf die Nerven.

1.Herr: Auch Fotos von Negerkindern gibt es und Fotos von nackten Negerinnen mit Brustwarzen, groß wie Thermosflaschen Verschlüsse.

2.Herr: Was die physisch aushalten. Es ist ergreifend, wie sie verhungern.

1.Herr: Und das verendende Vieh? Ein idealer Brutherd für Seuchen.

2.Herr: Die Prostitution vor den Touristen …

1.Herr: Die haben sie überall. Das ist keine typisch afrikanische Erscheinung. Sie brauchen sich nur umzusehen.

Mann im Tropenanzug, der mit gebeugtem Rücken aufmerksam zugehört hat: Danke vielmals meine Herren. Sie haben meine Simba also nicht gesehen. Sehr nette von ihnen. Heia Safari! (Geht suchend zwischen den Hindernissen auf und ab und verschwindet schließlich hinter der Maschine.)

Ein blütenweißes Kindermädchen schiebt einen blütenweißen Kinderwagen rasch über die Bühne. (Achtung beim Aufstellen der Hindernisse, ihr Weg muss frei sein.)

1.Herr: Die aufgetriebenen Bäuche unter den dünnen Rippen. Die offenen Wunden. Es fehlt ihnen eindeutig an Hygiene und gesunder Ernährung. Ich würde sagen sie leiden unter Nahrungsmangel.

2.Herr: Dabei bekommen sie aber wunderschöne, große Augen. Das Gesicht besteht nur mehr aus Augen.

1.Herr: Ich kenne die Plakate. Sie stören manchmal.

Das Kindermädchen schiebt den Kinderwagen über die Bühne zurück. Auf der Bühnenmitte angelangt holt sie eine bunte Rassel aus dem Wagen und scheppert damit.

Kindermädchen: Ist ja schon gut … guti … guti … ruhig, nur ruhig, ich bin ja da … ich bin ja bei dir. (Sie setzt den Weg fort. Das muss so natürlich wirken, wie wenn ein wirkliches Kindermädchen in die Szene geraten wäre. Die beiden Herren setzen unbeirrt ihr Gespräch fort.)

2.Herr: Sie sterben, erwiesenermaßen, an Entkräftung.

1.Herr: Das ist logisch.

Blonde Negerin, die aufgestanden ist und die Herren einmal umkreist: Ich trage ein Modell der Haute-Couture. Einmaliger Schnitt, beste Stoffqualität. Die Leute sagen ich bewege mich sehr graziös, aber das sei unserer Rasse eigen. Ein Privileg unsere Rasse. Schwarze Modells sind der letzte Schrei. Zwar nicht der allerletzte, aber schwarz ist “in“. Ich habe die schwarze Haut und die schwarze Seele einer Gazelle oder einer Wildkatze.

Regisseur, der hinter sie getreten ist: Oder die einer gutmütigen, dicken, schwarzen Mami, eine Glucke mit vielen Kindern.

Die meisten Schauspieler bewegen sich jetzt. Sie klopfen ihr Gewand aus, fahren sich übers Haar, sprechen leise miteinander oder verständigen sich durch Gesten. Das soll sehr privat und unbekümmert wirken.

1.Herr: Dabei sind sie trotz kultureller Mängel …

Negerin, zum Regisseur: Ihre Bemerkung war nicht sehr kultiviert, ich habe sie für charmanter gehalten.

1.Herr: Im Grunde genommen sehr charmant.

Regisseur: Ich protestiere. Ich bin Regisseur, also kulturell tätig. Ich nehme mir kein Blatt vor den Mund und nenne die Dinge beim Namen.

2.Herr: Obwohl sie komische Namen haben …

Negerin: Trotzdem sind sie ein netter Kerl.

2.Herr: Und es Riesenkerle unter ihnen gibt.

Regisseur: Danke, für den netten Kerl. Dann verstehen wir uns ja.

1.Herr: Auch die Verständigung fällt einem schwer. Die andere Mentalität spielt eine große Rolle.

Negerin: Ihre brutale Mentalität wirkt bei mir nicht. Die Masche zieht nicht. Sie sind zu direkt.

2.Herr: Direkt will ich ja mit ihnen nichts zu tun haben.

1.Herr: Wenn es nicht unbedingt sein muss.

Negerin, stellt einen Fuß auf den Schenkel des 1.Herrn und nestelt an ihren Netzstrümpfen. Zum Regisseur: Die Beine können sich sehen lassen. Sehen sie sich meine Fessel an. (Über die Köpfe der beiden Herren hinweg an die Balletteuse gewandt): Da, sehen sie, he da (schwingt ein Bein).

Balletteuse: Lassen sie mich in Ruhe! Lassen sie mich in Ruhe mit ihren unteren Extremitäten!

1.Herr, die Negerin nicht beachtend: Ja, Beweglichkeit und schlanke Glieder kann man ihnen nicht absprechen.

2.Herr: Obwohl manche Stämme ausgesprochen kurze Extremitäten ihr Eigentum nennen.

Balletteuse: Der Regisseur ist nicht ihr Eigentum. Schwarze Nutte, Schlange!

Negerin: Ballettratte!

1.Herr: Die Ratten fressen dreiviertel der am Hafen lagernden Hilfsgüter.

Regisseur: aber, aber meine Damen.

Balletteuse: Ich brauche ihre Hilfe nicht. Für sie bin ich keine Dame. Für sie bin ich Fräulein Mayer. Lassen sie mich ab heute in Ruhe. Belästigen sie mich nicht mehr. Ich komme immer pünktlich zur Probe, das wissen sie genauso gut wie ich. Ich erfülle meine Pflicht. Mehr können sie nicht von mir verlangen. Ihre privaten Interessen sind mir gleichgültig. Sie gehören nicht hierher. Aber ich lasse mir von der da (zeigt auf die Negerin) nichts mehr gefallen. (Wendet sich trotzig ab.)

Jung.Schausp.: Die Schwarze gefällt mir.

Alt.Schausp.: Psst!

Negerin: Das Fräulein schmollt. Das kleine Biest schmollt. Na ja. (Tritt an die Rampe, mit singender Stimme): Ich könnte nicht behaupten, dass es mir hier nicht gefällt. Auch wenn das Klima etwas rau ist. Doch am glücklichsten war ich in meiner Heimat, in meiner ewig sonnigen Heimat, wo ich wie eine scheue Gazelle durch den grünen Busch streifte, wo ich in durchsichtigen Flüssen badete, und mit den Fischen spielte, wo ich an heißen Abenden dem dunklen Klang der Trommeln lauschte, meine Hüften wie Palmen im Monsun wiegte, wenn wir die Kalabassen aufs Feld trugen, um die durstigen zu laben. Wie vermisste ich das ferne Gekreisch der Affen und das Grunzen der Kaffernbüffel, wenn sie in schlammigen Tümpeln faulenzen. Die Welt war in Ordnung bis zu dem Tag als die Sklavenhändler kamen, unser Dorf niederbrannten und mich – welch bitteres Schicksal – in Ketten wegschleppten. Sie bearbeiteten meinen zarten Körper mit der geflochtenen Peitsche. Ich musste für sie schön sein und tanzen. Ich, ein hochgewachsenes Kind der Wildnis mit dem Freiheitsdrang eines Raubtiers! Schließlich wurde ich an einen alten, lüsternen Scheich verkauft, der mich in seinem Harem einkerkerte. Dort saß ich wie ein gefangener Vogel, verweigerte die Nahrung, starrte durch die Gitter, siechte dahin und wurde kränker und kränker. Mein Leib wollte die Seele nicht mehr halten. Der geizige Besitzer beschloss mich zu verkaufen. Mein Wert hatte sich inzwischen so weit vermindert, dass ein gütiger, väterlicher Europäer mich billig erstand. Er nahm sich meiner, wie einer Tochter an und pflegte mich gesund. Ich war bald wieder im Besitz meiner früheren Schönheit. Ein Talentsucher der zufällig am Haus meines Gönners vorbei kam hörte meine Stimme und engagierte mich. So bin ich hier gelandet. Manchmal spüre ich noch den Gesang des Urwalds durch mein Blut brausen. Dann muss ich geschwind kaltes Wasser trinken. Ich bin ein Gewebe aus Elfenbein und schwarzem Samt. Die Innenflächen meiner Hände sind rosige Rosen. Aber fragen sie meinen Manager. (Dreht sich suchend um) leider ist er verhindert. Er könnte ihnen die Geschichte viel ergreifender erzählen.

Regisseur: Die alte Masche. Wenn ich das nur verhindern könnte. Sie macht sich lächerlich. Glauben sie ihr kein Wort. Sie hat den Busch nie gesehen. Sie wurde als Tochter eines Pfandleihers in den Slums von Harlem geboren. Ihr Vater, der im berechtigten Ruf eines gewissenlosen Ausbeuters stand, bereicherte sich an seiner eigenen Rasse. An den Ärmsten der Armen. Er hatte auch bei Rauschgift und Prostitution seine Hände im Spiel. Sie hat die Not nie gekannt. Sie wuchs wohlbehütet auf. Noch dazu ist sie ein außerordentlich geschäftstüchtiges Luxusgeschöpf.

Hauptmann zu den drei Soldaten: Antreten! (Soldaten treten an) Gewehr bei Fuß! (Soldaten tun es) Wir können uns den Luxus der Faulheit nicht leisten. (Er kommandiert währenddessen das Folgende): Rechts um, links um, gerade aus, halt, Gewehr ab, schultert das Gewehr … usw. (Darf nur als Geräuschkulisse dienen).

Negerin zum Regisseur: Nun verschaffen sie mir die Rolle?

Regisseur: Das kommt auf ihre stimmliche Verfassung an. Für die Gage bin ich nicht zuständig. Da müssen sie sich an den Direktor wenden. Kommen sie! (Die beiden gehen zu dem weiter hinten sitzenden Direktor. Er gleicht in seiner martialischen Pose eher einem Zirkusdirektor. Er könnte eine Peitsche in der Hand halten und Stiefel tragen.)

Regisseur: Darf ich ihnen diese Dame vorstellen, sehr verehrter Herr Direktor … sie würde ger …

Direktor sich strahlend erhebend: Dass sie uns beehren freut mich gnädige Frau … allerdings, ob die Gage ihren Ansprüchen genügt …

1.Herr: Dabei sind die Wilden völlig anspruchslos. Eine Hand voll Reis …

2.Herr: Sie verwechseln da etwas. Ich glaube den Kontinent.

1.Herr: Kann schon sein Herr Kollege. Das macht die Hitze. Wo waren wir stehen geblieben?

2.Herr: Bei der Evolution der Insekten, der selbst mit Insektiziden nicht beizukommen ist.

1.Herr, lüftet den Zylinder und wischt sich mit einem weißen Sacktuch den Schweiß von der Stirn: Richtig! Aber im Gegensatz zu ihrer werten und sicherlich fundierten Meinung, – dass sie fundiert ist will ich ja nicht leugnen – bin ich der Ansicht, dass auch der Mensch befähigt ist sich weiter zu entwickeln, ja diese Weiterentwicklung ein absolutes Muss für ihn darstellt.

2.Herr: Sie haben sich eben den Schweiß von der Stirne gewischt.

1.Herr: Ja und?

2.Herr: Die Urmenschen haben das Gleiche getan. Der einzige Unterschied besteht darin, dass sie den Arm oder den Handrücken dazu verwendet haben, während sie ein Taschentuch benutzten. Allein Sinn und Zweck der Bewegung bleibt der gleiche. (Nimmt die Brille und putzt sie.) Bedenken sie nur die Tatsache, dass man vor ein paar hundert Jahren als Mitteleuropäer durchaus im Ruf einer universellen Bildung stehen konnte, etwas, das heute unmöglich ist. Ich will damit sagen, das Wissen, aber nicht der Geist hat sich erweitert.

1.Herr: Als Mitteleuropäer über Mitteleuropa meinen sie?

2.Herr: Bitte, wenn sie das Gebiet so einschränken wollen … natürlich hatten Gebildete eine Ahnung von nahen und fernen

Orten, von Afrika usw., aber eben nur eine Ahnung. Es wurde nie das riesige Material an sie herangetragen, dass ein heutiger Mensch, wollte er sich tatsächlich universell bilden, bewältigen müsste, was selbstverständlich unmöglich ist. Wir sind durch die Fülle überwältigt.

1.Herr: Was – wir? Sie und ich? Wir haben unser Fachwissen. Wir sind Kapazitäten auf unserem Gebiet.

2.Herr: Nein, mein Lieber, wir haben uns nur spezialisiert. Wir sind spezielle Spezialisten geworden. Wir haben uns auf ein Teilwissen beschränkt. Das Gehirn ist keineswegs mitgewachsen. Wir gehören einer der vielen Gruppen an, die sich abermals teilt, wenn die Erkenntnisse wachsen. Das führt zu einer dauernden Abspaltung. Wir sind wieder zu Jägerhorden mit eigenem Jagdgebiet und speziellen Jagdmethoden geworden. Was kann ein sogenannter Kosmopolit von dem fassen was um ihn geschieht? Von allen Dingen und Ereignissen ein winziges Stückchen. Und selbst wenn sie drei Milliarden und achthunderttausend Jahre existieren würden, lieber Herr Kollege, und sich dabei tausendfach spalten könnten, die einzelnen Ereignisse wären nur bruchstückhaft für sie vorhanden. Sie müssten zugleich Künstler, Revolutionär, Staatsmann, Prostituierte, Lustknabe, Gattin, Leichenbestatter, Bauarbeiter, Astronaut, Unternehmer, Pädagoge, Hilfsschüler … ich kann alle menschlichen Erscheinungsformen nicht aufzählen … das alles zugleich müssten sie sein und zwar in jedem Land, zu jeder Stunde und an jedem Ort. Wie eine tausendköpfige Hydra.

Jung.Schausp.: Die quatschen was zusammen. Die Kleine vom Ballett ist ganz appetitlich.

1.Herr: Ein sehr interessanter Aspekt.

2.Herr: Aber nicht realisierbar. Das ist die Tragödie.

Mann im Tropenanzug tritt wieder zu ihnen: Ich habe drei Löwenbabys geschossen, wollt sagen geknipst. Sie liefen mir direkt vor die Kamera. Waren gar nicht scheu. Sehen sie sich die putzigen Dinger an. (Zeigt den beiden Fotos, die sie nicht beachten.) Sind sie nicht entzückend? Meine Frau wird sich freuen. Sie ist ganz verrückt nach Tierbabys. Da, das finde ich auch gelungen … wie der dreinschaut …

1.Herr, (laut in die Rede des Mannes hinein): Die vertrockneten Brüste der Negerin, an denen halbtote Säuglinge hängen.

Mann im Tropenanzug: Auch meine Kinder werden sich freuen. Da …

1.Herr: Ich habe schon Appetitlicheres gesehen. Die greinenden Münder sind eine offene Wunde. Weshalb verhungern sie so provokant? Muss das so auffällig geschehen? Sie müssen wissen, lieber Herr Kollege, dass ich ein empfindsamer Mensch und außerdem ein großer Ästhet bin. Ich hasse derart marktschreierisches Sterben. Ich hasse und verabscheue es, obwohl ich am menschlichen Skelett nichts auszusetzen habe. Weder an dem von Erwachsenen noch an dem von Säuglingen.

Mann im Tropenanzug, der ihnen ein Bild nach dem anderen hinhält: Sind sie nicht lieb? Es war ein voller Erfolg. Trotzdem ich nicht zum Schuss gekommen bin. Ich danke ihnen für ihren freundlichen Typ. (Geht nach hinten.)

Kindermädchen stürzt von rechts herein. Sie zerrt den Kinderwagen hinter sich her. Schreiend: Man hat mir das Baby gestohlen, man hat es entführt!

Hauptmann: Still gestanden! (Soldaten tun es, freundlich zum Kindermädchen) Was ist geschehen? Kann ich ihnen behilflich sein?

Kindermädchen: Mein Kind! Kidnapping! Man hat mir das Kind gestohlen.

Regisseur, der hinter der Maschine vorgetreten ist, nach vorne brüllend: Lassen sie sich gefälligst eine bessere Ausrede einfallen!

Kindermädchen: Entschuldigen sie! Sehr wohl, Herr Regisseur.

(Knickst) zum Hauptmann: Das Baby ist ins Wasser gefallen. Was soll ich nur tun? Was werden die Herrschaften sagen? Mein Gott, ich werde entlassen.

Hauptmann: Beruhigen sie sich vorerst. Wir müssen strategische Maßnahmen ergreifen. Sachliches Handeln ist wichtig. Allerdings ist der Fall Im Reglement nicht vorgesehen.

Kindermädchen: Dabei habe ich den Kleinen immer verwöhnt. Mich um ihn gesorgt wie eine Mutter – nein ärger – die weichsten Deckchen, die zartesten Windeln, damit das Ärschchen nicht wund wird … Wenn das Kleine geblinzelt hat hab‘ ich schon um seine Gesundheit gezittert … es war ja auch gar so winzig und zart … und dabei so ein lieber lustiger Kerl … was mach‘ ich nur … was kann man da bloß machen … bitte helfen sie mir doch … ich bin völlig verzweifelt …

Hauptmann: Ich stehe zu ihrer Verfügung. Bedienen sie sich meiner. Ich könnte ihnen ein … ich meine, das könnten sie dann als Kind ihrer Herrschaft ausgeben.

Kindermädchen: Ich weiß nicht so recht. Und wenn es kein Junge wird? Außerdem dauert es zu lange.

Jung.Schausp. zum alt.Schausp. in den letzten Satz des Kindermädchens hineinsprechend: Wir können uns ein paar Schillinge verdienen. (Steht auf.) Vielleicht kann ich ihnen helfen Fräulein?

Kindermädchen schluchzend: Sie?

Jung.Schausp.: Ja, Momentchen (Wickelt eine säuglingsgroße Puppe aus einem Bündel und hält sie ihr, an einem Bein, verkehrt hin.) Da nehmen sie.

Kindermädchen: Aber …

Alt.Schausp.(aufstehend): So geht das nicht. Zuerst müssen wir die Geburt einleiten.

Jung.Schausp.: Ich vergesse auch auf Alles. (Zum Kindermädchen) Agieren sie stellvertretend für die Mutter.

Alt.Schausp.: Werden sie Mutter. Werden sie Mutter ohne die Freuden der Lust aber mit den Schmerzen der Geburt. Das ist eine kleine Strafe für ihre Schlamperei. (Er dreht das Kindermädchen, sodass es halbseitig vom Publikum gesehen wird. Die folgende Szene darf keinesfalls obszön wirken. Zum jung. Schausp.) Ich überlasse das dir. Du hast sicherere Hände.

Jung.Schausp. zum Kindermädchen: Spreizen sie die Beine. Etwas weiter – ja, so. Halten sie sich fest. Ja, stützen sie sich.

(Das Kindermädchen steht zurückgebeugt, die Hände unter sich auf die Griffstange des Wagens gestützt. Der Schauspieler fährt ihr mit der Puppe unter das Kleid. Sie bäumt sich auf und stößt einen stöhnenden, langgezogenen Schrei aus. Der Schauspieler zieht die Puppe zwischen den Beinen hervor und schwenkt sie in der Luft. Einige Schauspieler klatschen.

Er schüttelt die Puppe fachgerecht, klopft auf ihren Popo. (Horcht) Nichts! (Schüttelt sie wieder.) Nichts!

Alt.Schausp.: Du hast vergessen das Tonband einzustellen.

Jung.Schausp.: Ja, richtig. (Öffnet eine Klappe am Rücken der Puppe und hantiert im Inneren herum. Es ertönt überlautes Babygeschrei.)

Alt.Schausp.: Stell sie ein bisschen leiser.

Junger Schausp. befolgt den Wunsch und reicht sie dann dem Kindermädchen: So junge Frau.

(Sie drückt die Puppe an sich, besinnt sich, holt aus dem Wagen Windeln und wickelt sie. Dabei geht sie mit der Puppe wie mit einer Puppe um, also nicht sorgsam, wie mit einem Kind.)

Alt.Schausp.: War doch ganz harmlos. Bis auf das bisschen Schmerze.

Kindermädchen: Das können …

Jung.Schausp.: Die normalste Sache der Welt. Ich weiß nicht warum die Weiber so einen Zirkus machen.

Kindermädchen: Das können sie …

Alt.Schausp.: Natürlich kann ich. Ich bin auch schmerzempfindlich. So ein Theater machen. Von wegen gesegneten Leibes und so. Möchte wissen, wo da der Segen ist. Was ist dran gesegnet? Und erst wenn der Balg da ist! Die tiefen Regungen des mütterlichen Herzens. Selbstverständlich treten die nur ein, wenn die Mutter in Bezug auf ihr Kind nicht kriminell ist oder als kriminell gilt. Dabei sehen Neugeborene aus wie blau gefrorene, verkrüppelte Greise. Ich finde das zumindest. Dieses idiotische Lächeln auf allen Gesichtern, wenn der Säugling primitive Lebenszeichen von sich gibt, oder nur rülpst, furzt, vor sich hin brabbelt oder ihm der Speichel übers Kinn rinnt. Diese verstehende, durch nichts gerechtfertigte Lächeln, das wie eine Epidemie über alle Gesichter schleicht, macht mich wahnsinnig. Entschuldigen sie meine aggressive Art. Aber was macht den Menschen, in diesem unwürdigen Stadium so liebenswert, so entzückend?

Kindermädchen: Aber … es ist doch mein Kind. (Sie schreit fest dazwischen.)

Alt.Schausp.: Schweigen sie! Sie sind voreingenommen! Was ist an diesem schlafenden oder schreienden Fleisch, das die Bezeichnung Mensch noch nicht verdient, entzückend? Der unförmig große Kopf? Die kaum tauglichen Händchen? Die gekrümmten Beinchen?

Kindermädchen: Aber …

Alt.Schausp.: Allein die Ausdrücke, süß, entzückend, reizend und putzig, sind doch erniedrigend für einen Menschen. So kann man junge Hunde bezeichnen. Erschreckend ist der Umstand, dass sie, von allen Unappetitlichkeiten abgesehen, wirklich nur süß und putzig sind. Trägt das Spiel mit Puppen daran Schuld? Ist es eine Wiederholung des Puppenspiels? Oder liegt der Reiz im Machtbewusstsein? Im einmaligen Machtbewusstsein einer völlig hilflosen Kreatur gegenüber? Manche Mütter wissen mit ihren Kindern nichts mehr anzufangen, sobald sie erwachsen werden und menschliche Regungen zeigen. Man hat ihnen die Puppe weggenommen. Die Puppe hat sich selbständig gemacht. Aber ich will nicht verallgemeinern.

Kindermädchen, zum jung.Schausp.: Wie kann ich ihnen danken?

Alt.Schausp.: Zuerst werde ich sie auf die Vorteile der Puppe aufmerksam machen. Erstens kann man ihre Lautstärke bestimmen. Wie sie gesehen haben, ist das ganz einfach. Zweitens kann man sie völlig abschalten. Drittens scheißt sie nicht uns schreit nicht nach dem Fläschchen. Viertens brauchen sie keine Sorgen zu haben, dass sie je an einer Kolik oder Erkältung leiden wird.

Jung.Schausp.: Wenn sie ein paar Schillinge für uns hätten?

Kindermädchen: Gern. (Kramt in der Handtasche.)

Alt.Schausp.: Außerdem können sie mit der Gewissheit nach Hause gehen, dass die gnädige Frau das Kind für ihr eigenes hält. Das könnte ihnen schon ein paar Schillinge wert sein.

Kindermädchen: Da haben sie. Es war mir ein Vergnügen. (Geht, den Kinderwagen vor sich herschiebend, schnell ab.)

Jung.Schausp., nachrufend: Danke, danke, herzlichen Dank.

Alt.Schausp.: Wie viel?

Jung.Schausp.: Da. (Streckt ihm die Hand hin.)

Alt.Schausp.: Es geht.

Jung.Schausp.: Hoffentlich besucht sie nie das Warenhaus, aus dem wir die Puppe geklaut haben.

Alt.Schausp.: Sieht doch eine wie die andere aus. Ein Serienprodukt.

Jung.Schausp.: Du hast Recht.

Alt.Schausp., zum Bühnenarbeiter, der in ihrer Nähe, die Hände in den Taschen, an der Wand lehnt: He, du!

Bühnenarbeiter: Meinen sie mich?

Alt.Schausp.: Ja, dich.

Bühnenarbeiter: Was ist?

Jung.Schausp.: Hol‘ uns eine Flasche Bier.

Bühnenarbeiter: Ich bin nicht euer Diener.

Jung.Schausp.: Hab‘ ich das gesagt? Bitte bring‘ uns eine Flasche Bier aus der Kantine. Wir sind fremd hier. Nimm dir auch eine mit. Für uns gleich zwei.

Bühnenarbeiter: Das ist was anderes. Ich wusste nicht, dass ihr hier fremd seid. (Jung.Schausp. gibt ihm Geld in die ausgestreckte Hand. Er holt das Gewünschte. Sie setzen sich mit dem Rücken zur Wand und trinken.)

Während der vergangenen Handlung – seit dem Auftritt des Kindermädchens – hat die Negerin mit großen Gästen eine kaum oder auch nicht hörbare Koloraturarie gesungen. Der Harlekin-Clown hat sich frisch geschminkt. Der Wissenschaftler an der Maschine gearbeitet. Die Balletteuse einige Tanzschritte geübt, und sich wieder gesetzt. Das alles darf die Handlung nicht stören.

Hauptmann zu den Soldaten: Ihr müsst leuchtende Vorbilder der Nation sein. Eure Pflicht ist es mit männlicher Entschlusskraft zu handeln, die auf Eigeninitiative und Training beruht. Ihr sollt die Befehle ausführen, ohne darüber nachzudenken. Ihr habt blindlings zu gehorchen. Wehrmachtszersetzter und Agitatoren werden an die Wand gestellt. Wer Agitator ist bestimmt die oberste Führung, die wie eine Mutter zu euch ist. Habt ihr verstanden?

Alle Drei: Ja.

Der Hauptmann, vor den 1. Soldaten tretend: Wiederholen sie!

1.Soldat, drückt die Brust heraus und spricht sehr schnell und monoton: Wir müssen mörderische Vorbilder der Nation sein. Wir müssen lernen Menschen zu töten und in ihnen Raubtiere sehen, da die Menschen lernen uns zu töten und in uns Raubtiere sehen. Wir müssen die Augen schließen und jeden Befehl blind ausführen. Nur in diesem Zustand ist individuelles Handeln erlaubt. Menschen die anders denken werden abgeknallt. Wer abgeknallt wird bestimmt eine Handvoll Ordensträger.

Hauptmann, zurücktretend: Sehr brav! (Räuspert sich. Mit leidenschaftlicher Stimme) Aber denkt auch an die wehende Fahne, den Trommelwirbel, die siegreiche Fahne, den Trommelwirbel, die flammende Fahne, den Trommelwirbel, die stumme Fahne, den gedämpften Trommelklang. (Noch weiter zurücktretend. Er steht die ganze Zeit über mit dem Rücken zum Publikum. Die Soldaten haben das Gesicht der Rampe zugewandt.)

Du Schwert in meiner Linken.

Was soll dein heiteres Blinken?

Schaust mich so freundlich an.

Ich hab‘ dir doch nicht … weggetreten … Blödsinn … ihre blöden Visagen bringen mich aus dem Konzept. Die Rührung bringt mich … so soll es heißen …

Schaust mich so freundlich an.

Hab‘ meine Freude dran, hurra!

Sie da im ersten Glied, haben sie etwa gelacht? Wagen sie es nicht zu lachen! Nein? In Ordnung. (Räuspert sich.) Aber denkt auch an die schwarzbraunen Mädchen, den abenteuerlichen Duft der Fremde, das Knistern des Lagerfeuers. All das könnt ihr kostenlos konsumieren. Wenn es schlimm hergeht, werdet ihr höchstens die Arme, die Beine, den Kopf, gegebenenfalls auch das Leben verliere. (Zum Soldaten Nr.3): Was war mein vorletztes Wort?

3.Soldat: Verlieren.

Hauptmann: Falsch, das war mein letztes Wort. (Zum zweiten Soldaten): Wissen sie es?

2.Soldat: Zu Befehl - Leben.

Hauptmann zum 1.Soldaten: Und das letzte?

1.Soldat: Verlieren.

Hauptmann: Also – (Zeigt auf den 2.Soldaten).

2.Soldat: Leben.

Zeigt auf den 3.Soldaten.

3.Soldat: Verlieren.

Der Hauptmann zeigt abwechselnd. Das muss sehr rasch gehen.

2.Soldat: Leben.

1.Soldat: Verlieren.

2.Soldat: Leben.

1.Soldat: Verlieren.

2.Soldat: Leben.

1.Soldat: Verlieren.

2.Soldat: Leben …

Hauptmann: Halt! Das klappt ja schon ausgezeichnet. Und nun zu ihnen. (Tritt vor den 3.Soldaten.) Ich versichere ihnen sie werden es auch noch lernen. Robben sie zweimal um den Platz. Aber ein bisschen Tempo, wenn ich bitten darf. (Soldat wirft sich zu Boden.) Sind sie einverstanden? Sehen sie die Richtigkeit meiner Entscheidung ein?

Soldat, zu dem knapp vor ihm stehenden Hauptmann, hinaufschreiend: Jawohl!

Hauptmann: Disziplin muss sein oder sind sie anderer Meinung?

Soldat: Nein!

Hauptmann: Würden sie mir die Stiefel küssen, wenn ich es befehle?

Soldat: Jawohl!

Hauptmann: Auch schleckend?

Soldat: Jawohl!

Hauptmann: Mit Vergnügen?

Soldat: Jawohl!

Hauptmann: Dann schlecken sie. (Hält ihm die Stiefel hin. Zu den beiden Andren): Bei der modernen Armee arbeitet man ohne Schikanen. Sie haben gesehen, wie sich ihr Kamerad darum reißt. (Zum Liegenden): Es genügt.

Soldat: Zu Befehl.

Hauptmann: Ich hoffe sie merken sich die Lektion. Robben sie.

Der Soldat robbt während des weiteren Geschehens über die Bühne. Er ist nicht die ganze Zeit sichtbar.

Hauptmann: Lassen sie sich das eine Warnung sein. Ja! Selbstverständlich werden wir auch in Friedenszeiten benötigt. Bei Unwetterkatastrophen oder beim Brückenbau werden unsere Pioniere oft eingesetzt. Aber das ist nicht unsere eigentliche Aufgabe. Das ist pervers! Verstanden?

Soldat: Ja.

Hauptmann: Gut! Kriegshandwerk hat eine lange Tradition. Auf einer Seite beschützen wir Frauen und Kinder, auf der anderen Seite vergewaltigen und morden wir sie. Das geschieht im Lauf des Krieges wechselseitig. Aber so viel Allgemeinbildung werdet ihr ja haben. Zusammenfassend. Die eigentliche Aufgabe des Soldaten ist der Krieg. Sonst wären sie ja unnütz. Die eigentliche Aufgabe des Soldaten ist es den Frieden zu schützen. Die Logik müsst ihr einsehen, meine Herren.

Harlekin-Clown, der sich langsam genähert hat: Darf ich mitmachen? Ich melde mich freiwillig.

Jung.Schausp.: Sei nicht blöd …

Alt.Schausp.: Misch dich nicht drein!

Hauptmann: Scher dich zum Teufel. Witzfiguren können wir nicht brauchen.

Clown, schüchtern: Was sie eben gesagt haben hat mein Zirkusblut in Wallung gebracht. Es klang nach Dressurakt. Ich roch Raubtiergestank. Wissen sie, diesen typischen, beißenden …

Hauptmann: Scher dich zum Teufel!

Der Clown stellt blitzschnell ein kleines Podium vor den Hauptmann. Er besteigt es. Der Bühnenarbeiter hängt ihm einen glänzenden Mantel um, der das Podium verdeckt. Der Clown steht so, dass er dem Publikum fast den Rücken zukehrt. Bei heftigen Bewegungen wird jeweils eine Seite seines Gesichtes sichtbar.

Clown (Mikrophon), den Hauptmann anbrüllend: Was erlauben sie sich? Sind sie wahnsinnig geworden? Wissen sie nicht wen sie vor sich haben? Das ist eine Unverschämtheit!

Hauptmann, salutierend: Zu Befehl! Verzeihung, ich habe sie nicht …

Clown: Sie erkennen ihren obersten Kriegsherren nicht? Sie sind degradiert! Man hat seinen obersten Kriegsherren selbst dann zu erkennen, wenn er inkognito reist! (Zu den Soldaten); Nehmen sie diesen Mann fest! (Die Soldaten nehmen den Hauptmann in die Mitte.) Stillgestanden! (Die Drei erstarren.) Ich will nach diesem unliebsamen Zwischenfall zum Grund meines Besuches kommen, der zugleich eine Inspektion ist, vor allem aber eurer Aufmunterung dienen soll. (Pause. Mit kläffendem Gebrüll:) Ihr seid die Stützen der Verfassung. Die meisten Putschversuche werden von den Militärs angezettelt. Die meisten Putschversuche werden von den Militärs niedergeschlagen. Wenn es keine Armee gäbe, gäbe es keine Kriege. Das ist das Ei des Kolumbus. In der glitzernden Pracht meiner Epauletten, in dem schmeichelnden Geklirr meiner Orden, im Takt meiner Stiefel, liegt meine Stärke. (Er brüllt, im Gegensatz zum kommenden Text, weiter.) Milde, welche Milde habe ich über meinen Feind ausgeschüttet. Strenge, fürwahr, welche Strenge für meine Freunde? Aber das war sinnvoll. Gerade seine Freunde muss man sieben, gerade bei ihnen muss man hart durchgreifen und sie zu brauchbarem Material formen. Wir müssen alle mehr Härte an den Tag legen. Denn unser stolzes, kühnes Volk soll nicht durch die Anwesenheit der schleimigen, von aller Welt verdammten Nachtschnecken und anderer Ungeziefer – so muss jeder treue, aufrechte Staatsbürger diese Elemente bezeichnen – verunsichert und verschneckt werden. Denkt an unsere prallen weißhäutigen Frauen, die uns mit geschminkten Lippen zujubeln und mit weichen Händen Beifall klatschen. (Aus dem Lautsprecher dringt dreimal unverständliches Volksgebrüll, das der Clown in starrer Haltung entgegennimmt.) Die Tageslosung lautet – niemals, aber auch niemals, verschnecken! (Abermaliges Gebrüll.) Ich persönlich bin der Garant dafür, dass unser Volk niemals verschneckt. (Gebrüll, er hebt besänftigend die Hände, der Lärm fällt zusammen.) Und das, solange ich hier (klopft ekstatisch auf eine imaginäre Brüstung, man hört das Klopfen überlaut) an der Spitze des Staates stehe und unsere Fahnen dem lieben Gott geweiht sind. (Stille. Clown zaghaft): Hab ich was falsches gesagt?

Regisseur: Lassen sie Gott aus dem Spiel.

Clown: Ich sprach von geweihten Fahnen. Gut, betrachten sie den Satz als gestrichen. Die Fahnenweihe ist für mich nicht existent, Herr Regisseur. Es kommen diesbezüglich noch einige Sätze, die ich lieber weglassen werde.

Regisseur: Reden sie stumm weiter.

Clown: Wie sie wünschen (gestikuliert).

1.Herr: Der Krieg hat auch sein Gutes. Denken sie an die glücklichen Jahre des Aufbaus.

2.Herr: Und an die derzeitige Sagnation der Wirtschaft. Die Kriegsopfer waren eben im Grunde genommen …

1.Herr: Wirtschaftsopfer.

Regisseur: Ich bitte um Ruhe!

Der Soldat ist inzwischen an seinen Ausgangspunkt zurückgerobbt.

In strammer Haltung zum Hauptmann: Befehl ausgeführt (salutiert).

Seine Kameraden weisen mit stummen Kopfbewegungen nach dem Clown.

Der Soldat dreht sich um und salutiert noch zackiger: Mein oberster Kriegsherr!

Clown: Das nenne ich militärische Schulung. Erkennen, begreifen und sofort reagieren. Bravo, junger Mann. Wie sehen sie denn aus? Was haben sie ausgefressen? Welches Regiment?

Dritter Soldat brüllt etwas Unverständliches.

Clown: Was wird ihnen zur Last gelegt?

3.Soldat: Herr Hauptmann haben mir den Befehl erteilt, um den Platz zu robben.

Clown: Das ist gut. Weshalb?

3.Soldat: Ich habe das vorletzte Wort seiner Ansprache nicht behalten.

Clown: So, so, der Herr Hauptmann hält Ansprachen. War sie bedeutend?

3.Soldat: Ich glaube nicht.

Clown: Sie hatten also nicht den Eindruck, dass er mit mir konkurrieren wollte?

3.Soldat: Nein.

Clown: Der Hauptmann steht unter Arrest. Sie sind ein tüchtiger Soldat. Intelligent und von rascher Auffassungsgabe. Ich übergebe ihnen das Kommando.

3.Soldat: Ich bitte meinen ehemaligen Vorgesetzten nicht hart zu bestrafen.

Clown: Eine edle Gesinnung. Tun sie mit ihm was sie für erforderlich halten.

Während der Clown, gestützt von Bühnenarbeitern, vom Podest steigt, sich den Mantel abnehmen lässt, der achtlos zu Boden geschleudert wird und anschließend das Podest langsam in eine Ecke trägt, die Soldaten strammstehen, der neu ernannte Hauptmann salutiert und die Balletteuse einige Schritte geht, der 1.Herr zum anderen: Eine gute Sache fordert eben ihre Opfer.

2.Herr: Lieber Herr Kollege, die Toten stanken bestialisch. Eine alte Frau lag drei Wochen vor meinem Haus, auf der gegenüberliegenden Straßenseite. Stellen sie sich das vor, ganze drei Wochen und das noch dazu im Sommer! Ein Bombensplitter, wissen sie, ein Splitter hatte sie erwischt. Und dann die Fliegen. Die fetten, grünen meine ich. Sie setzten sich auf die Speisen. Sie ertranken in der Suppe. Ekelhaft!

1.Herr: Bei der Verwesung handelt es sich um einen simplen Zersetzungsprozess … den gleichen Vorgang haben wir beispielsweise bei der Gärung …

2.Herr: Sie wollen mir doch nicht Vorlesungen halten.

1.Herr: Aber keinesfalls, nichts läge mir ferner … (gestikulieren oder flüstern, wobei ihre Gesten nicht dem Flüsterton entsprechen).

3.Soldat zum ehemaligen Hauptmann: Sie haben ihn also nicht erkannt. Antworten sie, sie Trottel!

Ehemaliger Hauptmann, jetzt 3.Soldat: Zu Befehl, nein.

Hauptmann: Stillgestanden! Nehmen sie Haltung an, wenn sie antworten!

3.Soldat: Zu Befehl!

Hauptmann: Sie schlafen ja. Ich werde für ihre Ermunterung sorgen. Robben sie um den Platz. Ein bisschen Tempo vorlegen, wenn ich bitten darf! (Soldat wirft sich zu Boden). Sehen sie die Richtigkeit meiner Entscheidung ein?

Soldat von unten: Jawohl!

Hauptmann: Ohne Disziplin kann die Armee nicht bestehen.

Soldat: Jawohl.

Hauptmann: Würden sie mir die Stiefel küssen, wenn ich es befehle?

Soldat: Befehl ist Befehl Herr Hauptmann!

Hauptmann: Auch schleckend!

Soldat: Mit Vergnügen?

Hauptmann: Dann schlecken sie.

Soldat: Es ist mir eine Ehre.

Hauptmann: Bei der modernen Ausbildung arbeitet man mit Fingerspitzengefühl. Sie sehen welche Freude ich ihren Kameraden bereite. (Nach unten sprechend) es genügt.

Soldat: Berauben sie mich nicht des Vergnügens.

Hauptmann: Nein, genug. Mein Entgegenkommen hat Grenze. Robben sie jetzt und kühlen sie ihre Leidenschaft.

Soldat: Gern (robbt).

Hauptmann zu den beiden Soldaten: Sind sie zur Wache eingeteilt.

Soldat: Zu Befehl! (Sie schultern die Gewehre und gehen auf der linken (rechten) Bühnenseite auf und ab. Der Hauptmann verschwindet unter den Arkaden.)

Jung.Schausp.: Das ist noch ein größeres Schwein als der andere.

Alt.Schausp.: Aus Lämmern wachsen Wölfe.

Jung.Schausp.: Wir brauchen dringend etwas zum Beißen. Wir brauchen Geld. Ich möchte mich wieder einmal besaufen. Ich möchte … glaubst du, dass man uns engagiert?

Alt.Schausp.: Gefällt dir der Laden?

Jung.Schausp.: Gefällt, gefällt – bei unserer Lage haben wir keine Wahl.

Negerin, die mit dem Direktor weiter in den Vordergrund getreten worden ist, zum Direktor: Gefalle ich ihnen wirklich? Sie geizen nicht mit Komplimenten.

Alt.Schausp.: Man müsste dem Direktor ein paar Komplimente machen. Von wegen Ruf dieses renommierten Theaters und so. Am besten du sprichst mit ihm. Du bist der bessere Rezitator. Seit der Bär krepiert ist geht es mit uns bergab.

Jung.Schausp.: Ein Maul weniger zu stopfen.

Alt.Schausp.: Ich bin sehr an ihm gehangen. Sein Tod stimmt mich traurig. Geh, stell dich vor. Und wenn es nur eine Nebenrolle ist. Vielleicht auch zwei.

Negerin: Eine Nebenrolle würde ich keinesfalls spielen.

Direktor: Wo denken sie hin, meine Liebe, wie könnte ich sowas von ihnen verlangen?

Alt.Schausp.: Geh schon.

Jung.Schausp.: Dabei würde ich den aufgeblasenen Kerl am liebsten in den Arsch treten.

Alt.Schausp.: Emotionen können wir uns nicht leisten.

Direktor zur Negerin: Darf ich ihnen eine … (kramt in den Taschen)

Bühnenarbeiter zu den beiden Schauspielern: Zigarette? (Betont lässig)

Direktor das Päckchen hinhaltend: Anbieten?

Jung.Schausp. fischt zwei aus der Schachtel des Bühnenarbeiters: Danke!

Negerin zum Direktor: Ah, die Sorte rauchen sie?

Jung.Schausp. zum Bühnenarbeiter: Sie schmeckt ausgezeichnet.

Negerin zum Direktor: Einfach wunderbar.

Alt.Schausp.: So ein Kraut habe ich schon lange vermisst … ich genieße es …

Negerin: Ich rauche nämlich selten aber wenn dann intensiv.

Alt.Schausp.: … und inhaliere jeden Zug mit Genuss.

Negerin: Da ich heute sowieso indisponiert bin kann ich mir's leisten.

Direktor: Davon habe ich nichts bemerkt gnädige Frau.

Negerin: Doch, doch, ich bin fürchterlich erkältet. Das macht das Klima. Ich bin die Tropen gewöhnt.

Jung.Schausp. der an den Direktor herangetreten ist: Pardon, wenn ich sie unterbreche. Ich will sie nicht lange aufhalten, Herr Direktor. Mein Kollege und ich sind … ich wollte sagen wir haben im Moment kein festes Engagement. Zumindest keines, das unseren Leistungen entspricht. Sicher, viele Bühnen reißen sich um uns aber für Chargenrollen sind wir uns zu schade, deshalb wäre es uns eine Ehre bei ihrem vorzüglichen Ensemble mitwirken zu dürfen.

Direktor: So?

Balletteuse zum Clown der ihre Schenkel tätschelt: Hör sofort auf! Gib die Pfoten weg! Du störst mich in meiner Meditation.

Direktor zum jung.Schausp.: Merken sie nicht, dass sie stören?

Jung.Schausp.: Entschuldigen sie, aber ich dachte sie hätten noch eine Nebenrolle unbesetzt oder zwei.

Direktor: Erstens einmal redet man mich nicht mit sie, sondern mit sehr verehrter Herr Direktor an, und das am Anfang jedes Satzes. Dabei deutet man eine Verneigung an und schließt demutsvoll die Augen. Zweitens reicht man vorher ein schriftliches Bittgesuch ein. Drittens unterbricht man mich nicht (schreiend). Weg mit ihnen, sie Flegel! Wenn man ihnen Manieren beigebracht hat, kommen sie wieder. Ich erwarte von meinen Ensemblemitgliedern eiserne Disziplin. Eine Tugend, die sie noch lernen müssen.

Jung.Schausp.: Sehr verehrter Herr Direktor …

Direktor: Was wollen sie noch, ich habe keine Zeit!

Jung.Schausp.: Eine Minute …

Direktor: Nicht eine Sekunde. Ich bin beschäftigt, das sehen sie doch. Ich weiß nicht, wo mir der Kopf steht. Ein Termin jagt den anderen. Jeder kommt mit seinen Problemen zu mir. Beleuchter, Regisseure, Bühnenbildner, Schauspieler. Die Entlüftung funktioniert nicht. Es regnet durchs Dach. Dann streikt wieder das technische Personal. Ich muss mit dem Betriebsrat verhandeln. Die Drehbühne klemmt. Ein Scheinwerfer fällt aus. Die Probe muss durch die Erkrankung des Hauptdarstellers verschoben werden. Die Premiere fällt ins Wasser. Einer alternden Diva muss die Gretchenrolle ausgeredet werden. Die Kostüme kommen zu spät aus der Schneiderei und erwecken noch dazu den Protest der Schauspieler. Der Vorhang klemmt. Die Requisiten reichen nicht, und was es da sonst noch an Verzögerungen und Unannehmlichkeiten gibt. Alles lastet auf meinem Rücken. Ich opfere mich auf. Ich tue mein Bestes. Ich schlichte, arrangiere, improvisiere. Natürlich ernte ich keinen Dank. Aber sie wissen ja selbst wie das ist. Sie sind ja vom Theater. Ein Laie hat nicht die blasseste Ahnung von diesem Betrieb. Sie sind doch kein Laie? Sie sind doch Schauspieler. Dann müssen sie mich verstehen. Ich setze das voraus. Was wollten sie eigentlich?

Jung.Schausp.: Ich wollte nur …

Direktor: Ach ja, ich erinnere mich … Sie wollten Ensemblemitglied werden. Ich habe jetzt keine Sekunde Zeit. Kommen sie ein andermal wieder.

Jung.Schausp.: Wann?

Direktor: Was … wann? Sagen wir morgen, übermorgen, wann immer sie Zeit haben. Hat mich sehr gefreut. (Zieht die Negerin beiseite.)

Der jung.Schausp. geht mit dem Wort “verdammt“ auf seinen Platz zurück.

Alt.Schausp.: Was war? Hast du was erreicht?

Jung.Schausp.: Wieder nichts.

Alt.Schausp.: Scheiße.

Direktor zur Negerin: Ich möchte sie gerne einladen, falls sie nichts besseres vorhaben. Ich kenne ein nettes Lokal. Dort könnten wir das Weitere in Ruhe besprechen.

Negerin: Gern. (Direktor bietet ihr den Arm an. Beide gehen hinter der Maschine ab.)

Jung.Schausp.: Hochnäsiger Affe. Rotzlöffel. Ich möchte ihm die Zähne einzeln ausbrechen. Aber langsam, damit er es genießt.

Der robbende Soldat ist bei den Schauspielern angekommen.

Soldat, weinerlich: Sehen sie mich an. Dabei habe ich nur meine Pflicht erfüllt. Als Vorgesetzter war ich streng aber gerecht. Vielleicht manchmal ein bisschen zu streng, aber das bringt der Beruf mit sich. Dabei bin ich privat der gutmütigste Mensch der Welt und ein vorbildlicher Familienvater. Ich kann keiner Fliege etwas zuleide tun. Wollen sie ein Familienfoto sehen? (Kramt in der Brusttasche. Die Suche wird durch Liegen erschwert.) Nein? Sie wollen nicht? Jedes Wochenende fahre ich mit meiner Familie ins Grüne. Im Herbst lassen wir Drachen steigen. Manchmal jausnen wir bei der Großmutter. Ich meine bei meiner Mutter und der Großmutter meiner

Kinder, die in einem Häuschen am Stadtrand lebt. Sie ist auch im Besitz eines Gärtchens und versorgt uns mit frischem Obst. Das ist sehr angenehm. Ich bin ein mäßiger Trinker. Ich rauche nicht. Am wohlsten fühle ich mich in meinem gemütlichen Heim. Wollen sie das Bild sehen? (Zeigt ihnen eine Photographie. Die beiden beachten ihn nicht. Sie zeigen abwechselnd auf die Balletteuse, die wieder übt, wobei der junge Schauspieler und der Clown obszöne Gebärden austauschen.) Also das (zeigt) ist mein ältester. Wie alt? Siebzehn, im Februar wird er siebzehn. Nächstes Jahr macht er das Examen. Ja, ein guter Schüler. Ich kann mich nicht beklagen. Da, rechts, das ist meine Frau. Neben ihr mein Zweitältester und daneben der Jüngste. Er ist erst fünf. Das ist Waldi, unser Dackel. Nein, das Licht ist zu schwach. Ich habe geglaubt die Sonne genügt. Das ist das Haus meiner Mutter. Ja, das ist meine Mutter. (Steckt die Fotos ein. Seine Antworten müssen selbstverständlich nach gewisser Zeit erfolgen. Er lauscht vor jeder Erwiderung, angestrengt. Wegkriechend.) Es ist nämlich schade um die Aufnahmen. Ich hatte kein Blitzlicht bei mir. (Er wendet den Schauspielern bereits den Rücken zu.) Nein, danke, wie gesagt, ich bin Nichtraucher. Ich habe mir das Rauchen vor Jahren abgewöhnt. (Schnaufend) Seitdem geht es mir gesundheitlich viel besser. Sie brauchen mich aber deswegen nicht für einen Gesundheitsapostel halten. Ja, anfangs habe ich zugenommen … aber da … (Er taucht in den Requisiten unter. Man hört nur Gemurmel.)

Jung.Schausp., sich lang ausstreckend: Ich werde ein Nickerchen machen. Die Erde dreht sich auch so weiter. Auch morgen und übermorgen. Der verdammte Hund. (Gähnt) Aber ich lasse nicht locker. Bis ich ihm so auf die Nerven falle, dass er mir eine Rolle gibt.

Alt.Schausp.: Wir haben kein Bier mehr. (Schwenkt die leere Flasche.)

Jung.Schausp.: Hab‘ keinen Durst. Ich möchte schlafe. Ich möchte den Ärger wegschlafen, nur eingehüllt in einen weichen, traumlosen Schlaf sein. In wattiger Leere, sonst nichts.

Alt.Schausp.: Die Erde dreht sich auch weiter, wenn er schläft. Vielleicht …

Jung.Schausp., schläfrig: Was?

Alt.Schausp.: Ist das Universum der ungeheure Rest eines Toten? Vielleicht ist unsere Galaxie ein Teil seines verwesenden Magens?

Jung.Schausp., schläfrig: Vielleicht ei Teil seines verwesenden Hirns? Die fantastische Reflexion eines irren Hirns.

Alt.Schausp.: Die fantastische Reflexion eines verwesenden Gehirns. Du meinst wir existieren gar nicht?

Jung.Schausp.: Kann sein.

Alt.Schausp. tritt ihn.

Jung.Schausp.: Au!

Alt.Schausp.: Du jedenfalls existierst.

Jung.Schausp.: Leider, mir knurrt der Magen. Ich kann nicht einmal schlafen.

Alt.Schausp.: Dann bleib so liegen. Du verbrauchst weniger Kalorien.

Wissenschaftler, hinter der Maschine auftauchend: Bald habe ich es geschafft. Die Entwicklung der Technik beruht auf einer immer komplexeren Verfeinerung der Grundideen. (Hantiert an der Maschine.)

Clown, nach hinten rufend: Wem interessiert das? Bleib in deinem Gehäuse! (Zur Balletteuse) Entzückend.

Balletteuse: Wie bitte?

Clown: Hast du ein süßes Ärschchen. Lass mich bitte nur einmal, nur einmal, hin greifen. Bitte. Ich führe dir zuliebe die tollsten Scherze auf. Du brauchst nur ja zu sagen.

Balletteuse: Aber nur einmal. Ehrenwort!

Clown: Ehrenwort!

(Balletteuse stützt die Hände gegen den Quader und streckt ihm die Kehrseite hin. Er kniet sich nieder und streichelt die Rundungen. Die Balletteuse stößt ihn mit dem Hinterteil zurück. Er fällt um.)

Balletteuse: Ich habe gesagt nur einmal. Wo bleibt dein Ehrenwort?

Clown: Ich bitte vielmals um Entschuldigung. Meine Hände haben sich selbständig gemacht, als sie über die köstlichen Rundungen glitten. Sie sind mir davongelaufen. Ich konnte sie nichtmehr einfangen. Ich bin schuldlos. (Überreicht ihr eine rote Papierblume.)

Balletteuse, die sich ihm zugewandt hat: Was soll ich damit? (Wirft sie achtlos über die Schulter.)

Clown: Du hast mein Herz in den Abfall geworfen. (Lautes, greinendes Weinen.)

Balletteuse: Ich will deine Späße sehen. Los! Ich möchte lachen. Spielen wir das uralte Spiel.

Clown, weinend: Muss das sein?

Balletteuse: Du hast es versprochen.

Pantomime.

Der Clown schlägt Purzelbäume, zaubert Blumensträuße aus dem Ärmel und streut sie über die Balletteuse. Spielt auf einer winzigen Geige, die er vorher unter grotesker Mimik stimmt. (Er setzt oft zum Spielen an, findet aber immer wieder Klangfehler. Die Geige ist natürlich stumm.) Er setzt sich mehrfach neben den Sessel, will der Balletteuse die Hand küssen und stolpert dabei. Er bindet sich am Boden sitzend die Masche seines Schuhs und kommt erst unter vielen Anstrengungen wieder hoch. Er fällt auf den Rücken und zappelt wie ein Käfer, zieht mit dem Zeigefinger den Mund zu einer lachenden Grimasse und verrenkt den Kopf.

Das alles vollführt er unter lautem Weinen, das anfangs komisch, später rührend und gegen Ende beängstigend echt wirken soll. Seine Bewegungen werden tragischer. Er verbeugt sich vor der Tänzerin, legt die Rechte aufs Herz, bietet es ihr an, hebt schmachtend die Arme, lässt sie resignierend wieder sinken, hebt sie abermals, diesmal schon zaghafter, lässt sie sinken, macht einen dritten, schwachen Ansatz zum Händeheben und schüttelt betrübt den Kopf. Steht mit hängendem Kopf und hängenden Armen da. Reißt sich mit einer jähen Bewegung das Herz aus der Brust und bietet es der Tänzerin in der flachen Schale seiner Hände dar. Sie zuckt die Achseln. Das Herz in den weit vorgestreckten Händen haltend rutscht er knieend auf sie zu. Sie macht eine hochmütige Geste. Er legt das unsichtbare aber durch seine Bewegungen fast greifbar gewordene Herz vorsichtig vor ihre Füße. (Das muss unglaublich zart und behutsam, fast zitternd geschehen. Sein Weinen geht dabei in stoßweises Schluchzen über. Die Balletteuse lehnt, bis zum Herzopfer, mit verschränkten Armen an dem Quader. Anfangs langweilt sie sich aber je tragischer die Gesten des Clowns werden umso mehr lacht sie. (Ihr Lachen muss passiven Charakter haben und darf das Weinen des Clowns keinesfalls übertönen.) Der dicht vor ihr knieende Clown hebt die Arme und weist auf sein Herz. Sie zerquetscht es mit der Ferse und schleudert die Reste mit der Fußspitze zur Seite. Gongschlag. Der Clown fällt aufs Gesicht und bleibt leblos liegen. Sie setzt den nach unten abgewinkelten Fuß zierlich auf seinen Rücken. Dabei stößt sie, in Siegesgöttinnen Pose, einen Arm nach vorne, streckt den anderen zurück und wölbt die Brust vor, sodass die Pose etwas sieghaft, vorwärtsstürmendes hat. Das lebende Bild dauert etwa eine halbe Minute. In der zweiten Hälfte der Pantomime kann leise Musik einsetzen.

Unterdessen hat der Wissenschaftler die Maschine geputzt, an Hebeln gedreht, Klappen inspiziert, Drähte zurechtgebogen, Lampen ausgetauscht. Das alles macht er mit ruhigen unauffälligen Bewegungen. Sein sachlich gesprochener Text kommt:

.1. Beim stummen Gegenspiel des Clowns.

.2. Während der Clown am Rücken liegt, wie ein Käfer zappelt und dabei manchmal erschöpft pausiert.

1.Text: Maschinen haben ihre Harmonien und Disharmonien, die einander ablösen. Ich würde sie als praktische Kunstwerke bezeichnen. Sie können dem Schöpfer genauso wie diese entgleiten. Sie können selbständig werden und sich gegen die Herrchen wenden, sie können beißen. Ah, zu locker. Gleich

Kindchen. Ihr erstes Surren schlägt den Erfindern und den Mitarbeitern, die sich begreiflicherweise mit den Erfindern identisch fühlen, wie das Geklingel von tausend Kinderstimmen, ans Ohr. (Pause). Die Schraube müsste noch angezogen werden … (Pause) ich muss mit größerer Akribie arbeiten … zum Wohl der Menschheit, im Sinn der Charité … so, das ist jetzt in Ordnung …

2.Text: Der Mensch bezeichnet sich als Krone der Schöpfung. Warum soll die technische Entwicklung nicht die Krone des Menschen sein? Eine Krone aus Gammastrahlen, Hunderttausendvolt, Milliarden von Pferdestärken, gebündelter Sonnenenergie, dem Gesang der Raketen und Benzinmotoren, einem glücklichen Leben mit Ventilatoren, Akkumulatoren, Sensoren, Rotoren. Eine Krone aus Anspruchssteigerung, die durch Produktionssteigerung befriedigt wird, eine Krone, die Hygiene, Tatendrang und Gesundheit ausstrahlt. Eine Krone, die nicht mehr mit sentimentalen, unberechenbaren, unpraktischen, sadistischen und masochistischen, mit von Mystizismus geschwängerten Bazillen der Vergangenheit behaftet ist. Der Mensch wird aufrecht und klar in die Welt blicke, die Natur und seine Gefühle beherrschen, sich in der von ihm geschaffenen Umgebung wohlfühlen und nur das Mögliche und Nutzbringende anstreben. Ich sehe Swimmingpools, leuchtende Wiesen, gläserne Meeresstädte, glückliche Kinder, Erwachsene, die bis ins hohe Alter aktiv bleiben, Mondfarmen, helle, hochgewachsene Menschen in sportlichen Anzügen, umweltfreundliche, lautlose Fortbewegungsmittel … Obstgärten, die dreimal im Jahr tragen, ein gemäßigtes Klima … (geht putzend hinter die Maschine).

Die Tänzerin wird von allen Schauspielern mit kurzem, dünnen Beifall bedacht. Sie nimmt den Fuß vom Rücken des Liegenden.

Der Clown springt auf und versetzt der Balletteuse eine schallende Ohrfeige: Du Luder, was erlaubst du dir eigentlich?

Balletteuse: Entschuldigung … ich, ich (schluchzend) habe sie nicht erkannt, Meister. (Leise weinend). Ich bitte sie vielmals um Entschuldigung. Bitte behalten sie mich trotzdem. Ich werde ab heute immer pünktlich zur Probe kommen. Das verspreche ich hoch und heilig.

Clown: Wirst du es wirklich, du Schlampe?

Balletteuse: Ich verspreche es ihnen, Meister.

Der Clown umkreiste, die Hände in die Hüften gestemmt, die Balletteuse: So, wirst du das? Deine Leistung ist miserabel. Du bist mittelmäßig begabt. Eine kleine, unbegabte Ballettratte. Ein Nichts, ein vollkommenes Nichts.

Balletteuse: Ich weiß, Meister.

Clown: Ah – du weißt es. Und da wagst du mir unter die Augen zu treten?

Balletteuse: Ich werde alles tun was sie wollen. Wirklich alles.

Clown: So, wirst du das? Nur ich kann aus dir eine Tänzerin machen. Wenn ich wollte eine Ballerina. Aber dazu wird deine kümmerliche Begabung kaum reichen. Bist du die Mühe überhaupt wert? Ich frage mich ernstlich ob du der Mühe wert bist?

Balletteuse: Wenn sie es nur versuchen würde.

Clown, vor ihr stehend: Gut, ich werde mit dir spielen. Wenn du nicht parierst, fliegst du.

Balletteuse, knicksend: Danke Meister.

Clown: Zeig deine Schenkel. (Befühlt sie.) Ich habe schon besseres Material in der Hand gehalten.

Balletteuse: Meine Schenkel, meine Hüften, meine Brust, mein Bauch, alles, alles steht zu ihrer Verfügung, Meister. Formen sie mich. Lassen sie mich nicht fallen.

Clown: So und du glaubst, dass du die nötige Begabung mitbringst?

Balletteuse: Ich hoffe auf ihr Genie.

Clown: Aha, du setzt also deine ganze Hoffnung auf mich. Na schön! Wir werden sehen, ob du was taugst. Den Grundschritt bitte! Schlecht, noch einmal! Lockerer, sie bewegen sich wie ein Trampeltier. (Er lässt sie unter den stereotypen Befehlen üben. Noch einmal, bitte. Lockerer den Grundschritt. (Seine Stimme ist leise, aber klar verständlich.)

2. Soldat, an dem Schauspieler vorbeirobbend: Die Pflichten des modernen Soldaten erfordern Entschlusskraft, Eigeninitiative und Verantwortungsbewusstsein. Jeder junge Mensch, der sich zu einer verantwortungsvollen Aufgabe berufen fühlt, sollte der Armee beitreten. Sie können sich auch als Lastkraftwagenfahrer, Ingenieur oder Techniker fortbilden, und zwar auf Kosten des Heeres. Der ideale Beruf für dynamische, junge Menschen. Wir bieten eine gesicherte Stellung und ein geregeltes Einkommen, aber sie dürfen nie vergessen, dass unsere gemütliche Kriegsspielerei … (Er robbt hinter die Requisiten.)

Clown wieder lauter: Noch einmal, bitte. Lockerer! Sie bewegen sich wie ein Nilpferd. Graziöser! Noch einmal, bitte, lockerer. Nein, so geht das nicht. (Die Balletteuse steht mit hängenden Armen verzweifelt da.) Sie müssen sich etwas anstrengen, Kindchen.

Balletteuse: Ich versuche ja mein Bestes.

Clown: Ihr Bestes ist nicht gut genug. Ich vergeude da meine Zeit.

Balletteuse: Ich bemühe mich ja.

Clown: Also. Grundschritt. Stellen sie die Beine anders, sie Trampel! Graziöser, anmutiger! Also, Grundschritt. Nein. Nein. Sehen sie, so macht man das. (Er macht ihr den Grundschritt vor. Clownesk, er rutscht aus, taumelt, flattert mit den Händen.)

Balletteuse, bewundernd: Meister!

Clown: Was?

Balletteuse: Ob ich ihn je so können werde, Meister?

Clown: So nicht, annähernd vielleicht. Aber sie haben gesehen, was man aus der Grundstellung machen kann.

Balletteuse: Ich bewundere sie.

Clown: Das ist mir egal. Von ihnen bewundert zu werden ist keine Auszeichnung.

Balletteuse: Selbstverständlich nicht, Meister!

Clown: Aber weiter, weiter. Also Grundstellung. Und Grundstellung. Und Grundstellung. Und Grundstellung. Und Grundstellung. Und Grundstellung. Sie sind erschöpft, nicht wahr?

Balletteuse: Nein Meister, ich bin nicht erschöpft.

Clown: Sie wagen mir zu widersprechen? (Rascher) Und Grundstellung. Und Grundstellung. Und Grundstellung. Und

Grundstellung. Und Grundstellung. Sind sie noch immer nicht erschöpft, liebes Kind?

Balletteuse: Etwas.

Clown: Umso besser. (Sehr rasch) Und Grundstellung. Und Grundstellung. Und Grundstellung. Und Grundstellung. Und Grundstellung.

Balletteuse: Ich kann nicht mehr.

Clown: Sehen sie, wie ich gesagt habe, sie taugen nichts.

Balletteuse: Aber ich bemühe mich doch so.

Clown: Mühen allein nützt nichts, wenn kein Talent vorhanden ist. Sehen sie mich an. Es wurde mir von einer gütigen Fee in die Wiege gelegt und trotzdem habe ich hart an mir gearbeitet. Oder glauben sie der Ruhm fällt einen in den Schoß? Nein, nein meine Beste dahinter steckt härteste Arbeit. Arbeit bis zur Selbstaufgabe. Sie haben mich erschöpft. Üben sie allein weiter.

Balletteuse: Darf ich hoffen?

Clown: Das kommt auf ihren Fortschritt an. Mit Sicherheit kann ich noch nichts sagen. (Er setzt sich auf die Bühne.)

Die Balletteuse bewegt sich während der ganzen Prozedur klarerweise mit Grazie und Geschmeidigkeit. Sie übt weiter aber sehr langsam (Zeitlupe) und mit großen Pausen. Die Pausen dauern jeweils ein paar Minuten.

Der Hauptmann tritt unter den Arkaden hervor. Er ist leicht angeheitert. Die Wachen salutieren stramm.

Hauptmann: Rührt euch! Wo ist die degradierte Kanaille?

1.Soldat: Robbt, Herr Hauptmann.

Hauptmann: Gut.

2.Soldat: Da kommt sie, Herr Hauptmann.

3.Soldat ist zu den Füßen des Hauptmanns gerobbt. Er hat grüne Zweige um den Helm gebunden.

Hauptmann: Wo? Ich sehe ihn nicht …

2.Soldat: Unter ihnen, Herr Hauptmann.

Hauptmann: Da sind sie ja endlich! Wo treiben sie sich herum?

3.Soldat, liegend: Befehl ausgeführt, Herr Hauptmann!

Hauptmann: Man soll nichts übertreiben. Stehen sie auf. (Nach den Zweigen greifend.) Sie sind wohl noch ein bisschen infantil? In dem Alter Indianer spielen! Welcher Häuptling sind sie?

3.Soldat: Zu Befehl Herr Hauptmann. Ich habe mich getarnt.

Hauptmann: Wie sie aussehen! Putzen sie den Dreck ab. Was für ein Objekt wollen sie überfallen? Eine Ranch? Oder ein Fort? Eine Wagenkolonne? He?

3.Soldat: Zu Befehl, Herr Hauptmann belieben zu scherzen.

Hauptmann: Ja, großer Häuptling. (Zu Allen.) Wir schalten eine Rastpause ein. Wir machen Rast. Wir machen … ja … Rast. Setzen sie sich. Ich habe ihnen etwas Erfreuliches mitzuteilen. Es wird bald Krieg geben.

Die Soldaten starren unter Gemurmel einander an, schütteln die Köpfe und beobachten den Hauptmann, der ihnen den Rücken zukehrt.

1.Herr zum 2.: Übrigens, Indianer sind der letzte Modeschrei. Die Büchereien sind voll von Publikationen über sie, seitdem es publik geworden ist, wie bestialisch diese Rasse ausgerottet wurde. Amerika klopft sich reuig an die Brust.

2.Herr: Ich habe gehört, dass teilweise bakteriologische Waffen eingesetzt wurden.

1.Herr: Amerika war uns schon immer weit voraus, verehrter Herr Kollege.

2.Herr: Vor allem wenn es um die Deportation von Frauen und Kinder ging.

1.Herr: Was oft einem Todesurteil gleichkam.

2.Herr: In vielen Fällen hat man sich nicht die Mühe gemacht, sondern sie gleich an Ort und Stelle niedergemetzelt.

1.Herr: Mit Südamerika müssen wir noch ein bisschen Geduld haben aber ich versichere ihnen, bald werden entsprechende Bücher auf den Markt kommen.

2.Herr: Wieso?

1.Herr: Dort dezimiert man die Indianer gerade. Aber warten sie ab, in einigen Jahren können wir uns in aller Ruhe darüber aufregen.

Regisseur, der hinter die Beiden getreten ist, ernst: Viele werden den Weg der Tränen gehen.

2.Herr: Übrigens, wie hoch steht der Kurs für einen Indianerskalp?

1.Herr: Ich habe noch keine Börsenberichte gelesen. Außerdem kommt es darauf an ob es sich um die Kopfhaut eines Mannes, einer Frau oder eines Kindes handelt.

2.Herr: Ob Bub oder Mädchen ist aber egal, nicht?

Der Hauptmann zündet sich eine Zigarette an, zieht eine Karte aus der Tasche, faltet sie auseinander und breitet sie am Boden aus.

1.Herr: Wie wollen sie das bei dem kleinen. Blutigen Stückchen Haut mit Haaren dran diagnostizieren?

2.Herr: Sie haben glänzendes, schwarzes Haar. Wie Krähenschwingen.

1.Herr: Man kann aber auch das Skelet eines getöteten Häuptlings im Büro platzieren. Das macht sich sehr attraktiv. Vor allem, wenn es sich um einen berühmten Häuptling handelt.

2.Herr: Oder den Kopf am Jahrmarkt ausstellen. Zehn Cents Eintritt. Kinder die Hälfte.

Regisseur: Ich spreche jetzt den Text von Motavato, Häuptling der Cheyenne. (Sehr ernst.) "Obwohl mir Unrecht geschehen ist, bin ich voll Hoffnung. Ich habe nicht zwei Herzen … Wir sind zusammengekommen, um Frieden zu machen. Meine Scham ist groß, wie die Erde." (Zieht sich zurück.)

1.Herr: Weil sie gerade vom Deportieren und Metzeln sprechen. Ist in Europa nicht vor kurzem etwas ähnliches passiert?

2.Herr: Ich kann mich an nichts erinnern. Ich habe von nichts gewusst. Lassen sie diese alten Geschichten ruhen.

Hauptmann zu den Soldaten: Freut ihr euch nicht? (Faltet die Karte zusammen und steckt sie ein.) Ihr seht so belämmert drein. Das Morgenrot des Krieges steht vor der Tür. Es rötet die Fensterscheiben. Es bricht herein in die gute Stube und reißt die Männer mit sich fort. Echte Männer natürlich. In einem Bad aus Blut und Stahl wird die Nation gesunden.

Ja, Kameraden, Stahl auf Fleisch und Fleisch auf Stahl. Das ist eine Bewährungsprobe Kameraden! Singt doch! (Brüllend) Ein Lied! Eins, zwei, drei. Die Drei singen zögernd: Sah ein Knab ein Röslein stehn, sah's mit vielen Freuden …

Hauptmann: Ihr Arschlöcher! Verrückt geworden? Ein Soldatenlied natürlich! So ein Lied (grölt):

Schön ists ein Soldat zu sein,

So schön, so schön.

Wir hauen allen den Schädel ein,

wie schön, wie schön.

Und wenn dem Feind das Auge bricht,

dann spucken wir ihm ins Angesicht,

wie schön, wie schön.

Und wenn dem Feind das Auge bricht,

dann treten wir ihm ins Angesicht,

wie … schö …

Na was? Habt ihr die Sprache verloren?

1.Soldat: Wir sind das Töten nicht gewöhnt.

Hauptmann: Was? Scheißkerle. Und sowas will Soldat sein! Du bist ein Schandfleck der Armee.

1.Soldat: Wenn wenigstens ein Schlückchen Cognac da wäre.

2.Soldat: Das kräftigt …

3.Soldat: Wärmt den Magen.

1.Soldat: Mord ist ein hässliches Wort.

Hauptmann, brüllend: Wer redet denn von Mord? Soll ich sie wegen Defätismus an die Wand stellen lassen?

1.Soldat: Ich habe mich versprochen.

Hauptmann: Das will ich hoffen! Das will ich sehr hoffen! Außerdem hat die oberste Heeresleitung für alles gesorgt. (Zieht eine Flasche aus der Tasche und öffnet sie. Überlautes Geräusch, wenn der Stoppel entfernt wird. Die Soldaten zucken zusammen.) Da Kamerad! (Reicht die Flasche einem Soldaten.) Trink Kamerad! (Der Soldat schnuppert.)

1.Soldat: Beste Sorte? Fusel. Echter Fusel!

Hauptmann: Kosten sie!

1.Soldat kostet und hustet: Ganz schön scharf.

Hauptmann: Hab' ich dir zu viel versprochen?

2.Soldat: Ich habe Frau und Kinder daheim, außerdem bin ich Tierfreund.

Hauptmann: Gerade Frau und Kind solltest du ja beschützen. Das ist deine Aufgabe.

3.Soldat: Ich hab' in meinem Leben noch nie jemanden umgebracht.

Hauptmann: Höchste Zeit, dass du's lernst. Vor allem, wenn es einem guten Zweck dient.

3.Soldat: Das behauptet der Feind auch.

Hauptmann: Der Feind lügt. Der Feind lügt grundsätzlich. Der Feind ist grausam, brutal und feig. Der Feind vergewaltigt, spießt Kinder auf frisst Menschenfleisch. Er zerstört wertvolle Kulturgüter und handelt nach dem Prinzip der verbrannten

Erde. Der Feind ist ein Untermensch. Ein Barbar. Eine minderwertige Kreatur.

1.Soldat, trinkend: Ausgezeichnet. Brennt wie Feuer.

Hauptmann: Gib die Flasche weiter. Da sind noch mehr trockene Kehlen.

1.Soldat: Zu Befehl. Reicht sie dem Zweiten.

Hauptmann: Jeder nur einen Schluck! Disziplin, Kameraden!

2.Soldat: Brrr (Gibt die Flasche dem Dritten).

3.Soldat: Das hatte ich nötig (schnalzt mit der Zunge und reicht sie dem Hauptmann)

Hauptmann: Danke Kamerad. Ich habe mich schon bedient. Während des … während … nach … nach der Lagebesprechung, weißt du … nach der Lagebesprechung … im Offizierskasino … in der Kantine …

3.Soldat: Dann du. (Reicht sie dem ersten. Die Flasche kreist während des folgenden Gespräches. Sie sollte tatsächlich Flüssigkeit enthalten, damit der Vorgang echt wirkt.)

1.Soldat: Wir tun also nur unsere heilige Pflicht. Wir stehen nur zum Eid, den wir geschworen haben. Also kann uns nichts daran hindern, unsere heilige Pflicht zu tun, aber auch gar nichts.

Man hört Panzerkettengeklirr, das immer lauter wird. Die Soldaten blicken erst ängstlich umher und springen dann auf. Sie rufen. Man kann ihre Worte nicht verstehen. Sie deuten über die Köpfe des Publikums hinweg. Das sollte sehr zwingend wirken. Am besten wäre es, wenn sich ein Lautsprecher im Rücken des Publikums befinden würde. Ihre Kopfbewegungen folgen den einzelnen Panzern. Auch der Clown hat sich umgedreht. Der Bühnenarbeiter erklärt den beiden Schauspielern die einzelnen Typen. Er antwortet auf Fragen, verneint, streitet fast mit dem älteren, besteht auf die Richtigkeit seiner Behauptungen, verneint wieder und erklärt von neuem. Der Lärm hat seinen Höhepunkt erreicht. Der Direktor und die Negerin tauchen hinter der Maschine auf und starren fassungslos. Die Tänzerin unterbricht ihre Übung und hält sich die Ohren zu. Der Direktor schüttelt empört den Kopf, sagt etwas zur Negerin und zieht sich mit ihr zurück. Der Regisseur hebt die Arme und fuchtelt verneinend mit den Händen. Der Lärm erstirbt langsam.

Hauptmann, in den absterbenden Lärm hinein: Es waren die unseren.

1.Soldat: Gott sei Dank.

Hauptmann: Habt ihr gezählt?

2.Soldat: Soweit es ging. Die Staubwolke war zu dicht.

Hauptmann: Beruhigt euch das? Glaubt ihr nun an die Stärke unserer Waffen?

2.Soldat: Gepanzerte Urweltungetüme.

Hauptmann: Setzen wir uns wieder.

1.Soldat: Ich dachte schon …

2.Soldat: Beklemmend

1.Soldat: Da werden wir rennen … wie die Hasen.

Hauptmann: Selbstverständlich. Uns bleibt nur der Rest.

2.Soldat: Werden sich die Zähne ausbeißen.

1.Soldat, schüchtern: Klar.

Hauptmann: Setzen!

Sie lassen sich nieder.

1.Soldat: Ein imposantes Schauspiel. Die walzen jeden zu Brei.

Hauptmann: Die Aggressoren verdienen nichts Besseres. Aber Kinder, die Flasche ist ja halb voll. Weitermachen! (Sie trinken.)

Clown, zur Balletteuse, die ihre Übungen inzwischen wiederaufgenommen hat: Hören sie jetzt auf mein Fräulein. Es genügt für heute.

Balletteuse: Wie finden Sie mich?

Clown: Gut. Sie müssen nur noch etwas mehr Courage zeigen.

3.Soldat: Ich fühle mich stark wie ein Löwe.

Clown: Im Großen und Ganzen bin ich mit ihnen zufrieden.

2.Soldat: Ja, auch ich fühle mich schon besser.

Balletteuse: Danke. (Knickst, nimmt ein Buch und beginnt darin zu blättern. Erklärend zum Clown.) Ich studiere nämlich noch

Clown: Es fehlt ihnen nur noch ein bisschen Courage.

Die Balletteuse beachtet ihn nicht. Sie ist in die Lektüre vertieft.

2.Soldat: Ich schlag‘ der Welt den Schädel ein!

1.Soldat: Der reinste Nektar. (Trinkt) Nektar mit Spirituosengeschmack. Ich glaube, Petroleum ist auch dabei.

Clown: Alles braucht natürlich seine Zeit und viel Übung.

3.Soldat: Ich fühle wie ein alter Soldat, ein geübter Kämpfer.

Clown: Üben, üben und wieder üben.

3.Soldat, brüllend: Ich bin ein geübter Kämpfer!

Clown: Bei ihrem Talent kommt es nur auf die Übung an.

3.Soldat: Ich bin ein Kämpfer!

Clown: Und schonen sie sich in der Freizeit.

1.Soldat: Ich kenne keine Schonung. Weder für mich noch für andere.

Clown: Schonen sie sich und meiden sie den Alkohol.

1.Soldat: Ich schone niemanden. Ich bin besoffen!

2.Soldat, träumerisch: Ich auch …

3.Soldat: Ich fühle mich wie Gott … beschwipst …

Hauptmann: Der Vergleich hinkt.

3.Soldat: Sie haben prinzipiell recht.

1.Soldat: Bei meinem Husten! Wenn ich huste, springt das Weltall in Stücke!

2.Soldat zum Hauptmann: Er … er war früher Schauspieler (vertraulich) ein … ein miserabler Schauspieler.

Clown: Außerdem sollten sie sich vor Nässe und Erkältungen hüten. Eine rheumatischer Erk …

1.Soldat: Wer quatscht da immer dazwischen? (Stiert zum Clown hinüber.) Was geht dich mein Rheuma an?

Alle begaffen den Clown.

Jung.Schausp.: Besoffene Bande.

Alt.Schausp.: Sei ruhig!

Clown, sich den Soldaten zuwendend, gelassen: Ich habe nicht mit ihnen gesprochen.

Hauptmann: Kommen sie einmal her!

Clown zur Balletteuse: Das kostbare Instrument, auf dem sie spielen ist ihr Körper. Er darf nicht unnötigen Belastungen ausgesetzt werden.

Hauptmann: Sind sie taub? Sie sollen herkommen!

Clown: Das ist ein väterlicher Rat.

Hauptmann: He, wird's bald? Kommen sie schon. Das ist ein Befehl.

Clown: Sie haben mir nichts zu befehlen. Ich bin ein freier Mensch.

Hauptmann: Soll ich ihnen eine Einladung schicken? Na los!

(Winkt den Clown lässig her. Der reagiert nicht.)

Clown: Wenn sie etwas von mir wollen müssen sie schon herkommen.

Regisseur, der zum Clown getreten ist: Um Gottes Willen, reden sie nicht so! Das bringt uns ärger.

Hauptmann, brüllend: Na, wird's bald!

Regisseur: Gehen sie hin und entschuldigen sie sich.

Hauptmann: Ich warte.

Regisseur: Sagen sie es handelt sich um ein Missverständnis.

1.Soldat, mit schwerer Zunge: Trink einen Schluck mit uns! (Hebt die Flasche.) Komm!

2.Soldat: Mein Kamerad ladet dich ein. Hast du nicht gehört?

Regisseur: Gehen sie hin, solange es sich noch gütlich regeln …

Clown: Danke, ich trinke nicht.

1.Soldat: So komm schon her, du verdammter Zivilist!

3.Soldat: Willst du mich und meine Kameraden beleidigen?

Clown zum Regisseur: Es wird Zeit. (Hebt einen am Boden liegenden Regenmantel auf und zieht ihn an.)

2.Soldat: Wohin denn so eilig?

1.Soldat: He, dageblieben!

Regisseur: Beeilen sie sich!

3.Soldat: Was ist denn, nicht so hastig, alles mit der Ruhe, di bleibst noch da!

Regisseur: Schnell!

Hauptmann, aufspringend: Nehmt ihn fest!

Soldaten aufspringend, nicht gleichzeitig: Zu Befehl!

Regisseur: Ich habe sie gewarnt. (Schnell ab.)

Die Soldaten haben inzwischen die Bühne überquert und packen den Clown der nach rechts (links) strebt an den Armen.

Clown: Lassen sie mich los!

1.Soldat: Sie kommen mit! Sie sind verhaftet!

Clown: Wo ist der schriftliche Befehl? Lassen sie mich los!

1.Soldat: Nur nicht frech werden … lasst ihn los! (Die Soldaten treten zurück und flankieren ihn.)

1.Soldat: Vorwärts! (Der Clown zögert. Der zweite Soldat packt ihn am Ärmel.)

Clown: Lassen sie das! Ich kann allein gehen.

Hauptmann: Schneller! Macht ihm Beine!

Die Soldaten packen den Clown und schleifen ihn über die Bühne.

Hauptmann: Da sind sie ja endlich. Schade, dass sie nicht freiwillig gekommen sind. Es tut mir leid, dass ich sie abholen lassen musste. Hoffentlich hat man sie mit gebührender Ehrfurcht behandelt.

Clown: Ich bin ein freier Bürger. Ich protestiere.

Hauptmann: Aber selbstverständlich.

Clown: Lassen sie mich gehen! Ich habe nichts verbrochen.

Hauptmann: Sachte, sachte. (Nähertretend.) Warum wollen sie nicht mit uns trinken? Meine Kameraden haben sie doch freundlich eingeladen. Oder etwa nicht? Ist ihnen unsere Gesellschaft zu minderwertig?

Der Wissenschaftler setzt die Maschine in Gang. Aufleuchten der Glühlampen, rasseln, surren, pfeifen. Erst leise, später steigert sich die Lautstärke und endet in durchdringendem Sirenengeheul am Ende der Szene.

Clown schweigt.

Hauptmann: Ich habe sie was gefragt!

Clown, gequält: Das habe ich nicht behauptet.

Hauptmann: Ah, das haben sie nicht behauptet. Aber wahrscheinlich gedacht. Ich hatte schon gedacht sie wären stumm. Plötzlich verstummt. Eine momentane Verkrampfung der

Stimmbänder … Das kann dem intelligentesten Menschen passieren … (Hält ihm die Flasche hin.) Trinken sie!

Clown: Nein.

Hauptmann: So … hm … so also steht die Sache. Kameraden, dieses Individuum findet es unter seiner Würde mit uns zu trinken.

Clown: Ich trinke nie.

Hauptmann: Uns zuliebe hätten sie eine Ausnahme machen können. Sie wären nicht gestorben. Kommt ihnen ihr Verhalten nicht selbst etwas sonderbar vor? Ich glaube sie haben was gegen uns …

Clown: Keineswegs …

Hauptmann, ohne zu unterbrechen: Ja, sie haben was gegen uns. Schießen sie los, klären sie uns auf. Haben wir einen Fehler gemacht? Sind wir ihnen zu nahegetreten? (Clown schweigt.)

Hauptmann zu den Soldaten: Wir sind ihm nicht fein genug. Der Herr wünscht von uns nicht belästigt zu werden. Ist es nicht so? (Schweigen.) Übrigens, sind sie für den Krieg? Um es zu präzisieren, lieben sie den Krieg? Ich frage noch einmal. Lieben sie ihn?

Clown: Als freier Mensch muss ich ihnen keine …

Hauptmann: Was? Weiter … weiter …

Clown: Rechenschaft geben.

Hauptmann: Maul halten! (Geht um ihn herum.) Hm. Sie glauben wir wissen nichts von ihnen? (Pause.) Sie fühlen sich sicher. (Pause.) Aber sie sind uns kein Unbekannter. (Bleibt vor ihm stehen.) Sie stehen schon seit langem unter Beobachtung. Hm. (Zündet sich eine Zigarette an.) Da staunen sie, was?

Clown: Aber ich …

Hauptmann: Schweigen sie! Sie haben überhaupt nichts zu reden. Wir kennen ihre Entwicklung. Wir kennen ihre Affären, ihre Schulden und ihre Freunde. Selbst ihre Kinderkrankheiten. Sie haben drei Goldplomben. Zwei auf der rechten und eine auf der linken Seite. Voriges Jahr konnten sie wegen einer schweren Erkältung vierzehn Tage nicht zum Dienst erscheinen. Sie haben sich im Laufe des letzten Jahres auffällig über unsere Regierung geäußert. Zweimal ihrem Dienstmädchen gegenüber, einmal in angeheitertem Zustand und dreimal in einem öffentlichen Lokal. Seht euch diese Sau an! Ihr einziges Ziel ist es die Seele unseres Volkes in ihrem Unflat zu ersticken. Wenn er wenigstens Manns genug wäre an die Öffentlichkeit zu treten. Aber nein, er wühlt im Geheimen und gibt sich offiziell als braver Bürger. Seht euch nur die Verbrecherphysiognomie an! Die unedle Haltung seines Körpers. Du miese Dreckseele! Du geistige Jauchegrube! Dein Gesicht schreit nach Ohrfeigen! Sprich mir nach … ich bin eine geistige Jauchegrube. Los, mach's Maul auf!

Clown: Ich weiß nicht was sie woll …

Hauptmann: Ich bin eine geistige Jauchegrube!

Clown: Ich …

Hauptmann: Weiter …

Clown: Ich sage nichts mehr.

Hauptmann: Ach so. Wie du willst. (Tritt ihn ins Schienbein.)

Clown: Au …

Hauptmann: Und wehleidig auch noch. Wehleidig und feig. So seid ihr alle. (Tritt ihn noch einmal. Clown schreit auf.) Schlag ihn!

1.Soldat: Ich?

Hauptmann: Schlag ihm aufs Maul!

Soldat schlägt zögernd.

Hauptmann: Fester!

1.Soldat schlägt noch einmal.

Hauptmann: Schlag ihn zu Brei! Er glaubt noch immer nicht! Er lacht noch! (Der Soldat ohrfeigt den Clown. Die beiden anderen halten ihn mit einer Art von Polizeigriff fest.) Dir wird das Lachen noch vergehen! Fester, nicht so zaghaft! (Die Schläge prasseln ins Gesicht des Clowns. Er weint leise.) Gut so, ja …

Der Clown reißt sich los und stürzt zur Rampe: Ich will … (Er bekommt einen Schlag, der ihn zu Boden wirft.) … eine Verhandlung … eine … (Sie zerren ihn von der Rampe weg.)

Hauptmann: Was für Geschichten? Schlagt ihn nieder! Schlagt die Drecksau nieder!

Die Soldaten werfen den Clown auf die Bretter. Sie bearbeiten ihn mit Händen und Füßen. Er schreit.

1.Soldat: Dir werd ich's geben …

2.Soldat: Du Hund …

3.Soldat: Er wehrt sich … der feige Hund beißt …

Keuchen Geschrei und Stöhnen des Clowns. Unverständliche Laute von Seiten der Soldaten. Das soll sehr realistisch wirken und von kaum ertragbarer Brutalität sein.

Hauptmann: Gebt es ihm! Gebt ihm die Freiheit, die er braucht! … Hast du nicht irgendwelche intellektuellen Phrasen bei der Hand? … Dabei waren wir so nett zu ihm!

Die Soldaten haben den Clown in die Mitte genommen. Sie treten ihn wie einen Ball hin und her. Er rollt über den Boden. Das Ziel ihrer Tritte ist hauptsächlich Kopf und Unterleib. Der Clown krümmt sich in embryonaler Stellung. Er blutet und winselt.

Hauptmann: Hast du noch Fragen? (Grinsend.) Wir stehen zu Diensten. (Schreiend.) Macht ihn fertig! (Die Soldaten sind eng zusammengerückt. Der Clown liegt als zuckendes Bündel unter einem Klumpen Brutalität.)

Hauptmann: Kastriert das Schwein!

Erster Soldat zieht das Messer aus der Scheide. Die anderen halten den sich Windenden, knien halb auf ihm. Man sieht nur die zuckenden Füße des Clowns und hört seine gurgelnden Schreie. Der Soldat sticht ihm mehrmals zwischen die Beine. Das Sirenengeräusch hat volle Lautstärke erreicht und erstickt jedes andere Geräusch. Das Messer ist blutig. Das Sirenengeheul wird etwas leiser.

Regisseur, herbeilaufend: Hören sie auf! Sind sie wahnsinnig geworden? (Man versteht ihn infolge des Geheuls schlecht. Der Ton fällt schlagartig zusammen. Die Soldaten erheben sich erschöpft und schwer atmend.) Macht Platz! Ihr seid zu weit gegangen! So war das nicht vereinbart! (Er hebt den blutigen Clown auf, dessen Gurgeln bei der Berührung verstummt und führt ihn, nein, trägt ihn fast auf seinen alten Platz zurück. Über den Unterleib des Clowns breitet sich ein Blutfleck aus. Der Regisseur lässt ihn vorsichtig auf die Bretter gleiten. Er sitzt mit dem Rücken zum Publikum und schaut zur Balletteuse hinauf, die ihn nicht sieht. Die Soldaten machen verlegene, ratlose Bewegungen.

Wissenschaftler, halb von der Maschine verdeckt: Es klappt. Sie funktioniert. Ein paar Korrekturen noch und sie wird ein Segen für die Menschheit; (verschwindet).

Negerin, die sich inzwischen an den Bühnenrand gesetzt hat, die Beine herabbaumeln lässt und strickt, zum vorrübergehenden Regisseur: Kommt bald mein Auftritt?

Regisseur, der sich auf dem Rückweg zu den Soldaten befindet: Bald, gnädige Frau. Es dauert noch ein bisschen.

Negerin: Haben sie sich verletzt?

Regisseur: Warum?

Negerin: Ihre rechte Hand blutet. Hatten sie einen Unfall?

Regisseur: Ach, das ist nichts. Ich habe mich ein bisschen geschnitten mit einem Dosenöffner, vielmehr an der Dose selbst.

Negerin: Zeigen sie her.

Regisseur: Nicht der Rede wert. (Nimmt mit der Linken ein Taschentuch und wickelt es um die rechte Hand.)

Negerin: Moment noch. Ich wollte sie gern … (Der Regisseur beugt sich zu ihr herab. Die beiden flüstern.)

Der Hauptmann deutet den Soldaten sich zu setzen. Sie ziehen sich von der Blutlache zurück und plumpsen apathisch zu Boden. Erster Soldat bietet dem Dritten die Flasche an. Der verneint. Der Erste wirft die Flasche weg.

Clown, sein Text setzt beim Flüstern der Negerin ein: Üben, üben und wieder üben. (Er spricht schleppend.) Üben sie. Es fehlt ihnen nichts als ein wenig Courage. Aber im Großen und Ganzen bin ich mit ihnen zufrieden. Alles braucht, natürlich, seine Zeit, und vor allem viel Übung. Bei ihrem Talent kommt es nur auf die nötige Sicherheit an. Schonen sie sich in ihrer Freizeit. Schonen sie sich und meiden sie den Alkohol. Außerdem sollten sie sich vor Nässe und Verkühlung hüten. (Sehr leise, aber deutlich.) Den Grundschritt, bitte … (Seine Worte gehen in unverständliches Flüstern über, das langsam ausklingt.)

Der Regisseur hat inzwischen die Negerin verlassen und steht vor den Soldaten: Was ist ihnen da eingefallen, meine Herrn?

1.Soldat: Es ist so über uns gekommen.

2.Soldat: Er war frech.

3.Soldat: Er hat uns provoziert. Wir können nichts dafür.

Regisseur: Das wird ihnen ein Disziplinarverfahren einbringen. Ich hoffe das wissen sie.

2.Soldat: Wir haben nur einen Befehl ausgeführt.

1.Soldat: Sonst nichts.

Regisseur zum Hauptmann: Sie stehen unter Arrest. Ich weiß zwar, dass das nichts ändert. Es werden Andere kommen und ihren Platz einnehmen aber im Moment bereitet es mir Genugtuung. Am liebsten würde ich sagen: robben sie! Robben sie bis ich mich wieder daran erinnere, falls ich sie nicht überhaupt vergesse und an Erschöpfung krepieren lasse. Selbstverständlich würde ich ihnen einen Beobachter mitgeben, damit sie nicht mogeln.

Hauptmann: Zu Befehl! (Salutiert.) Ich habe kein Blut an meinen Händen.

Regisseur: Ja, sie haben sich nicht dreckig gemacht. Sie sind bei der Drecksarbeit sauber geblieben. Würden sie die

Liebenswürdigkeit haben mir zu folgen? Sie bekommen eine saubere Zelle mit Klimaanlage. Außerdem können sie auf eine ordentliche Verhandlung hoffen. Wir wissen was wir gefangenen Offizieren schuldig sind. (Zu den Soldaten.) Ihr seid Kriminelle. Gebt die Waffen ab! Das dicke Ende folgt noch. (Zum Bühnenarbeiter.) Nehmen sie den Plunder!

Bühnenarbeiter: Wohin damit die Arsenale sind schon voll.

Regisseur: Irgendwann vernichten sie den Mist.

Bühnenarbeiter: Wozu unsereins alles kommt. (Räumt die Waffen zusammen und trägt sie hinter die Bühne. Man hört ihr polterndes Aufschlagen.)

Regisseur zu den Soldaten: Sie können sich ruhig setzen. In ihrer Haut möchte ich nicht stecken. (Zum Hauptmann.) Kommen sie! (Geht mit ihm hinter die Arkaden.)

1.Soldat: Ich weiß gar nicht was der will? Ich bin doch ein anständiger Mensch.

2.Soldat: Ah, und ich nicht? Du warst auch dabei.

1.Soldat: Dabei … na und? Wir waren alle dabei.

2.Soldat: Du hast ganz schön hin gedroschen. Wenn das jemand wüsste. Wenn das an die Öffentlichkeit dringt bist du erledigt!

1.Soldat: Lass‘ meine Familie aus dem Spiel. Krieg ist Krieg.

2.Soldat: Wer spricht denn von deiner Familie? Was scheiß‘ ich mich um deine Familie?

Jung.Schausp. zum Alt.Schausp.: Schau dir die Dämmerung an!

1.Soldat: Ich will nichts mehr hören. Musst du mich demütigen? Was geschehen ist, ist geschehen. (Zuckt die Achseln.) Basta!

3.Soldat: Hört endlich auf. Dadurch wird nichts besser. Wir Kleinen zahlen immer drauf. (Sie sitzen mit gesenkten Köpfen.)

Jung.Schausp.: Wenn die Sonne, die Leuchte meines Lebens sinkt, werde ich immer ein wenig sentimental. Ich bemitleide mich und schiebe die Schuld an meinem Versagen anderen zu.

Alt.Schausp.: Das tut jeder. Wie könnten wir sonst das Leben aushalten? Aber, du hast nicht ganz so unrecht. Wir sind ein Opfer der Umstände.

Jung.Schausp.: Dabei könnten wir glücklich sein, wenn ich in der Welt Regie führen könnte … lach nicht! Also, ich würde vor Probenbeginn zu den Mitwirkenden sagen: Meine Damen und Herren! Ich stelle mir eine Welt vor in der einer dem anderen hilft, - um nicht zu sagen liebt – und das Geld zu dem wird was es eigentlich ist, nämlich zu einem notwendigen, praktischen Übel.

Alt.Schausp.: Eine ideale Welt.

Jung.Schausp.: Die egoistischste Welt aller Welten. Die Menschen würden aus Egoismus einander lieben. Sie würden das geben, was sie von anderen erwarten und der wiederum von ihnen erwartet. Einander helfen wäre das Gebot der Vernunft. Zweitens kann der einzelne Mensch nur im begrenzten Maß konsumieren. Der Überfluss würde den Bedürftigen zugutekommen, die im Laufe der Entwicklung verschwinden. Ich müsste zum nächsten Millionär gehen können und sagen: "Ich bin völlig abgebrannt. Ich brauche Geld, Bruder." (Mit veränderter Stimme:) "Setz dich erst, lieber Freund! Ruh dich aus! Willst du eine Erfrischung? Bitte bedien' dich! Wieviel darf es sein?" (Mit veränderter Stimme:) "So und so viel, lieber Bruder.“ (Mit veränderter Stimme:) “Was nur so eine geringe Summe? Du bist zu bescheiden. Ich flehe dich an, verlang‘ mehr! Falls du es nicht tust fühle ich mich schuldig,“ (Mit veränderter Stimme:) “Wenn es sein muss. Du weißt, dass ich nicht auf dich angewiesen bin.“ (Mit veränderter Stimme:) “Ich bitte dich darum. Es ist unverschämt aber ich bitte dich darum. Mein Ruf steht am Spiel. (Mit natürlicher Stimme:) Na gut, bevor ich mich schlagen lasse … usw.

Alt.Schausp.: Der Wunschtraum eines Hungrigen. Dabei sind dir Denkfehler unterlaufen. Erstens müssten alle Menschen arbeitsam sein und es dürfte keine Parasiten geben. Zweitens ist mir ein Millionär in dieser Gesellschaft undenkbar. Drittens möchte … der Millionär ist mir sehr sympathisch.

Jung.Schausp.: Ich habe mich schlecht ausgedrückt … es ist die Sehnsucht.

Alt.Schausp.: nach einer heilen Welt.

Bühnenarbeiter, der hinzugetreten ist: Was sie da reden ist vollkommener Unsinn! Ich brauche weder Hilfe noch Nächstenliebe! Ich möchte nur so behandelt werden, wie es mir zusteht. Was glaubt ihr wie viele ich in die Tasche stecken würde. Jeder soll seinen Fähigkeiten nach behandelt werden und den ihm entsprechenden Platz einnehmen. Ich will nur Gerechtigkeit, sonst nichts.

Jung.Schausp.: Das ist völlig absurd!

Alt.Schausp.: Wer soll denn der unbestechliche Schiedsrichter sein? Ha?

Bühnenarbeiter: Ich … ich meine, das wäre doch richtig.

Jung.Schausp.: Weltfremde Ideen. Wie lange sind sie schon beim Theater?

Alt.Schausp.: Streitet nicht! Wir sind ein Opfer der Umstände. Sie zum Beispiel fühlen sich erniedrigt und beleidigt. Auch ich leide (gähnt). Ich leide so ungeheuer, dass ich davon müde werde. Wir werden der Welt keine anderen Gesetze aufzwingen.

Jung.Schausp.: Gesetze! Nur weil die Menschen Bestien sind, muss man sie in den Käfig der Gesetze sperren. Wehe du nimmst die Gitter weg! Patsch, bist du schon erschlagen. Dabei könnte das Leben himmlisch sein. Meiner Theorie gemäß, meine ich.

Alt.Schausp.: Ausnahmen bestätigen die Regel.

Jung.Schausp.: Ich spreche nicht von Heiligen. Ich spreche von Menschen!

Alt.Schausp.: Lassen wir das; (winkt ab).

1.Soldat: Aber schön war es doch! Selbstverständlich gab es Situationen, die ich nicht gerne erwähne, aber das entsprach dem Stil der Zeit.

2.Soldat: Und wie haben wir damals gesoffen! Erinnerst du dich noch an den kleinen Weinkeller? Der ganze Zug war blau. Mein Jüngster wird der ganze Papa.

3.Soldat: Ich besitze eine Kakteenzucht. Die müsst ihr euch einmal ansehen. Hundertdreissigtausend Sorten. Tausend blühen gerade. Es gibt nichts schöneres als blühende Kakteen. Ich liebe sie. Man muss viel Einfühlungsvermögen haben. Man darf ihnen auf keinen Fall zu viel Wasser geben. Die Erde muss selbstverständlicher Weise sandig und trocken sein.

Wissenschaftler: Und da soll einer den Fortschritt leugnen. In mir ist der Zwang zu erfinden. Ich muss erfinden. Die Bombe ist eine geniale Erfindung. Auch die biologischen und chemischen Waffen. Mir geht es um die tolle Ausschöpfung der Möglichkeiten. Ich würde die Hälfte der Menschheit für eine phänomenale … Menschheit, das Wort klingt fern und abstrakt. Menschheit, Menge, Masse. Das ist ein verwachsenes Gesicht. Ein Gesicht, das aus vielen Gesichtern zusammenfließt, auseinanderfließt und nie feste Form annimmt. Ich experimentiere. Ich forsche zielbewusst, den logischen Verstand aufs Ziel gerichtet, das ins Unendliche wächst. Ich kann nicht aufhören. Wenn ich etwas entdeckt habe, muss ich weitermachen. Aufdecken, sezieren, analysieren, neue Variationen finden. Selbstverständlich wird die Arbeit gut dotiert. Ich habe mein Landhaus, mein Flugzeug und … na, aber … Und, wenn die Regierung meine Erfindungen missbraucht, bzw. ich mich missbrauchen lasse, was soll ich in meiner Zwangslage tun? Nur sie kann mir diesen teuren Arbeitsplatz zur Verfügung stellen. Ich bin moralisch nicht gebunden. Dazu habe ich keine Zeit. Ich absorbiere Ideen, wie andere Sauerstoff. Ich bin ein bisschen größenwahnsinnig und außerdem ein unscheinbarer Titan. Ich bin die Bombe. Ich erleuchte eure Ställe, die ihr Häuser nennt. Zugegeben, es ist letztlich die Elektrizität, aber ich habe sie gezähmt … und …

Jung.Schausp.: Auch ein Arschloch.

Wissenschaftler: Nutzbringend angewendet. Ich bin das Neonlicht, ich bin die Lichtreklame auf euren Straßen. Ich habe tausend Pferdestärken und mehr. Ich bin der Satellit, die Rakete, das Fernsehgerät, ein Auto, eine Eisenbahn, ein Unterseebot, das Rad, die Schaufel. Ich gebe zu, man kann jemanden mit dem Rad überfahren und jemanden mit der Schaufel erschlage. Aber das ist nicht meine Schuld. (Geht würdevoll hinter die Maschine.)

Kindermädchen, aufgeregt aus den Arkaden stürzend: Ich habe das Kind verloren! Es ist ins Wasser gefallen! Hilft mir denn niemand? Was werden die Herrschaften sagen? Mein Gott, ich werde entlassen!

Alt.Schausp. stößt den jung. Schauspieler mit dem Ellbogen.

Jung.Schausp.: Nehmen sie es nicht so tragisch.

Kindermädchen: Sie haben leicht reden!

Jung.Schausp.: Ich helfe ihnen. Ich habe ihnen schon einmal geholfen.

Kindermädchen: Kann sein, aber ich erinnere mich nicht.

Alt.Schausp.: Wo ist es passiert? Wie ist das Kind abhandengekommen?

Kindermädchen: Warten sie; (überlegt).

Jung.Schausp.: Sie müssen doch die Stelle wissen.

Kindermädchen, wie wenn es einen Traum erzählen würde: Ich weiß es nicht genau. Es war ein schöner Frühlingstag. Die Luft war ganz blau und die Blätter grün. Die Sonne stand über meinem Scheitel. Nicht das leiseste Lüftchen regte sich. Der Park war fast leer. Der Kies knirschte unter meinen Füßen. Tauben gurrten. Trotz der keimenden Triebe herrschte tödlicher Friede. Nicht das leiseste Lüftchen … Es war so als ob ich tot wäre. Aber ich konnte nicht fallen. Die warme Luft war dick wie Aspik, sie hielt mich.

Alt.Schausp.: Weiter!

Kindermädchen: Die Tauben … dort war ich schon … ich ging, und werde gegangen, vielmehr schwamm ich … wurde getrieben.

Alt.Schausp.: Weiter …

Kindermädchen: Die Täuberiche gurrten und umtanzten die Weibchen. Ihr Gurren hatte nichts Aufdringliches, es verstärkte die Stille … machte sie noch fühlbarer …

Jung.Schausp.: Und was war mit dem Kind?

Kindermädchen: Welches Kind? Von welchem Kind reden sie?

Alt.Schausp.: Von ihrem Zögling.

Kindermädchen: Ach richtig, den hätte ich beinahe vergessen. Sie kennen ja, die träg zwinkernde Frühlingsluft. Das Auge ist noch nicht an die grelle Sonne gewöhnt. Die Bäume sind noch halb kahl und der Schatten ist kalt. Die Umrisse der Gegenstände sind schärfer als sonst. Man ist geblendet. Und auf einmal war das Kind weg. Es war da und plötzlich war es weg. Ich habe es nicht vermisst. Das wäre gelogen. Ich konnte mich kaum mehr daran erinnern. Ich suchte es, freilich. Genauer gesagt, ich suchte irgendetwas, ohne tatsächliches Verlangen danach. Ist das nicht komisch? Dann erinnerte ich mich an die Herrschaft und bekam Angst.

Alt.Schausp.: Sie sind eine schlampige Person. Ihnen möchte ich kein Kind anvertrauen.

Kindermädchen: Es war da irgendetwas. Es war wie ein Blitz … so ähnlich, wie ein Blitz … und die ganze Welt war leer, die Blätter rührten sich nicht und die Statuen standen auffallend still. Selbst die Sonne bewegte sich nicht. Ich war völlig allein.

Alt.Schausp.: Sie stehen unter Schock. Sie haben sich abgekapselt. Ich will ihnen helfen. (Zum jung. Schauspieler:) Ein Glück, dass wir gestern im Kaufhaus die beiden Puppen gesto …

Jung.Schausp.: Gekauft haben.

Alt.Schausp.: Ja! (Schnürt das andere Bündel auf. Zum Kindermädchen:) Warten sie!

2.Herr zum ersten: Wir sind Ausbeuter. Wir beuten die Erde aus, bis sie keine Milch mehr gibt. Es leben zu viele Menschen auf dem Globus. Ich freue mich über jede Katastrophe. Ich denke mir- wieder weniger, wieder mehr Platz für mich.

1.Herr: Sie haben recht. Wir explodieren.

Alt.Schausp. zieht eine ungefähr fünfjährige Puppe aus dem Bündel. Sie ist mit der neuesten Kindermode bekleidet. Es handelt sich um ein Mädchen: Da, nehmen sie!

Kindermädchen: Herzlichen Dank … (zögernd) … aber meine war ein Bub.

Alt.Schausp.: Das ist doch egal. Oder sind sie noch immer mit Vorurteilen belastet?

Jung.Schausp.: Eine ausgezeichnete Puppe. Das neueste Modell. Sie kann gehen und sprechen. Man kann sie auch füttern.

Kindermädchen: Sie haben mich überzeugt. Wie kann ich ihnen danken?

Jung.Schausp.: Aber ich bitte sie. Nicht der Rede wert. Das ist doch selbstverständlich.

Kindermädchen: Sie sind zu gütig.

Jung.Schausp.: Gegenüber lebendigen Fratzen hat die Puppe den Vorteil, dass sie nur die vorprogrammierten Bewegungen macht und den aufgezeichneten Text spricht. Dadurch gibt es keine Entgleisungen. Sie verbirgt keine unangenehmen Überraschungen. Sie funktioniert, wie sie es wünschen. Ein ausgesprochen braves Kind.

Alt. Schausp.: Stell sie einmal auf.

Jung.Schausp.: Der Mechanismus ist denkbar einfach. Man bespricht ein Band und lässt es bei passender Gelegenheit ablaufen.

Kindermädchen: Da werden sich die Herrschaften aber freun. Vor allem die Gnädigste. Sie war immer echauffiert, wenn der Bub etwas unpassendes sagte.

Jung.Schausp.: Gehen sie einige Schritte zurück!

Kindermädchen: So?

Jung.Schausp.: Noch weiter! (Er dreht die Puppe in Richtung des Kindermädchens.) Los marschier meine Kleine!

Die Puppe, sehr langsam auf das Kindermädchen zu zappelnd, mit überlauter süßer Hollywood-Kinderstimme, sehr penetrant: Ich werde immer brav sein. Ein Kind das brav und fleißig ist, sich ordentlich wäscht, die Zähne putzt, das Gewand nicht schmutzig macht, pünktlich von der Schule kommt, brav beim Mittagessen sitzt, seine Hausaufgaben macht und abends brav ins Bettchen geht, wird von Eltern und Lehrern gelobt. Außerdem soll ich immer gut gelaunt und sauber sein. Wenn ich die Gesetze beachte und bei grünem Licht über die Straße gehe, komme ich nie mit dem Gesetz in Konflikt. Immer höflich sein, und bitte und danke sagen. Danke liebe Omama, danke lieber Opa, danke liebe Tante, danke lieber Onkel. Danke liebe Tante, danke liebe Omama, lieber Opa. Das Taschentuch nicht vergessen. Es dient zum Winken und Schnäuzen. Tüchtigkeit, Anständigkeit und Fleiß sind der Weg zum Erfolg. Wenn ich brav durchs Leben gehe und etwas Anständiges gelernt habe, kann mir Garnichts mehr passiere. Ich soll immer freundlich sein.

Die Puppe wird vom Kindermädchen abgefangen; sie verstummt.

Kindermädchen: Bezaubernd. Wie kann ich das je wiedergutmachen?

Jung.Schausp.: Wenn sie ein paar Schilling übrig hätten … Ich glaube das müsste ihnen sie Sache schon wert sein.

Alt. Schausp.: Wir haben schon längere Zeit nichts gegessen …

Kindermädchen: Das kann man nicht bezahlen. Was sie für mich getan haben ist unbezahlbar. Glauben sie mir, ich weiß es zu schätzen und bin ihnen unendlich dankbar. Ich bin für ewig ihre Schuldnerin.

Jung.Schausp.: Aber wir …

Kindermädchen: Ich weiß es hundertprozentig zu schätzen …

Jung.Schausp.: Wenn sie …

Kindermädchen: Nein, sagen sie nichts mehr. Jedes Wort würde alles zerstören. (Geht mit der Puppe ab.)

Jung.Schausp.: Zum Teufel!

Alt.Schausp., lächelnd: Sie hat dich angeschmiert. Wir sind die Dummen. Man merkt, dass du ein miserabler Komödiant bist.

Jung.Schausp.: Küß mich in Krakau!

Alt.Schausp., heftig lachend: Danke. Das hast du wirklich prächtig gemacht. Der geborene Geschäftsmann! Der Händler par excellence!

Jung.Schausp.: Du hättest es nicht besser gemacht. Es wird mir nichts übrigbleiben. Ich spreche noch einmal mit dem Direktor.

Alt.Schausp.: Tu das!

Die Maschine bewegt sich stoßweise. Sie zittert. Sirenengeheul, das immer stärker anschwillt. Dazwischen Flugzeugmotoren. Ihr Lärm kommt immer näher, erfüllt den Platz. Das Geheul der Sirenen hört auf. Nur der Flugzeuglärm bleibt. Die Darsteller flüchten von der Bühne und drücken sich gegen die Wand oder verschwinden hinter den Arkaden.

Balletteuse, schreiend: Jetzt kommen sie schon am helllichten Tag.

1.Herr: Schnell, schnell, machen sie …

Das Geräusch von Einschlägen. Die Schauspieler drücken sich tiefer in die Wand, kauern sich, die Hände schützend über den Kopf gelegt, zusammen. Der Clown, er ist langsamer als die anderen, taumelt, fällt auf den Rücken und bleibt bewegungslos mit weit ausgebreiteten Armen liegen. Die Schauspieler zucken bei jedem Einschlag zusammen. Die Flieger entfernen sich. Entwarnung. Die Schauspieler strömen langsam auf die Bühne, putzen ihre Kleider ab, rücken Requisiten zurecht und unterhalten sich.

Negerin: Am helllichten Tag! Eine Frechheit.

Direktor: Ist ihnen etwas geschehen?

Negerin: Nein.

Mann im Tropenanzug: Ich habe meinen Tropenhelm verloren. Hat ihn jemand von den Herrschaften gesehen? Das kommt davon, wenn man die Wilden bewaffnet.

Regisseur: Nein, ich habe keinen gesehen.

Die Balletteuse schlägt die Hände vors Gesicht und bekommt einen Weinkrampf. Man hört das Prasseln des Feuers.

Negerin, die Balletteuse liebevoll umarmend: Beruhige dich Kindchen. Es ist schon alles vorbei. Ist ja nichts geschehen. Ruhig, ruhig, beruhige dich. (Sie flüstert weiter auf sie ein. Das Schreien geht in Schluchzen über, das leiser wird.)

Balletteuse, schluchzend: Danke.

Negerin: Na, siehts du, es geht schon. (Die Balletteuse wischt die Tränen ab und schnäuzt sich.)

Negerin: Alles in Ordnung, Kleines?

Balletteuse: Ja …

1.Herr zum anderen: Sind sie verletzt Herr Kollege?

2.Herr: Sie?

1.Herr: Nein, aber ich finde es unerhört.

Jung.Schausp.: So eine Scheiße. Schmeißen ihren Dreck auf lebendige Menschen.

Negerin: Das nennt sich Kulturvolk.

1.Soldat, den Clown entdeckend: Da liegt ja einer. (Schreiend) Sanität!

Negerin: Ja wirklich, da liegt einer.

Die Anwesenden umringen den Clown.

Wissenschaftler: Lassen sie mich durch, ich bin Arzt!

Bühnenarbeiter: Lasst ihn durch, er ist Arzt!

Jung.Schausp. zum Mann im Tropenanzug: Gehen sie zur Seite, damit der Doktor Platz hat!

Die Schauspieler weichen zurück. Der Wissenschaftler kniet neben dem Clown: Er ist ohnmächtig. Puls normal. Hat viel Blut verloren.

1.Soldat, 2.Soldat, Balletteuse, 1.Herr im Frack, Direktor, durcheinander: Was ist? Was ist? Was hat er gesagt?

Herr im Tropenanzug, nach hinten: Er hat viel Blut verloren.

Wissenschaftler: Er braucht sofort eine Transfusion. Wer meldet sich freiwillig als Blutspender?

1.Soldat: Ich!

2.Soldat: Ich auch.

Mann im Tropenanzug: Ich auch, selbstverständlich.

Negerin: Ich!

Balletteuse: Ich melde mich.

Bühnenarbeiter: Klar.

Regisseur: Kann ich ihnen als Assistent behilflich sein?

Wissenschaftler: Verstehen sie was davon?

Regisseur: Ich habe einige Semester Medizin …

Wissenschaftler: Gut. Tragen wir ihn dorthin. (Zeigt auf die Maschine.) Hoffentlich hat der Angriff die Instrumente nicht beschädigt.

Der Mann im Tropenanzug, der Bühnenarbeiter, die Balletteuse und der junge Schauspieler tragen den Clown, dessen

Hände am Boden schleifen, hinter die Maschine. 1.Soldat, 2.Soldat und die Negerin folgen ihnen.

Wissenschaftler: Vorsicht, bitte.

Regisseur: Ich werde inzwischen eine Nährlösung vorbereiten.

Wissenschaftler: Bitte, Herr Kollege!

Der Arzt, der Assistent und die Träger werden von der Maschine verdeckt. Die zwei Soldaten und die Negerin warten vor ihr.

Stimme des Wissenschaftlers: Warten sie bitte draußen!

(Die Träger gesellen sich zu den Blutspendern.)

Regisseur, auftauchend: Bitte der oder die Erste!

Mann im Tropenanzug geht hinter die Maschine.

Die beiden Herren haben sich gesetzt. Auch der alte Schauspieler und der Direktor sind auf ihren Platz zurückgekehrt. Letzterer sitzt mit dem Rücken zu den Spendern und beachtet sie nicht. Der Mann im Tropenanzug kommt hinter der Maschine hervor, die jetzt leise summt.

Mann im Tropenanzug … Regisseur, ihm nachrufend: Na, hat's weh getan?

Mann im Tropenanzug: Wo denken sie hin? Das ist nicht das erste Mal.

Regisseur: Der nächste bitte. (Das wiederholt er bei jedem Spender.)

Die Schauspieler gehen nach der Blutabnahme mit entblößtem, abgewinkeltem Arm an ihren Platz zurück und setzen sich.

Unterdessen der 1.Herr zum 2.Herr: Ich finde das skandalös. Dass die Regierung nichts unternimmt. Wo bleibt die Armee?

Dabei haben wir genug Waffen um das halbe Weltall zu entvölkern. Weshalb wenden wir sie nicht an. Ich habe diese Gefühlsduselei satt.

1.Herr: Ich auch. Man wird nicht umhin kommen ihnen zu zeigen wer der Herr ist. Die bessere Rasse überlebt. Das ist ein Naturgesetz.

2.Herr: Was ich bezweifeln möchte, Herr Kollege. Denn zwischen besserer und stärkerer Rasse besteht ein Unterschied. Jeder durchtrainierte Halbidiot ist stärker als sie - verzeihen sie mir, verehrter Herr Kollege, - ohne dabei an ihre geistige Potenz heranreichen zu können.

Jung. Schauspiel., der an seinen Platz geht: Ihre geistige Potenz kann mir gestohlen bleiben. (Schreiend) Hochnäsige Affen! Armleuchter! (Er beugt sich dabei zu ihnen hinab. Sein Gesicht ruht zwischen ihren Gesichtern.)

1.Herr: Das wirft meine Theorie über den Haufen, Nein, nein, sie irren. Ich habe Waffen. Waffen, die ich nötigenfalls benutzen werde. Technische Waffen, die meiner Intelligenz entsprungen sind.

Jung.Schausp., brüllend: Dann stellen sie sich auf die gleiche Stufe mit den Halbidioten. Ich hasse euer kaltes Ignorieren der Tatsachen. Ihr seid verkalkte Theoretiker, übertünchte Gräber …

2.Herr: Ja, das stimmt. Ich gebe mich geschlagen. Ich gratuliere ihnen zu ihrem Erfolg. Ihre Maschinen können mehr vernichten als animalische Kraft.

Jung.Schausp.: Sehen sie nicht was sie angerichtet haben? (Zieht den Kopf zurück.) Völlig sinnlos. (Geht an seinen Platz.)

Die Beiden haben ihn selbstverständlich nicht beachtet.

1.Herr: Wo verbringen sie heuer ihren Urlaub?

2.Herr: Ich weiß noch nicht so recht, lieber Herr Kollege. Ich arbeite gerade an einer Abhandlung, ob die Übertragung von Juden- oder Negerblut gefährliche Folgen für den Patienten hat.

Die Negerin setzt sich mit abgewinkeltem Arm an die Rampe.

1.Herr: Ihr Ergebnis?

2.Herr: Ich rate auf jeden Fall zur Vorsicht.

Alle Spender haben ihre Plätze eingenommen. Der Regisseur tritt hervor, zieht den weißen, blutbefleckten Arbeitsmantel aus und wirft ihn über die Maschine.

Wissenschaftler: Aber Herr Kollege!

Regisseur: Entschuldigen sie, Herr Medizinalrat. Die Anstrengungen der letzten Tage, die vielen Verwundeten … sie müssen schon verzeihen.

Wissenschaftler: Das kann ich verstehen … ruhen sie sich aus.

Regisseur: Sie brauchen den Schlaf nötiger als ich.

Wissenschaftler: Ich bin ein alter Mann. Alte Männer brauchen nichtmehr viel Schlaf. (Nimmt den Arbeitsmantel von der Maschine.)

Regisseur: Aber, wenn ich …

Wissenschaftler: Gehen sie nur, ich komme allein zurecht.

2.Herr: Trotz der großen Belastung zieht es mich in den sonnigen Süden. Ich muss mich endlich entspannen.

1.Herr: Das habe ich schon lange vor.

Jung.Schausp.: Ich versuche es.

Alt.Schausp.: Du willst?

Jung.Schausp.: Ich versuche es.

Alt.Schausp.: Meinen Segen hast du.

Jung.Schausp.: Geht auf die Mittelbühne. Zum Regisseur, der auf dem Weg zur Negerin ist: Könnte ich den Direktor sprechen?

Regisseur: Wen darf ich melden?

Jung.Schausp.: Mein Name tut nichts zur Sache. Ich bin Charakterdarsteller.

Regisseur, erfreut: Ach sie sind es. Verzeihung, dass ich sie nicht gleich erkannt habe. Das macht die Dämmerung. Es ist mir eine Ehre. Ich habe schon lange davon geträumt sie kennen zu lernen. Ich gehöre zu ihren glühendsten Bewunderern. Vor allem ihre Sprechtechnik … aber, was rede ich … hatten sie nicht einen Bären?

Jung.Schausp.: Der ist krepiert.

Regisseur: Wie bedauerlich. Umso mehr freut es mich, dass sie den Weg zu uns gefunden haben. Einen Moment bitte. (Nach hinten rufend) Herr Direktor!

Direktor, ohne sich ihnen zuzuwenden: Ja!

Regisseur, gestikuliert in seine Richtung. Zum Schauspieler: Er kommt sofort. Bitte gedulden sie sich. (Geht zur Negerin.)

Direktor, vor sich hin rufend: Ich komme gleich! (Er blättert in imaginären Büchern.)

Der Clown kommt leise hinter der Maschine hervor und setzt sich, mit dem Rücken zum Publikum, vor die Füße der Balletteuse. Sie steht auf, richtet sich ihr Kleidchen, setzt sich wieder und liest weiter. Der jung. Schausp. geht auf und ab, nimmt Requisiten vom Boden, betrachtet sie, lässt sie fallen, zieht der Balletteuse das Buch aus der Hand und blättert darin. Die Balletteuse liest ohne Buch weiter. Er gibt es ihr zurück.

Regisseur zur Negerin: Ich habe eine Aufgabe für sie.

Negerin, aufstehend: Na endlich!

Regisseur: Verzeihen sie, dass es so lange gedauert hat.

Negerin, schmollend: Das werde ich mir noch gut überlegen. Ich bin eine bevorzugte Behandlung gewöhnt.

Regisseur: Es ging leider nicht anders, gnädige Frau. Die vielen Verwundeten. Sie hätten die Schreie hören müssen. Und es war nicht genug Morphium da … nicht einmal genügend Verbandszeug.

Negerin: Wovon reden sie, junger Mann?

Regisseur, heftiger: Ich trage keine Schuld an ihrer Behandlung, gnädige Frau. Da müssen sie sich bei jemandem anderen beschweren.

Negerin: Ich weiß, sie wollen mein Beste.

Regisseur, sanft: Das halte ich für meine Pflicht.

Negerin: Worum geht es?

Regisseur: Sofort! (Zum jung. Schausp.) Bitte kommen sie her! (Zum Clown) Sie auch.

Der Clown reagiert erst als der jung. Schausp. ihm auf die Schulter klopft und etwas in sein Ohr flüstert. Die beiden begeben sich an die Rampe. Die Hose des Clowns ist über dem Geschlechtsteil rot.

Negerin, inzwischen: Sie sorgen für Spannung, junger Mann.

Regisseur: Es handelt sich um eine Werbedurchsage.

Negerin: Meinetwegen, wenn es gut bezahlt wird. Ich weiß schon, meine Dinge sind tütü tata … ich bin so glücklich, seitdem tütü tata unfehlbar wirkt. Eine echte Erleichterung. Ich kann ohne tütü tata nicht mehr lebe. Manche Blödiane fallen tütü tata drauf rein. Das blabla, bla, bla-bla, bla.

Alt. Schausp., in den Spott der Negerin hinein: Das blabla, bla, bla-bla, bla. Ich fühle mich einsam. Ich bin in eine versteinerte Sekunde eingeschlossen, wie ein Insekt im Bernstein. Die Zeit vergeht nicht, nein, die Zeiten laufen parallel nebeneinander. Manchmal durchbricht einer die Mauer nach drüben und verschwindet. Manchmal bekommen wir von drüben Besuch. Manchmal durchbrechen wir selbst die Mauern und erleben Erlebtes. Ich sehne mich nach dem Jungen. Ich vermisse ihn. Vielleicht ist er tot. Nein, das ist alles Unsinn, ein billiger Trost. Ich werde auch meine Bären nicht wiedersehen. Ich kann die Schläge nichtmehr gut machen. Wenn die Toten wenigstens ahnten, dass wir bereuen.

Regisseur, die drei Kandidaten nebeneinander ausrichtend: So. Näher! Ja. Das ist zu eng so. (Seine Anweisungen dürfen die Rede des alt.Schausp. nicht stören.) Ja, so. Gut! Gut, so. (Der alt. Schausp. hat den Monolog beendet.) Also, wie gesagt, es handelt sich um eine Werbedurchsage. Es kommt darauf an wer schneller seinen Text spricht. (Die Bewerber stehen jetzt mit dem Gesicht zum Publikum.) Der Gewinner oder die Gewinnerin (knappe Verbeugung vor der Negerin) wird engagiert.

Negerin: Wie lautet das erste Gebot der Werbung? Wie heißt das schnell? (Ungeduldig zum Clown.) Helfen sie mir doch!

Mann im Tropenanzug, der auf der Suche nach seinem Helm, (er bewegt sich sehr unaufdringlich) nähergekommen ist: Das Bedürfnis zum Bedarf erheben bzw. zu steigern, gnädige Frau. Man verabreicht den Opfern so lange kleine Dosen Opium, bis sie süchtig werden und ihnen ein Dasein ohne Opium nichtmehr wünschenswert erscheint. Ich bin ein Kenner exotischer Sitten. (Die Negerin beachtet ihn nicht.) Selbstverständlich kann das Opfer ruhig über einen blöden Werbeslogan lachen. Das Gift muss das Unterbewusstsein ansprechen und zum Kaufzwang führen. Nicht umsonst beschäftigen große Konzerne ihre Psychologen.

Negerin zum Clown: Überlegen sie! Es liegt mir auf der Zunge.

Mann im Tropenanzug: Das ideale Endprodukt ist eine Kreatur, die dauernd unter Kaufzwangspsychose steht.

Regisseur: Unterbrechen sie die Probe nicht!

Mann im Tropenanzug: Verzeihung! (Bleibt stehen.)

Regisseur, der sich den Kandidaten zugewandt hat, dreht sich abrupt wieder um: Was wollen sie noch?

Negerin zum Clown: Na, wissen sie noch?

Mann im Tropenanzug: Haben sie zufällig meinen Hut gesehen?

Clown: Nein.

Mann im Tropenanzug: Durch die überaus starke Bestrahlung in dieser Gegend kann ein Aufenthalt in der Sonne, bei fehlender Kopfbedeckung, einen Sonnenstich nach sich ziehen

Negerin zum Clown: Das ärgert mich.

Regisseur zum Mann im Tropenanzug: Ich glaube ihnen, dass es ärgerlich ist, aber ich habe ihren Helm nicht gesehen. Bitte verschwinden sie jetzt, aber rasch.

Mann im Tropenanzug: Verbindlichsten Dank! (Verbeugt sich, fährt mit der Rechten automatisch zur Stirn, zuckt bedauernd die Achseln und entfernt sich in Richtung der Hinterbühne.)

Regisseur: Ich spreche ihnen den Text vor …

Negerin: Sollen wir dann alle auf einmal …

Regisseur: Nein. Mir würde der Überblick fehlen. Außerdem würden sie sich gegenseitig behindern. Also – es kommt auf die Schnelligkeit und klare Diktion an. Ich stoppe die Zeit ab.

Jung.Schausp.: Wenn ich richtig verstanden habe, handelt es sich um eine akrobatische Leistung?

Regisseur: Sie haben verstanden.

Clown: Ich spreche außer Konkurrenz.

Regisseur: Wie sie wünschen.

Negerin: Den Text, bitte.

Regisseur, langsam: Die Welt ist so schön, dass man darüber weinen könnte. Das ist nichts von Bedeutung und daher kein Verbrechen.

Negerin: Ist das alles?

Regisseur: Ja,

Negerin: Fangen wir an.

Regisseur: Am besten sie fangen gleich an. (Die Schauspieler sprechen normal.)

Negerin: Die Welt ist so schön, dass man darüber lachen könnte. Das ist etwas Bedeutendes und daher kein Verbrechen.

Regisseur: Ausgezeichnet! Eine Minute drei hundertstel Sekunden! Das ist eine gute Zeit! Das ist bis jetzt Bestzeit! Warten wir ab, wie schnell der zweite Kandidat spricht. (Zum Schausp.) Bitte!

Jung.Schausp.: Die Welt ist so traurig und tot, dass man darüber weinen könnte. Wir sitzen in einem Boot ohne Boden und steuern den Himmel an.

Regisseur: Eine Minute zwei hundertstel Sekunden. Das ist der erste Platz! Das ist eine kaum mehr zu überbietende Bestzeit! Sie waren um eine hundertstel Sekunde schneller als die Gnädigste!

Negerin: Verdammte Scheiße!

Regisseur zum Clown: Und nun zu ihnen!

Clown langsam: Die Welt ist eine Träne. Wir sind das Ungeziefer einer Träne. (Pause. Mit veränderter Stimme, schnell.) Außerdem möchte ich ihnen unsere neue Hautcreme vorstellen. Sie ist mein einziger Trost.

Regisseur: Das war eine etwas schwächere Leistung. Das war die bisher langsamste Zeit. Aber sie sprechen ja außer Konkurrenz.

Negerin: Ich weiß nicht was das soll. Ich sehe keinen Sinn. Erstens klingt es nicht besonders schön, zweitens ist es gefährlich und drittens besteht immer die Gefahr des Zungenbruchs.

Jung.Schausp.: Ich gestehe, die hundertstel Sekunde ist unwesentlich.

Negerin: Geradezu lächerlich!

Clown: Bin ich unter Erwachsenen oder im Kindergarten? Was sind das für sonderbare Werte?

Regisseur zum jung.Schausp.: Finden sie es auch kindisch?

Jung.Schausp.: Als Gewinner kann ich das nicht behaupten. Ich hoffe auf reichliches Honorar.

Regisseur: Haben sie schon am Anfang der Rede gefühlt, dass sie heute einen guten Tag haben? Waren sie nervös?

Jung.Schausp.: Nein, eigentlich nicht.

Regisseur: Die Entscheidung ist gefallen. Ich gratuliere ihnen.

Jung.Schausp.: Wo ist der Direktor?

Direktor, der herangetreten ist: Sie sind disqualifiziert, sie Flegel! Es muss heißen: "Wo befindet sich der sehr geehrte Herr Direktor? Diese Anrede muss in jedem Satz verwendet werden! Ihr Text hätte folgendermaßen lauten müssen: "Die Welt ist so traurig, dass man darüber weinen könnte, sehr geehrter Herr Direktor …". Noch dazu sind sie über das Wort "traurig" gestolpert. (Zum Regisseur): Sie haben das natürlich überhört!

Jung.Schausp.: Ich mache sie …

Direktor, brüllend: Ich wünsche die Anrede "sehr geehrter Herr Direktor"! Wie oft muss ich das noch wiederholen! Ihre Disziplinlosigkeit fällt mir schon seit langem auf. Außerdem sind sie ein miserabler Schauspieler. Hören sie sich nur den Satz an: "Die Welt ist so traurig und tot, dass man darüber weinen könnte" … und vergleichen sie damit das von ihnen gelallte Resultat. Das ist Pfusch! Stümperei! Und da wagen sie es mir unter die Augen zu treten und um eine Rolle zu bitten?

Nicht einmal, wenn sie hier vor mir auf den Knien gelegen hätte ich ihnen eine gegeben. Solche Versager kann ich an unserem Theater nicht brauchen. Und dann ihr freches Auftreten. Ihre durch nichts zu begründende Arroganz! Sie sind in meinen Augen erledigt. Eine Null. Eine Doppelnull!

Jung.Schausp. akzentuierend: Sie sind der größte Blödian, den ich kenne.

Direktor: Wa … was? (Brüllend) Sie sind wahnsinnig geworden … sie sind verrückt! (Greift sich an die Brust.) Mein Herz.

Regisseur: Aber … aber es handelt sich hier bestimmt um ein Missverständnis …

Direktor: Luft … mein Herz …

Regisseur zum Schauspieler: Ich verstehe sie nicht. Sind sie betrunken?

Direktor: Mein Herz. So etwas ist mir noch nie passiert. Ich bekomme keine Luft. Ich sterbe. (Atmet krampfhaft.)

Jung.Schausp.: Dann kann man sie wenigstens als Requisite verwenden.

Direktor, stöhnend: Gehen sie, aber sofort!

Regisseur, energisch: Gehen sie! Verschwinden sie und kommen sie mir nicht mehr unter die Augen!

Jung.Schausp.: Ihr könnt mich alle … kreuzweise … (Geht langsam zum alt. Schausp.).

Bühnenarbeiter zum Direktor tretend: Ich hätte eine Bitte.

Direktor erfreut, einen Arm um seine Schulter legend: Wird erfüllt. Endlich bitten sie mich um was. Wenn wir länger gewartet hätten … wären sie früher gekommen. Los reden sie! (Nimmt den Arm von der Schulter und schiebt ihn zur Rampe.)

Bühnenarbeiter, mit dem Gesicht zum Publikum, bescheiden: Ich hatte einmal einen kleinen Hund. Es war kein ungewöhnlicher Hund, aber er hatte ein ungewöhnlich weiches Fell. Das stimmt mich traurig.

Direktor, begeistert: Hören sie nur!

Bühnenarbeiter: Er hatte putzige, lange Ohren. Manchmal bewegte er sie, manchmal auch nicht. Dann hingen sie nur schlaff herab. Er hatte auch große beseelte Augen.

Direktor: Hören sie nur!

Bühnenarbeiter: Sie waren so schön, wie die einer Kuh. Lachen sie nicht! Im antiken Rom nannte man Frauen mit besonders schön geschnittenen, braunen Augen, die Kuhäugigen. Haben sie Kuhaugen schon beobachtet? (Aggressiver) Oder lieben sie Rinder nur wenn sie zerteilt und zubereitet vor ihnen am Teller liegen? Ich weiß sie sind Fleischfresser, Allesfresser. Der Mensch wird erst gut, wenn er nichts mehr isst. Selbst Pflanzen sollen schmerzen empfinden. Also essen sie nichts mehr. Dann hört jede Aggression auf. Sie werden sich besser fühlen. Es ist der Weg zur Unsterblichkeit. (Wieder sehr bescheiden und traurig.) Um auf meinen kleinen Hund zurückzukommen. Er hatte eine feuchte Schnauze, sie war immer feucht. Seine Zunge war lang, rosenrot und rau. Manchmal kratzte er sich, aber nur selten … mehr wollte ich eigentlich nicht sagen …

Direktor: Sie waren, wie immer, großartig. (Schüttelt ihm die Hand.)

Bühnenarbeiter: Danke. (Geht auf seinen Platz neben die Schauspieler und flüstert mit ihnen.)

Direktor: Wir haben ein großartiges Personal! Lauter liebe, hilfsbereite, junge Menschen! (Zur Negerin:) Sie bekommen selbstverständlich die Rolle. Es bleibt bei unserer Abmachung.

Negerin: Und wenn ich sie nichtmehr will?

Direktor: Aber Kindchen, das werden sie mir doch nicht antun? Ich bitte sie auf den Knien die Rolle anzunehmen!

Negerin: Das ist etwas anderes.

Direktor, erfreut: Ich habe gleich gewusst, dass wir zu einer Einigung kommen.

Aus dem Flüstern des Bühnenarbeiters schälen sich inzwischen folgende Fragmente: Der hat … gegeben, dem hab' ich's aber … gründlich … Augen gemacht … das ließ ich mir nicht gefallen … halb angeschissen hat er sich … aber ich … kalt und warm … ich … da nichts … da kennt ihr mich schlecht.

Clown: Brauchen sie mich noch?

Regisseur: Nein.

Der Clown setzt sich wieder vor die Balletteuse, das Flüstern der Drei verstummt.

Negerin: Ich mache mich zurecht. (Geht zu ihrem Sessel und schminkt sich.)

Direktor zum Regisseur: Dieser junge Schauspieler hat sich wohl für Orpheus gehalten.

Regisseur: Es war Orpheus persönlich.

Direktor: Na und wenn schon, was macht das aus? Wir kriegen genug andere Kräfte. Disziplinlosigkeit vertrage ich eben nicht!

Regisseur: Ich bin ganz ihrer Auffassung.

Der alte und der junge Schauspieler diskutieren stumm. Der Wissenschaftler setzt die Maschine in Gang. Sie leuchtet, surrt und klingelt leise. Einzelne Teile bewegen sich. Die Balletteuse steht auf, macht ein paar Schritte und setzt sich wieder.

Clown, langsam, zu sich: Ich erinnere mich daran, dass ich einmal von irgendwelchen Übungen sprach. Das muss schon lange her gewesen sein. Es ist eigentlich keine greifbare Erinnerung, sondern nur ein Hauch, der mich streift.

Balletteuse: Ich habe das Examen bestanden. Als ich noch ein Kind war wollte ich Tänzerin werden.

Direktor: Ich habe diese Nacht geweint. Ich hatte meine Schularbeiten nicht gemacht. Ich bin einfach dagesessen und habe sie nicht gemacht. Habe schlechte Noten bekommen. In allen Fächern. Also tausendfünfhundertfünfundfünfzig. Ich fühle mich innerlich leer. Das ist ein seltsamer Zustand. Dabei bin ich so stark wie eh und je. Ich stehe neben mir und beobachte mich gleichgültig.

Mann im Tropenanzug: Mein Anzug hat unter der tropischen Witterung gelitten. Ich werde mich zu meiner Familie begeben und im Kreis der Lieben dinieren.

Negerin: Mich kotzt alles an. (Wirft die blonde Perücke weg.) Ich weiß nicht mehr, wo ich hingehöre.

Die Schauspieler nehmen ihre ursprüngliche Haltung, wie am Anfang des Stückes, ein. Das soll langsam vor sich gehen.

Ihre Bewegungen werden steifer, schwerfälliger. Es herrscht große Müdigkeit. Ausgenommen davon sind die beiden Schauspieler.

Negerin: Ich möchte in einer sonnigen Nacht nackt baden. Nackt baden möchte ich in einer schwarzen Nacht, die voll Sonne ist.

Kindermädchen, halb sichtbar unter den Arkaden: Du bist ein braves Kind. Du wirst viel erreichen. Du gehst den richtigen Weg. Unfälle sollten ein Ansporn sein.

Hauptmann: Es wird kalt. Wo sind die Siege, die mich wärmten? Meine Ärmel sind abgewetzt. Die Stiefel löchrig. Die Orden müssten wieder einmal geputzt werden.

1.Herr: Ich versichere ihnen, sehr verehrter Herr Kollege, die Insekten haben die größere Überlebenschance.

2.Herr: Ja, der Mond ist sehr blau.

Regisseur: Es ist alles bestens geregelt. Wenn sie sich lächerlich machen wollen können sie mitspielen.

1.Herr zu sich: Sie haben recht, wir werden der Rattenplage auch noch Herr werden. Sie kriechen auf allen Seiten aus ihren Löchern. Dabei sind es so intelligente Tiere. Leider Parasiten und Seuchenträger. Aber ich versichere ihnen, wir werden …

Bühnenarbeiter: Ich hatte einmal einen kleinen Hund. Jetzt ist er tot. Vielleicht ist er auch nicht tot, sondern nur verschwunden. Ich bin sehr traurig. Aber das war es nicht, was ich sagen wollte. Ich kann die Worte nichtmehr finden.

Die Anwesenden sind erstarrt.

Jung.Schausp. zum Bühnenarbeiter: Du gehörst auch dazu? Das hätte ich nicht gedacht. (Er geht von einem zum anderen.) Was für eine unterhaltsame Gesellschaft! Starr desinteressiert. (Stößt den Clown mit dem Fuß gegen das Schienbein; lautes hohlklingendes Geräusch.) Nichts. Er rührt sich nicht mehr. (Klopft dem 1. Herrn gegen die Stirn. Ebenfalls lautes, hohles Geräusch. Es klingt so als würde man gegen eine Holztür oder einen Sargdeckel klopfen.) Auch nichts. (Geht zur Balletteuse.) Die Kleine wäre hübsch, wenn sie nicht so bewegungslos wäre. (Hebt prüfend einen Arm. Er fällt schlaff herab.)

Alt.Schausp., der sein Bündel geschultert hat: Wir wollen gehen.

Jung.Schausp., zum Direktor: Buuu. (Probiert den Homburg.)

Alt.Schausp.: Na, komm schon!

Jung.Schausp.: Du hast recht. Da ist nichts zu machen.

Alt.Schausp.: Ich bin kein Hungerkünstler! Ich habe Hunger! Wir brauchen einen Job. Wir sind Schauspieler. Unser Beruf schreit nach dem Spiel. Wir müssen spielen solange wir leben. Leben und Betätigung sind für uns dasselbe. Und wenn es nichts anderes wäre als den Mond anzustarren. Immerhin muss man manchmal die Augen schließen. Komm!

Jung.Schausp.: Ja, sofort! (Nimmt die von der Balletteuse weggeworfene Papierblume und riecht daran.) Trotzdem ist es schade. (Wirft die Blume weg.)

Alt.Schausp.: Komm endlich! (Sie gehen durch die Arkaden ab.)

Ende.

# About the Editor – Translator

During the 1980s I met Gerhard Waizmann in Vienna (Austria) via a common friend of ours. Gerhard, who was at that time not a renowned or professional author, has at one point handed over to me two of his plays in exchange for funds I have lent to him earlier. These two plays were "The Alternation / Die Ablöse" and "The Confusion / Die Verwirrung". Now, after more than forty years and a bit of history in between, the two plays are being published for the first time.

**Harald A. Osel** has been employed with an integrated oil and gas company since 1991 and has worked for it as a member of the Branch Management in various countries worldwide. He holds a PhD in Economics from the University of Vienna. By 2023 he retired from work and is living again in Vienna.

www.ingramcontent.com/pod-product-compliance
Lightning Source LLC
Chambersburg PA
CBHW021500090426
42739CB00007B/393

*9781922913371*